ROMANTICISM AND EVOLUTION

GENERAL EDITOR
Charles M. Sherover

I. THE SPIRIT OF THE CLASSICAL WORLD
WADE C. STEPHENS

II. THE REBIRTH OF LEARNING
The First Twelve Centuries
WILLIAM BRYAR
and
GEORGE L. STENGREN

III. SACRED AND SECULAR
1200–1500
GEORGE L. STENGREN

IV. SEPARATION AND RECONSTRUCTION
1500–1700
GEORGE L. STENGREN

V. THE ENLIGHTENMENT
The Proper Study of Mankind
NICHOLAS CAPALDI

VI. ROMANTICISM AND EVOLUTION
The Nineteenth Century
BRUCE WILSHIRE

VII. CRISIS IN MEANING
Dilemmas of 20th-Century Civilization
EDWARD C. CELL
and
JACK F. PADGETT

VIII. THE SPIRIT OF AMERICAN CULTURE
GERALD E. MYERS

The Spirit of Western Civilization

Romanticism and Evolution

The Nineteenth Century

AN ANTHOLOGY

SELECTED, EDITED AND WITH AN INTRODUCTION BY

Bruce Wilshire

CAPRICORN BOOKS : NEW YORK

Contents

V. EVOLUTION AND ANXIETY: TRANSITION TO THE PRESENT AGE

VI. EPILOGUE: SELF-LIMITATION AS THE GROUND OF HOPE

Flower in the crannied wall,
I pluck you out of the crannies,
I hold you here, root and all, in my hand,
Little flower—but if I could understand
What you are, root and all, and all in all,
I should know what God and Man is.

—Alfred Lord Tennyson

Acknowledgments

I T is not possible to express my thanks to all those persons who have, directly and indirectly, helped me to think through and prepare this volume. I owe deepest thanks to my parents for their encouragement and to my wife for her active assistance. I am deeply indebted to Professors William Barrett, Sidney Hook, Clyde Kilby and Alexander Gode von Aesche for arousing my interest in the movements of thought which marked the nineteenth century. My colleague, Professor Frederick Weiss, has given me valuable advice regarding the section on Hegel, and Professor Werner Beyer, chairman of the English Department of Butler University, has read large portions of the manuscript. Needless to say, I alone am responsible for the orientation of the volume as a whole and for the opinions expressed in it.

BRUCE WILSHIRE

Purdue University
Indianapolis Campus
March, 1967

Introduction

IT is common knowledge that romanticism arose in opposition to the rationalism and so-called Enlightenment of the seventeenth and eighteenth centuries. To point out the exact nature of the conflict, however, is the difficult and crucial thing. Two ages do not clash in the way combatants do who confront each other for the first time. Only because the newer age grows up with the older and learns to love the same themes does it quarrel so violently over the exact formulation of the themes and their mode of advancement. Family quarrels are the hottest, and this is not only true of the romantics in conflict with their spiritual fathers, but it is a truth which the romantics themselves first helped us see. To appear is not to appear out of nowhere; to appear is to evolve.

The freedom of the individual is a theme common to both ages. Alexander Pope, the Enlightenment poet, spoke words congenial to much of the postmedieval world when he declared that the proper study of mankind is man. Man—that is, not God. No matter if he is a creation of God, this creature can be understood independently of his Creator. No matter if he is embedded in a great "chain of being" which terminates in God at one end, man's immediate end is to attain his own individual perfection, not to glorify God.

But at no time in history has individualism and the quest for freedom been more intense than with the romantics. Their quarrel with the rationalists of the Enlightenment broke out over the proper formulation of the theme of freedom. The romantics and those they influenced claim that man had been cut away from his roots—by the rationalists in their search for freedom and individualism and by the scientist-prophets of the new age and the new birth; the romantics feared he would wither with overhandling. They claimed that man, although free and individual, cannot be understood in isolation from his world; man's world can not be understood in isolation from the past out of which it has evolved. For example, Hegel, no hysteric, maintained that the rationalists of the Enlightenment (Voltaire, for one) who ridiculed the religion of the past and cut themselves off from it in the name of freedom could never fill up the resulting void with their brilliant and witty talk; though time cannot be reversed and the past repeated, we have become what we are through the life of the past. Only within the seamless tissue of evolving civilization are productive tensions generated. We are dependent even upon our primitive ancestors; indeed, we are dependent even upon our opponents.

In the tangle of meanings around the word "romantic" we usually find the suggestion of escapism: the romantic thinker escapes from the present and its problems and seeks solace in the past and far away, in sentimentality and daydreams. Now, cases of this can be cited, particularly in the early "storm and stress" period (around 1770-80) when praise was given the "original genius" who would defy all rules and conventions and, in a storm of self-indulgence, go his own way. But the implication of escapism marks an exception to the rule; it is a shame for us to take it for the rule, especially since our problems are still very much like those of the romantics. We should not call a man an escapist who is trying to escape from what he thinks is a trap.

The main thrust of the romantic age and its aftermath is not an attempt to escape from the perennial problems of human existence. It is an attempt to solve them in a new context, not to obliterate them in daydreams but to establish human identity. The romantics' romanticizing (literally "modernizing") of traditional concepts comes from their conviction that such renewal is essential for the survival of our civilization.

The romantics maintained that the real interests of the individual had been misunderstood by rationalism; that the development of the individual has been impeded by a short-sighted egoism which had lost touch with the real potentialities for world-involvement and the sympathetic range of the ego itself. Heinrich von Kleist (1777–1811) expressed the romantics' need to seek for ". . . something, not Truth; something, not Love; something, not God." The fact that it was a seeking for something in general, rather than something in particular, suggests that what was lacking was a whole world, a whole context in which the individual could find himself and be at home. "Home is where the heart is"—a very romantic notion—and the heart was lost. Homesickness reverberates throughout the age; it cannot be construed as simply the personal problem of a particular man like Kleist. We might call it a sense of world loss.

Their plaint is understandable. It was not self-evident that three centuries of new birth, new learning, new continents, new science, new humanist ideology—the fruits of science shared by all—had actually enhanced the dignity and value of human life. Nietzsche, very late in the game, summed up the feeling: "We knowers are unknown to ourselves." It dawned on the romantics that scientific knowledge with its power over nature had been used by man to change the world before he had determined what his real interests were; as if he had wielded a fabulous weapon but, unaware of the position of his own feet, had begun to hack them off.

Care must be taken to distinguish the sort of science to which the romantics objected. It was mathematical physics which conceived of nature as a machine and which denied descriptive relevance to any but its own terms. To the romantic, human life seemed intrinsically purposive and goal-directed; a science which construed man as a body in space, as a machine within a machine, seemed not only false but dangerously demoralizing. We do not explain a machine's behavior by alluding to a goal *it* wishes to obtain; if we believe that man is really a machine, we must also believe that man's goal-directed efforts are a mere appearance, a sham. The danger is that man becomes a stranger to himself and loses his power to act.

The romantics were inclined to champion biology as the basic science. They thought of organisms as being vastly different from mechanisms. Not only did they intuit certain biological truths which were only later empirically confirmed, but the notion of "organism" became a root metaphor for much of their large-scale speculative thought. No consistent body of biological doctrine was built up; rather we find a junglelike profusion of ideas, amongst which must be counted such questionable notions as animism or hylozooism (*i.e.,* all the universe is alive), animal magnetism (*i.e.,* all living phenomena are the result of a single electromagnetic force-field or fluid), and certain dubious metaphorical notions (for example, the sexual organs not only resemble the whole organism, but the key to their behavior must be sought in the similarity).

Yet when we strip these peripheral notions away, we find a core idea that is certainly significant: organism is different from mechanism. In a mechanism the parts can be understood independently of the whole, or at most they require an understanding merely of adjacent parts. In an organism the parts can be understood only in relation to the whole; and each part exists not only by the means of all others, but also for *the sake of* all the others and the whole—that is, as an instrument or organ. The romantic tendency is to view the universe as an organism with organs, with each organ in turn an organism.

The total mechanism of the seventeenth-century English philosopher Thomas Hobbes is an obvious example of that to which the romantics objected. A less obvious example, but more instructive of the romantic rebellion in the long run, is the partial mechanism of his French contemporary, René Descartes. It is partial mechanism because only man's body and the external world which houses it are viewed as mechanisms; his mind is not—at least not a physical one. The romantic attitude toward Descartes is most instructive, because it indicates their belief that any mechanistic theses, given enough time and elaboration, will permeate and infect a whole world view.

Descartes thought that what a man immediately perceives is a bit of mental stuff, a sensation, inside his own mind; it cannot be something in the outer world, since there is nothing there but matter and mechanism, the causal machinery that produced the sensation inside himself. The self, the ego, is a thing that thinks, a hermetically sealed, spaceless point from which inferences are made concerning the existence of an outer world (all-that-is-not-self). The ego first finds itself cut off from the world, and this world is conceived in the most colorless, impersonal and abstract of all terms: those of mechanics and mathematical physics.

It is difficult to overestimate the importance of this theory of knowledge and this metaphysics. Momentous consequences are generated for ethics and social philosophy. If The Good is the good life for man, and if the life of man in its immediacy is a hermetically sealed container of sensations, then there is a tendency to infer that the good life consists of the largest amount of good (pleasant) sensations, and the elimination of painful ones. The danger of this position is that the immediately obvious and privately satisfying will crowd out the long-range, subtle and communal; that the ego will become grasping and cramped in its self-involvement. For the romantics there is no more wretched and distorted being than Descartes' "economic man"—a creature that calculates the return in pleasant sensations to be produced by a particular act and then acts accordingly. Despite having a nonphysical mind, he is like a machine.

For centuries after Descartes' death, however, philosophy (particularly English philosophy) was influenced by his metaphysics and theory of mind. John Locke, though a many-sided seventeenth-century thinker, also believed that the prime building blocks of knowledge were discrete sensations perceived in the mind; some of these sensations happened to be correlated, he supposed, to characteristics of physical things in the outer world. From this thesis it is a short step to Bishop Berkeley's radical position that the outer "correlated" world of matter does not exist at all; for, he argued, if all knowing is done with a mind which employs only mental resources, then only mind can be known to exist, and all the rest can be known not to—an ironic consequence of a position which began with Descartes as a partial mechanism and materialism

With David Hume, whose death in 1776 marks the outer threshold of the romantic era, this introspective and reductive analysis reached an eerie void: all that we know is a sequence of sensations—worldless and selfless mental bits. The romantic poet and artist William Blake, for one, expressed total contempt for this analysis of mind and human experience.

When Wordsworth proclaimed "We murder to dissect," the romantic movement was in full swing. So strong ran the conviction that "the whole is greater than the mere sum of its parts," that they even discarded the religious mechanism of the great Newton: "The universe is a machine. But God is in the wheels thereof." For the romantics this was nonsense. Wheels are still wheels; God must have something to do with *personality*. In Wordsworth's proclamation we find the hallmark of a generation of new thinkers: parts are meaningful as parts only because of the whole of which they are parts; analysis into parts is possible only because of a presupposed synthesis, or view of the whole, even if this synthesis be unacknowledged or inadequate. The new generation of thinkers, aided by Immanuel Kant, denied the validity of the contention that immediately perceived mental bits are the primordial building blocks of knowledge. Such a contention is possible, they maintained, only because of a failure to see that we perceive a sensation of a red tabletop, say, only because we already know where and when to look, only because we already know (whether we know that we know it or not) the world of space and time which contains us. That *World* is our "container," not the envelope of our skin which generates pleasant and painful sensations!

Furthermore, before we can mentally register a sensation we must already know *what* to look for. This knowledge of stable essence— the kind, the universal, the "what" that can be shared by an indefinite number of particular things—together with the use of language and the command of the institutions of civilization which language involves, profoundly complicates what is meant by "world."'

Descartes' philosophical successors on the Continent, rather than the English, provided a more fertile philosophical ground for the emergence of romanticism. For the seventeenth-century Spinoza there is only one building block of knowledge and only one real individual: the whole universe itself, the single substance. Pure reason steps directly to ultimate reality, the whole, and straddles the distinction of mind and matter. For Leibniz the general contours of the whole are likewise accessible to reason, and the secret of the realization of the individual self follows accordingly: man, the microcosm, becomes a whole, integrated being through reflecting the whole universe, the macrocosm. Moreover, in both thinkers the ideals of liberalism and individualism are advanced in a way more nearly congenial to romanticism. For Spinoza, parts are merely an infinity of attributes of the single divine substance ("it takes all kinds. . ."), and for Leibniz, the parts are a myriad of all mutually possible minds.

Interpretations of Spinoza in particular play a significant role for the trailblazing romanticist Johann Herder, as well as for Goethe and Hegel. Herder wrote, "The more life and reality, that is, the more rational, powerful and perfect energy a being has for the maintenance of a whole to which it feels itself belong, and to which it imparts itself inwardly and entirely, the more it is an individual, a self."* The philosophical synthesis of Hegel is the consummating bloom of an intellectual tendency which regards the whole as primordial and irreducible.

Yet much more lies behind the emergence of romanticism than Descartes' rationalist philosophical successors on the Continent. Here we only mention the revolutionary events which mark a decisive turning point in the history of the West. With the revolutions in America and France, the emotions, the irritations, the yearnings for power and freedom experienced by individuals as individuals break into historically decisive action. In Paris, in 1789, the poor poured into the street, never to be completely suppressed.

---

* See Johann Herder, *God: Some Conversations* (New York: Hafner Publishing Co.), p. 575.

Is there any possible way of summing all this up? Only with an audacity equal to the audaciousness of the subject matter itself: a spirit of the times, a something new in the air, stirred men of every rank to come to grips with the actual environment and to find a new home for man within it.

Can Kant's intellectual revolution, spawned in a study, be part of this spirit too? Yes—with similar audacity: Speculative philosophy is effective only when it limits itself to the range of sense experience; ethical philosophy is effective only when it regards the individual's purposive, goal-directed activity as autonomous, irreducible, and perfectly unimpeachable. The individual's self-imposed obligation is to will the good for all men, and by prescribing moral standards to himself a man finds his freedom.

What is this spirit which is romanticism? Sensuousness, concreteness, action, community, democracy, and a sense of history. We must be good and we must create beautiful things. It is the *activity* of art, and of life itself, which is as little grasped in the sheer intellectuality of rationalists as in the notion of a passive mind, acting only in introspection or in frivolous fantasy, which was espoused by the English "Empiricists." In a word, the stress placed on unity by the Continental rationalists was necessary for romanticism, but alone it was insufficient. Even Leibniz's concept of a minutely graduated and ascending chain of being was strangely static and failed to express the possibility that both individual and species could achieve higher levels on the chain.* For the romantic, the individual acts for the sake of the whole and finds himself the greater individual. For the romantic, reality is unity *and* time: evolution.

Not just the concept of the whole, but the whole in its concrete immediacy or nature; not just accurate knowledge about nature, but sensuous intuition of it and active involvement within it as a process—that is the earmark of the romantic. According to Wordsworth, the natural world can restore us to ourselves, can restore us to health, if we act with and not against its grain. The poet contem-

---

* For Leibniz the ultimate reality, the monad, is not an entity but a law of process. Yet there is a suggestion of fatalism in his doctrine that for a supreme intelligence all one's future possibilities are, in principle, discernible in his present actual state of being. Thus process *qua* evolution is hard to conceive in Leibnizian terms. He was similar to Pope in this respect, I think: "On superior powers/Were we to press, inferior might on ours:/Or in the full creation leave a void,/Where, one step broken, the great scale's destroy'd."

plates the harmony and fitness of the natural world that encompasses, directs and situates man; this contemplation prompts the "spontaneous overflow of powerful feeling."

From this follows a major thesis of romanticism: Although this spontaneous overflow of feeling is directed immediately upon the world (the not-self in some real sense),—yet it is nevertheless a revelation of the self to itself. The same idea is found in Byron: "I live not in myself, but I become/Portion of that around me; and to me/High mountains are a feeling." More emphatically: "Are not the mountains, waves and skies, a part/Of me and of my soul, as I of them?" Not only does he discover his feelings in discovering mountains; the mountains *are* his feelings in some sense of the troublesome verb, "to be." This romantic thesis is possible only because of an implicit conception of the structure of consciousness (or mind) and a heavy stress on the importance of this structure in human behavior: consciousness is primarily and immediately consciousness *of* a world; but consciousness is also reflective and knows it; consciousness is self-consciousness and knows that it is bound up in the world. More: the world is known as a part of consciousness. More yet: consciousness is also the core of the personal self.

This is a key, I think, to understanding the romantics: self-conscious man first finds himself beyond himself. He finds himself in nature predominantly, but also in civilizations of the past and in possible ones of the future; for his knowledge of nature is a function of his learning, and his learning is a function of civilization. For example, Shelley hears what he must certainly know is a bird ("To a Skylark") and declares, "Bird thou never wert." It is something more, or something beside, or . . . ? Again, Keats hears a bird ("Ode to a Nightingale"), and straightway establishes a bond of continuity with the past by calling it an "immortal bird" whose voice was heard ". . . In ancient days by emperor and clown:/Perhaps the self-same song that found a path/Through the sad heart of Ruth, when,/sick for home,/ She stood in tears amid the alien corn. . . ."

Once the bogey of anthropomorphism is shooed away (and it has become a bogey through chronic overemphasis by "scientific" commentators), these lines of the poets catch us up in a number of valuable suggestions: There is nothing known without a knower, and that is man; the sense of the known, of the real, is a sense for ourselves which we must confer upon the real; sense and meaning is supplied by language, art, the wellsprings of civilization; in discover-

ing the meaning of things we also discover our own meaning–for man ✔
is the giver of meaning. That bird is not just a particular, mortal
organism; it is the same *kind* of bird (essence, sense) as the one
whose "self-same" song found a path through the sad heart of
Ruth long ago. That is, the bird is known as part of, and in terms of,
man's evolving world; and in knowing what it is known as, we also
know about ourselves as its knower. Shelley's simile directly links
the human and inhuman world: the skylark is "Like a poet hidden/in
the light of thought/Singing hymns unbidden. . . ." This suggests that
metaphor and personification, as unfitting as they may be for certain
human projects (mathematical physics, for example), are nevertheless to some degree a foundation and point of departure for all
meaning, no matter how refined and impersonal this meaning ultimately becomes. As some romantics thought, language itself is metaphor. The world is like man and his experience, and *that* is how it is.
And man is like the world he knows, and that is how he is.

Some of this is completely explicit in the Germans of the same period and even slightly earlier. Herder declared that everything that
the Spirit of the world moves and nurtures has its meaning pressed
into our hearts by Him. Less dramatically, it is only in self-knowledge
that world-knowledge can be attained, for the external can act upon
a man only through and within him; or since the essence of all existence is life, the essence of the knowledge of life is self-knowledge. This
is explicit in certain poets like Novalis, although the fact that it is
explicit does not necessarily make their poetry any greater.

The spontaneous self-revelation which is poetry comes not in
crabbed reflections and analytic introspection but in a flood poured
out toward the not-self. The self is determined by the not-self (how
broad and strange the term "self" becomes!); the nature of what is
seen as the not-self is determined by the self. In this fluid interaction
of self and not-self, subject and object, in this "living center" as the
philosopher Schelling put it, we see beyond incipient Platonism
(essence, form) and detect the germ of Schelling's and even to a
greater extent Hegel's logic; so strongly is the interdependence of
opposites affirmed that the revolutionary denial of the law of contradiction follows: A is both A and not-A, at least insofar as concrete, historical reality of the world is concerned. We glimpse here
the inchoate philosophical synthesis typical of much of romanticism: Protagoreanism ("Man is the measure of all things") blends
with Platonism (impersonal form is the measure). Hence there is a

temptation for some romantics to think that man, insofar as he knows the universe, is divine.

But the romantic poets are more than incomplete romantic philosophers. It is in their poetry that their superb sensuousness and disdain for abstractions is best revealed. They want to give us not just accurate knowledge about persons and things but intimate acquaintance with them, intuitions of them, involvement with them. For example when we come upon wild animals or birds which are quiet and still in the still forest, the poets teach us that we can not only know that they are still, but that in sensuous intuition we can participate in their stillness—become a part of it and be stilled ourselves. A person who knows all *about* animals, who possesses the best scientific knowledge in one sense of that term, may be as nervous as ever; but then he does not possess full knowledge. Full knowing is being.

The past of each individual as well as the past of the race engaged the romantics' concern. Again the microcosm mirrors the macrocosm; the little organism, the big one; and—most fundamentally in process—time, change. It is the child from which the man springs that determines how the man springs and how far. Childhood is not the mere prelude to adulthood, but its foundation. Wordsworth's phrase, "The child is father to the man," sounded a new note in a rationalistic age which depicted children as little, incomplete adults in its paintings. For Wordsworth, the child is not a half-made-up adult, but a full-fledged entity in its own right that determines, in the fullness of time, just what the adult will be.

Again, it is Herder—with some prefigurations in Vico—who first saw the correlation between the evolution of the individual and that of the race. As with the adulthood of the individual, the adulthood of the race is not its childhood and never can be; time is irreversible; but the adulthood of the race, as with the individual, will be forever incomplete without a vigorous childhood, and without the ongoing recognition, appropriation and, indeed, transcendence of it. Childhood must be acknowledged and loved in order to be transcended. For Herder, our hold on the world is language, and language did not come about through arbitrary convention or as a gift from God; it evolved out of the ejaculatory cries and the biting metaphors employed by the children of the race to make the world their own. It is myth which gathers the world up into one, relates it to man and makes him feel at home within it. For a language to lose this mythical and metaphorical drive is for a language to become desiccated and artificial; the same drive must be retained in the evolving whole of civilization. Thus the emphasis in the romantic period upon folk songs and ballads and ancient, half-forgotten national religions (Richard Wagner's work, for example); romantics were convinced that if a language were to lose the mythical, it would lose its potency for the user of language.

Everywhere in romanticism we find a striving for wholeness, what today we would call (with some loss of meaning, I think) integration of personality. The romantics gained the insight that the primal inclinations of the child—toward exploration, toward the successful completion of tasks, toward the satisfactions of the senses—can be smothered under a load of conventional morality, economic prudence and the social decorum of the day. And if the child is thus prevented from making his own mark on the world and reading off the meaning of the mark, he will be cut off from his own sources of power and control, indeed his own personality; he will be a fragment, without foundation, at the mercy of every wind and pressure.

We find in Rousseau, and in the majority of the thinkers who followed him, the idea that autonomy is the true meaning of freedom. To be free is to be in control of one's destiny, and that means to be in charge of one's life: to have the ability and the desire to act intelligently and effectively in the world. Freedom is not just freedom *from*, say, deprivation and restraint (negative freedom); it is also freedom *to do*—which involves the ability and opportunity to do (positive freedom). Full, positive freedom is just the opposite of acting capriciously, or in such a way that no assignable cause can be found for the behavior. Thus, if anything, a suprarationalism emerges with the romantics: an attempt to fashion a concept of reason sufficiently broad and flexible to cover the purposive, goal-directed, nonmechanical nature of human behavior. That the attempt sometimes results in vague and sweeping pronouncements is true, but one thing is sure: in combating "the Age of Reason," the romantics did *not* become irrationalists.

Intimately connected with this ideal of positive freedom is a dominant ideal of society: Society is that context in which free and intelligent action is possible. Only in cooperative social relationships can the individual realize his own potentials. For Rousseau, for

Kant, and for others, the ideal society is a society of autonomous men, each one freely desiring the autonomy of every other, and thus freely accepting the limitations on his own behavior which the company with other autonomous men inevitably entails. It is only the positively free, the autonomous man, who attains goodness and real dignity—a value for which there is no substitute. The good man is the one who can be free, and the good society is the one which promotes, through education, for example, the self-imposed directions and limitations of individual autonomy.

Just exactly what constitutes this promotion was a ground for dispute. For Kant the state is important for the good life, but not absolutely essential; for Hegel it is only the state that can guarantee freedom and provide positive opportunities and instrumentalities for the realization and maintenance of it; for Marx it is only the economically and socially revolutionized state that can provide the opportunity for real autonomy and individual power. For Mill (who was influenced by the romantics in spite of himself) the democratic state protects individual liberty of thought; for Green the democratic state guards the channels of individual opportunity and positive freedom. However different their formulations, the overall equation of autonomy and freedom is fundamentally the same for each of these thinkers.

There is an obvious feature in the romantics' championing of nature and in their attack on newly industrialized society. Landscapes were destroyed and replaced by factories, streams were being polluted, and towns blackened by soot and grime. The profusion, the spontaneity, the revelry-in-the-accidental which is nature was being annihilated by industry. The romantics were acutely aware of what was slipping away. But the Industrial Revolution was a revolution of man's whole world—his civilization. While increasing the pcwer of the few, it decreased the power and autonomy of the many; it uprooted them socially and imperiled their freedom and selfhood.

The attack on industrialized society reached its shrill crescendo in Karl Marx: To work in a factory instead of at home or in a closely knit guild is simply to lose control over what is produced, when and where it is produced, and with whom it is produced. And since man's freedom, indeed his personality or self, is a function of what he can actually control in the world, his self must shrink accordingly. No single individual worker can afford the means of production in an industrialized society, for example a steam operated machine, with the fuel it demands and the vast system of distribution its products require. So the worker must be uprooted from his ancestral home and brought to the new cities where the means of production and distribution are located; when he gets there, he is unable to control the use to which these means of production and distribution are put; because he works on an isolated part of the goods produced, he may even have no idea of what the end-product is. His work leaves no individual intelligible mark on the world. Therefore, Marx reasoned, the worker cannot assess the meaning and value of his own actions and cannot determine his own identity as a personality. The result of this social and economic alienation is man's alienation from himself.

In Marx's view, this alienation can be overcome only through a revolutionary restructuring of the industrialized society. For man to regain himself, he must regain control over the products of his labor, and must achieve a new community with his fellows which shall allow him to blossom in freedom as a social being. The new man of the industrial and scientific age requires a new world; and it is only when we understand romantic passion that we understand why the strident Marx as well as the mellifluous Wordsworth emerged from the same movement of thought.

For the romantics, ideals are real; and any viewpoint which fails to account for their function in human behavior fails to be realistic. The morally, socially and esthetically ideal are really inspiring; if we fail to see this we fail to see that human beings really suffer without this inspiration. If a human life is somehow limited to the present and the actual, it is a stunted and withered life. Self-conscious man—this creature before our eyes—is a being of distances. The ideal, the not-yet, the merely possible are real *as such* for him. The limits of human behavior cannot be assigned until the limits of human imagination have been set as well. It might be argued that this is impossible: since that which sets the limits could only be imagination itself, and to do this we would have to imagine the unimaginable—an absurdity.

For the romantics, moreover, ideals spring from a sense of values, and values from the satisfactions which things are expected to give. The value of a thing is as real a part of it as its breadth and length. If we love something, it is a beloved thing; if we fear something, it is a fearful thing. Self-conscious man, conscious of the world both in its actuality and possibility, becomes what he is as a function of what he values. He is a coward because of what he values; he is a lover because of what he values. Wordsworth best expresses the fundamental role which evaluation plays in his doctrine of "the feeling intellect." Because of a man's feeling awareness of the value of things, things really are, say, dangerous, and he really is a being-coping-with-danger. The world in which he actually lives is the world which makes sense to him as an acting, feeling, evaluating being: the reality of that world lies in its *relationship* to men, in its appearing *to him*, in its meaning *for him*; it is not a world describable exclusively in terms of mathematical physics—world "out there." The world is personal because it affects him personally—as expressed in the first book of Wordsworth's *The Prelude*:

> Ye Presences of Nature in the sky
> And on the earth! Ye visions of the hills!
> And souls of lonely places! Can I think
> A vulgar hope was yours when ye employed
> Such ministry, when ye through many a year
> Haunting me thus among my boyish sports,
> On caves and trees, upon the woods and hills,
> Impressed upon all forms the characters
> Of danger or desire; and thus did make
> The surface of the universal earth,
> With triumph and delight, with hope and fear,
> Work like a sea? . . .

But the sword cuts both ways. If a man is what he is as a function of what he values, and if his values are corrupted, or if his evaluational life simply diminshes, then he will be corrupted or he will diminish. The inevitable corollary follows: what Schiller called "the disenchantment of the world."

We sense in many romantics the anxiety that man's emotional and evaluational life is in danger; that modern civilization has outrun its own lines of communication; that man no longer communicates with his own heart. They are aware that traditional values and ideals have suffered displacement or fragmentation: the ideal of the family and of the agricultural town; the ideal of manual labor in accord with the rhythm of nature, day and night, work and replenishment; the potent and naïve ideal of God as the supreme perfection for human life as mediated by Jesus Christ. Values must be revivified and reclaimed, for if we cease to care deeply, we will cease to *be* deeply, cease to be in our depths . . . put it as you will.

For the romantic, philosophy tended to become ideology—that is, a program for salvation. The word "salvation" is used literally, since for the romantic to be diminished in being is for him to be damned here and now, and to be free without valued goals is to be lost. Either traditional values were to be modified to fit the changing sensibility and circumstances of the time, or new values were to be discovered. The first way of salvation was the one more heavily traveled at first. The modification of religious values is a prime example; the stress was shifted from God's transcendence to his immanence: the historical process and nature itself were thought to be the Divine, struggling to unfold its own perfection in time, and inviting our support. Evil was no longer thought to be nothing or surdlike, but rather an exciting challenge. That this modification in doctrine imperiled God's omnipotence was not felt until later.

The second alternative, to discover or invent values, loomed larger and more portentously as the age progressed. The problem: Which possibilities for action in the broad new gamut of possibilities opened up by science, technology and revolutionary new learning are in fact viable ideals for man, ideals which actually motivate him to self-realizing and satisfying action? The problem is compounded immeasurably by the fact that for the first time in history the primacy of *the actual* over *the possible* was being doubted (compare Aristotle's ancient notion that it is *possible* for a knife to cut only because it is *actually* sharp, etc.). The doubt springs from the new possibilities opened to thought by science, from the new social plans advanced by inspired revolutionaries, and in the depths of thought from Kant's influential doctrine that the specification of an actual thing is a function of the possibilities of knowing that thing allowed by human experience. The world must be discussed as it is relative to man, not the reverse, and a doctrine of relativity becomes itself a possibility of thought. When man is discussed, the point is most disturbing: He must be discussed relative to himself—or so it would seem. But what on earth does this mean? Does the human self possess any actual structure which determines the range of possible human actions, and amongst them those that are best?

This problem is, I think, central to understanding the romantics and those who followed them in the nineteenth century. The whole age stresses process, individual personality, and full realization of that personality through striving after, and perhaps achieving, particular values, goals and ideals. We should begin with Rousseau, who displays his belief that our hope for man rests most securely in the education and development of his natural and actual "inclinations"—tendencies to explore, to build, to feel pleasure. But we notice a vagueness in his formulation of these inclinations. Later we can see Hegel display his belief that hope for man rests in the state which includes him as a number, and in a universally coherent network of actual relations discoverable by philosophy. But most of Hegel's followers were not content with his system, and it disintegrated in their hands, Especially in Europe we find radical ideals advanced which to the traditional eye could only seem chaotic—radical individualism (Stirner), radical communism (Marx), radical traditionalism (Kierkegaard) and radical futurism and new-moralism (Nietzsche).

We can now be more precise in our formulation of the problem. Granted that man is the forward-looking being, that he will be hopelessly incomplete without an ideal, a not-yet, to strive after; how is he to discover viable ideals—ideals which will satisfy his whole being both in the striving and in the attainment? Granted, consciousness and imagination—particularly the modern, emancipated consciousness and imagination—can project for our forward-looking gaze the most fantastic and enticing possibilities. But they have not been realized yet. How do we know they will satisfy? Moreover, these possibilities and ideals often clash, and often in the same personality.

But most of all—and here we get to the nub—what assurance do we have that consciousness, the very generator in man of the ideal and the possible, is reliable? That is, how do we know that consciousness will generate ideals which answer to the many needs of the personality? We might get some assurance if we could believe that self-conscious man is fully aware of all his own needs and tendencies. Or, on a more general level, we might get some assurance if we could believe that the range of possibility-posing consciousness is limited by some actual structure of the self which is conscious.

It is the chief agony of the age that neither of these assurances were forthcoming for a great number of thinkers in the West. First, the integrity of consciousness was impugned, in part through depth psychology with its doctrine of the subconscious: Consciousness conceals as much as it reveals, and it purposely masks off portions of the personality. Second, and more generally, it was hard for many thinkers to believe that the productions of consciousness, its fantasies and all, were limited and shaped by any actual tendencies or structures or "real potentialities" that had been built into the species *Homo sapiens* from the beginning. It might be very well for Aristotle to speak of an acorn as potentially an oak tree, and of an oak tree as the form and natural end of the acorn which guides and limits its process of growth. But the romantics, concerned with process, ends and development, traveled on a different philosophical ground, partially because of Kant; the analogy of acorn-oak to child-man was difficult to swallow. How can there be ends for *man* without his conscious recognition of these ends as ends? And if there happen to be such subconscious or nonconscious tendencies or ends, cannot consciousness misidentify them, or fail to identify them altogether? Thus there would be the possibility of chronic splitting in the personality. Or more likely, does not consciousness encompass the whole personality with an array of pure and original possibilities—possibilities which are not merely unfulfilled actualities (forms) but which stand by themselves as irreducibles? If so, the ends and guidelines of personal development are not fixed.

All evolves, all is in process, but where is it going? This is the anxiety that grows with the age. The skepticism concerning Aristotle's doctrine that actuality logically precedes potentiality generates the apprehension that there are no fixed canons of rationality (for what is fixed to be rational about? Any particular possibility just may be unattainable!), and this skepticism further prompts the giddy or distressing conjecture that the universe itself is open-ended, that the boundaries of its process are not even fixed.

It is this open universe, without fixed standards, transcendent of history, which most disturbed Johann Wolfgang von Goethe after his early romanticism, and which sent him in search of form, symmetry and balance between subject and object, person and world, imagination and reality. The works which radiate from his long life (1749–1832) provide an invaluable, if brillantly slanted, commentary on the course of western civilization during that period. Goethe contrasts his modern world to the closed world of the ancients in which man's place was defined and delimited by stable actualities and necessities—physical, social and moral. This conception of enclosure generated a supportive ethics: one ought to act in a certain way because ultimately one must, whether one wills to or not. The ancient person was shielded from both the paralyzing fear and the seductive fascination in the face of his own freedom, simply because his free will was not conceived as being very potent and his possibilities for action were conceived as limited. To Goethe's mind, the modern world exhibits an incommensurability between will and world: one wills because one is able to will, but what one *ought* to do remains in doubt. The modern will brings disruption because it is an impulsive and unstable reaching out toward untried possibilities. The problem, as he saw it, is to find "objective correlatives" (to borrow the phraseology of T. S. Eliot) for the will and its acts: justifications for actions in terms of satisfactions gained and goals won; a true "return" on actions which would be the "inner form" of the act, its equilibration and completion. Goethe seems to have thought that wholeness in the modern age is still possible, because man is a part of nature, and new knowledge of the forms of nature, gained through right-minded natural science, could not itself be disruptive; furthermore, a disciplined will which seeks and patiently awaits new satisfactions and objective correlatives is also possible.

We must underline the difficulties of Goethe's quest. In the dominant thought of the nineteenth century, transcendent superstructure for the world is absent: immanence and relativity are the hallmarks. When God is discussed, it is His immanence in the world process which is central; when ideals are discussed, it is their anticipated realization in the temporal flow of the secular world. When wholeness is marked as the object of yearning, it is the wholeness of this world, not the next or another. If existence cannot be oriented and values discovered in the evolving stream of history itself, then the tendency is to conclude that orientation and values are not to be discovered.

Regarded as a program for the reconstruction of civilization, the romantic movement was a disappointment. Regarded as a program still to be pursued ("The books on the romantics have not yet been closed," writes William Barrett), it remains a disappointment. Goethe's hope was not realized. Scientific knowledge did not provide a conceptual structure sufficiently broad for us to comprehend our place in the universe. Science could not formulate new values by which to mark out satisfactions which would contain the will, direct it, and bring it to equilibrium.

For the tide of science and technology swept around, rather than through, Goethe and the romantics and despite all its gifts brought disruption to our sense of the whole (how is the natural-scientific interpretation of human life comparable to Shakespeare's or the Bible's?), and most ironically of all, brought depression to our sense of our own worth, autonomy and power. Charles Darwin's work on the evolution of the species cast light on biology, but a shadow on man's ability to control his own destiny through purposive acts, rational choice and beneficence. The romantic ideal of spontaneity became something of a nightmare, because it was viewed in an altered context. Darwin claimed that most significant advances of the human species are brought about by chance and natural selection, not rational choice, and the real powers at work in natural selection are the instinctual, spontaneous and apparently brutish forces of survival. The impression is unavoidable: since deliberate volition and rational choice are not ultimately decisive, and since such conscious volition and choice are involved in what we *mean* by the self (as the romantics made crystal clear), the self is not its own master. The depreciation of purposive action marks a reversion to one aspect of mechanism. And despite scientific caution and at least a halfway respect for the dangers of the genetic fallacy, authoritative allegations of man's subhuman genesis did little to breed confidence that the reconstruction of the distinctly human or humane world was a discernible and attainable value.

To undermine the importance of volition, choice and ends is to undermine the importance of consciousness; man's confidence in himself was shaken in direct ratio to his confidence in his own consciousness. Moreover, it was shaken not only by Darwin, but from many sides at once, dating from about the middle of the nineteenth century.

Influential physiologists asserted that the fundamental laws of consciousness are really laws of matter (the brain); since the laws of his brain are not usually known by the person, the conclusion follows that the causal conditions of his consciousness fall beyond the scope of his consciousness. The impression is left that consciousness is limited and dependent; and because our sense of ourselves is involved with our sense of the efficacy of our consciousness, the impression is left that we are like puppets.

Marx's contention that the chief effects of an economy are not consciously intended added its own note to the attack.

Philosophers such as the long-neglected Schopenhauer gained attention with the doctrine that the instinctual will to survival does not serve conscious reason, but just the reverse: conscious reason is mainly the servant of the will; it expends itself in rationalization and the disguising decoration of foregone impulses of the will. Only in art and in the will's denial of itself is salvation possible through ascetic withdrawal from the world.

To be noted also is the advancement of what we know today as existentialism and, related in some ways to this, depth psychology— particularly in the persons, of Kierkegaard, Dostoevsky and Nietzsche. Each of these men was influenced by the romantics, but in each a profound anxiety took root. Each was committed to the value of human freedom as autonomy and to the belief that man is a being projected toward the possible, the future; but without some point to the freedom, some purpose, some obtainable and satisfying value that makes the striving worthwhile, there can only be wayward and destructive lashings out of the will. For it is our being, our nature—if anything is—to be projected toward *something*.

As Nietzsche put it, man can endure any *how* if he has a *why*, if he has a valued goal that justifies his striving; but he would rather have the void for his purpose than be void of purpose. And for Nietzsche this is no mere play on words, since he sees mass destruction and nihilism as real possibilities. He proclaimed the death of God and with Him all eternal values transcendent of history. He said we must discover new tablets, new rules, new values, a new civilization. He said the good and the true will be that which is viable, that which works out, in a new era of human existence, assuming human existence itself works out.

Kierkegaard maintained that whatever is eternal must appear to us temporal men as elusive and paradoxical, yet indispensably important to embrace. Dostoevsky's statement of values is not clear; at times it is a kind of belated worship of nature and vitality, and at others a prescription of suffering for the attainment of sympathy. The thought of each of these three men is in marked contrast to Schiller's notion that every human has his values prescribed for him because each has the ideal man engraved within himself.* In a word, crucial.

Most important of all, these thinkers all find a darkness and ambiguity at the heart of any human project—that is, at the heart of we have a crisis of values in systems of thought where values are

---

* "Every individual human being . . . bears within himself, as his potential and destiny, the pure ideal image of men. To be in accord with its immutable oneness through all changes is the great task of his life."

consciousness. For Kierkegaard the prospect of the possible framed in consciousness, the not-yet, the *nothing*, as he calls it, is dreadful and unclear; the only thing of which we can be sure is that we must make a choice (for not choosing is itself a choice) and that each choice entails a multitude of rejections. To approach wholeness we must make radical choices and thus become narrower—a strange predicament. Indeed, for Kierkegaard the possible is so dreadful that if it is the good life that is not yet incorporated in our being—if the good life is the not-yet, the nothing—then we will dread the good life. This is the demoniacal, the perverted spirit or corrupted consciousness, the dialectics of which Kierkegaard elaborates (1843) in passages that make Freud's crypto-mechanistic account of human behavior look like nursery rhymes devised for budding biologists.

For Nietzsche, the deepest human motive is the will to power, to mastery; but through fear of it, or resentment of those strong persons who possess it, we can mask it from our sight and pretend that meekness and humility are the true values. Of course, these values are used to curb the strong; they are the dishonest and sneaking expression of the same will to power. Consciousness can easily be corrupted and men easily dominated by ulterior motives. Although Nietzsche maintains that the will to power can create profound values, he calls it "evil" because its exercise is dangerous. This is reminiscent of the early romantic William Blake, who contended in his "Marriage of Heaven and Hell" that there is a dark, turbulent and demonic side to the divine powers of creativity—except that Blake's framework of mystical Christianity is missing in Nietzsche. Now, when the creation of a new civilization is essential, and a new man ("Super-man") required, the outcome for Nietzsche is doubtful. His heralding of the new man is a challenge, not a prediction.

For Dostoevsky, in his clearest and most pursuasive writings, freedom cannot find an adequate object and turns in upon itself in a sickness of consciousness. It may be true that man was once a monkey, that $2+2 = 4$ and that prudence is good, but a person *need not* accept these truths; as a matter of fact, the willful and perhaps destructive refusal to accept them may be the only demonstration of his freedom that the person can find. The refusal is not to be construed as a mere whim, for it proves his right to have a whim.

It would be misleading to leave the impression that this dark trinity of thinkers comprises the entire end product of the romantic age. Marxists who have proliferated, for example, regard these three as cases of a decadent bourgeois class; men whose expertise is limited to a few points of abnormal psychology—what they could observe at close range in themselves. Furthermore, we find at this time a largely optimistic Emerson in America, who suffers no great disillusionment of spirit, and a wonderfully liberal William James a little later, who gives us a glimpse of what a reconciliation of the sciences and humanities might look like. We find, moreover, a philosopher like John Fiske, who has a quasi-religious experience looking at a steam locomotive (perhaps some today feel the same way about rockets). And a later Hegelian thinker, Thomas Hill Green in England, broadcasts a sanguine future for liberalism and the democratic welfare state.

Still and all, *fin de siècle* pessimism is indicative and understandable. Attacks on the efficacy of consciousness and reason cast doubt on the whole project of civilization itself. It can be asked, of course, how Darwin, Marx, Schopenhauer, Kierkegaard *know* that consciousness and reason are defective and unreliable if it is not through the use of that very consciousness and reason. Perhaps an initial overconfidence in reason was a factor in the ensuing loss of confidence. In any case, confidence in a single phalanx of rational endeavor was shattered, and we labor today not knowing what the various uses and competencies of reason are. How is the use of reason in physics related to its use in psychology? And how is the latter related to its use in the pursuit of the morally good life? These are questions that haunt the most respectable houses today.

The hangover from the romantics is lengthy and heavy, and it can at least be argued that no new positive cycle has yet begun. Most of their problems are still our problems. It remains to be proved that we can achieve dignity, respect others' rights, or even attain a minimal zest and skill for ordinary living. The welfare state leaves the central problem of human motivation untouched; communism serves up a strangely gray paradise; machines save us work and commonly bore us to tears; new "freedoms" are too often frenzied flailings which degrade us; and we are prey to grave and difficult-to-explain depressions and outbursts of hatred. We have unfinished business with the heart.

The nineteenth century was an opulent and hard-to-digest intellectual feast from which our own century is still taking its nourishment. In order to gain a clear view of it we must restrict and limit our focus (as Kant himself might have suggested). I think we can best view it from the perspective of the present. Accordingly the orientation of this presentation has been determined by the prime strands that have been absorbed and woven into the fabric of our own time. Even so, it is not possible to give due attention to everything that is relevant to us. There is really not very much verse and that is the unkindest cut of all. There is nothing about the nineteenth century's music and only little of its science, theology, economic theory, and drama. Were our focus less comprehensive and general some of its other leading thinkers would be present: its eighteenth-century precursors, its own spokesmen such as Lessing, Tetens, Winckelmann, Wieland, Feuerbach, Lotze, Bradley, Bosanquet, Bruno Bauer, David Strauss, Alfred Russell Wallace, Auguste Comte, Wilhelm Wundt, Ernst Mach, Josiah Royce and Charles Sanders Peirce. Each of these contributed in specialized ways to our inheritance from their time. Heine and Tennyson, who perhaps best epitomize its poetic expression have not been given their due.

The focus has been the development of the period's philosophical ideas. There are many reasons for this, the best one is the presumption that, especially in a philosophic age, philosophy offers the most general of all views and thus offers the greatest mileage from the smallest amount of material. Philosophy not only takes up and reflects, as does a Leibnizian monad, the outlook of its time; in so doing it contributes to the further development of the art and science that follow. On this level, an alternative procedure would have to use part of Kant's *Critique of Pure Reason* and to trace its influence through the pragmatists, Mach and later positivists. To some minds, that would have given a more hopeful and reconstructionist tone to the volume. Limitations of space together with my own belief that such a tone is not entirely justified ruled out such a course.

I do not confess, however, to what I take to be fairly widespread and current academic-philosophical bias which has only recently shown signs of abatement: that of the exclusive, detached technician. I have tried to take my cue from Kant: He did not feel above and beyond the oddball literary man Rousseau, but rather learned from him. Moreover, the relationship between Kant and the rest of the cultured public was a genuine interaction: Beethoven is said to have been deeply moved by Kant's ethics. To think that such an interaction between philosophers and the rest of mankind might happen is either to laugh or to cry. May such a community of intellect soon return to us.

I.

Beyond the Enlightenment:
Recovery of the Whole Man

1. ROUSSEAU: The Natural Individual

The main thrust of the romantics thinkers of the nineteenth century is the attempt to recover the dignity and integrity of the whole man: the person who is willingly and ungrudgingly communal; who is free when he acts autonomously and effectively within his environment; who is spontaneously and emotionally involved in his action. Freedom, society, autonomy, inwardness and emotion are the interrelated themes.

"Rousseau and romanticism"—the phrase falls together with ease. At least his work is an approach to the movement. Competing in an essay contest on the topic of the contribution of science to civilization, Jean Jacques Rousseau (1712–1788) wrote on the destructive aspects of that contribution. To the "enlightened" Diderot, the company of his friend Rousseau was "like having a damned soul at his elbow." In part, Rousseau was disturbing because his rich and unpredictable inner life overflowed the tidy categories of Diderot's *Encyclopaedia*.

The Encyclopaedists taunted Rousseau for writing about society while fleeing from it to live in the country. But he believed that a valuable contribution to society could be made only if the contributor had achieved something of value in his own life, and to achieve this he might have to be by himself. Furthermore, Rousseau thought that the urban society of his time had corrupted its citizens by confusing mores and morality, by forcing an artificial direction on natural and good inclinations, by miseducating so profoundly that the artificial had practically become an instinctual second nature.

Rousseau called the natural man who lives in harmony with his original inclinations the good man. Vagueness in Rousseau's formulation of these inclinations accounts for vagueness in his ideal. He says that as creatures of sensation we naturally seek pleasant sensations and avoid painful ones, and as creatures of reason we naturally seek ideals of perfection. This covers a great deal of ground, and on one side is suspiciously like the sensationalistic psychology inherited from Descartes and Locke. Indeed, the parts do not fit neatly together in Rousseau, and we must view him as a transititional figure, not neatly settled on either side.

But we can make some sense of Rousseau's idea of original inclinations if we try, and its importance repays the effort. First is his insight into development: The good man grows from the child who is allowed by ∨

the educator and society at large to be honest about his own sensations and desires. With this honesty as a basis, the child then finds standards of perfection which are appropriate and realistic for him. Echoing Aristotle, The good is the realization of man's natural tendencies and capacities. Different, however, is the suspicion that consciousness, which must recognize and intend this natural consummation, is not (as it was for Aristotle) an integral and determinate part of nature; it is boundless and wild. It is not until later in the age that this difference becomes troublesome.

We need simply note that Rousseau had a fundamental insight which penetrated beyond a psychology of atomistic sense data: the self is not just a bundle of sensations; it is an intentional, directed, original activity. We become a self by doing, and no one else can do our doing for us. The teacher must know when to leave the child alone. If the child's actions are dangerous, then he is simply prevented from acting in that way, but prevented with a minimum of talk; otherwise he is allowed the opportunity to make his own mistakes and to achieve the satisfactions of recognizing and surmounting them. The child is in the world along with us, and he will be naturally inclined to mimic what we do— not what we preach at him.

Rousseau is permissive but not soft; for example, "To expect to be always listened to is a form of domination which a child has no right to enjoy." The child becomes a self, one of worth and dignity, when he masters the world independently of the complicity of parents, servants, or knaves. To be pinned down by others' stares, demands, or even assistance, is to be robbed of one's world. Only by seeing the mark which he makes on the world does the child become respectable and intelligible in his own eyes. Insofar as Rousseau equates self and activity in the world, he escapes the egoism of a psychology of sensations.

Rousseau's *Emile* was published in 1762. It caused a scandal among those who thought of the child as a little adult to be reasoned with and preached at.

Rousseau advocates no hermit ideal: The child is to be educated to be social. It is only society *as it stands* which has so corrupted the educational process that the child must be removed from it until he has been armed by a proper education to enter it.

Given the present products of society's education, there is no hope for a valid social contract, *i.e.*, a free acceptance of the limitations involved in being an autonomous person who lives in a society among autonomous fellows. Each man must be taught to will the good of every other (the "general will"); this constitutes each man's dignity and true freedom as a rational being and the basis of the democracy which Rousseau's *Social Contract* proclaims as the only type of social order for morally free men. Freedom for the present social product of his time can mean only tyranny, license and intolerance.

It has been argued that Rousseau's advocacy of the free individual was a causal factor in producing the French Revolution.* But Rousseau himself shuddered at the prospects of revolution since no one was taking the time which the first step toward true freedom required—a new education. The revolutionaries were as miseducated in their own way as those they killed, for they had all been educated under the old regime. Too fast, too fast it all went, and Rousseau, one of the first romantics, was one of the first to taste its disappointment.

In reading the selection,† we should not fail to note that Rousseau's desire to produce a self-confident, autonomous man is linked with the general romantic belief in the efficacy of the esthetic sense in bringing this about. He writes, "My chief aim in teaching him to feel and love beauty in every form is to fix his affections and his tastes on it and prevent his natural appetites from deteriorating so that he begins to look for the means of happiness in his wealth instead of finding it in himself."

We know nothing about childhood, and with our false ideas the more we do, the more we botch. Even the wisest writers are so much concerned with what adults ought to know, that they never ask what children are capable of learning. They look for the man in the child and do not think of what he is before he becomes a man. . . .

The Maker of the world makes everything good, but man meddles and things degenerate. Man forces one soil to yield the products of another, one tree to yield another's fruit; he mixes up time, place and natural conditions; he mutilates his dog, horse and slave. Loving all that is deformed and monstrous, he disfigures all things. He will leave nothing as nature made it, not even man himself . . . who must be shaped to his master's taste like the trees in his garden.

Still, under present conditions, humans would be even worse than they are without this education. A man left to himself from birth would be more of a monster than the rest. Prejudice, force, authority, example, all the social conditions which swamp us, would destroy nature in him and put nothing in its place. He would be like a plant that has grown up by chance in the middle of a road, and got crushed under foot by the passersby. . . .

Plants are fashioned by cultivation, men by education. If a man

* See Karl Löwith, *From Hegel to Nietzsche* (London: Constable & Co., 1963), p. 283.

† The selection which follows is from Book I of *Emile* and was translated by Bruce Wilshire.

were born tall and strong, his strength and size would be of no use to him until he had learned to use them; they would even harm him by preventing others from coming to his aid; left to himself he would die before he knew his needs. We lament the helplessness of infancy only because we fail to see that the race would be extinct had not man begun by being a child. . . . All that we lack at birth and all that we need when we come to man's estate is the gift of education.

Education comes to us from nature, from men, or from things. The inner growth of our organs and capacities is the education of nature. The use we learn to make of this growth is the education of men. What we gain by our experience of our environment is the education of things. Hence we are taught by three teachers. If their teaching conflicts we are never at peace with ourselves and are badly educated; if their teaching agrees we are in harmony with ourselves and are directed straight to our goal. . . .

Of these three factors in education nature is wholly beyond our control, things are only partly so, and only the education of men is controlled by us. Even here our power is mainly illusory, since who can hope to control every word and deed of everyone with whom the child comes in contact. Viewed as an art, education is almost impossible; . . . only good luck enables us to reach its goal.

What is its goal? As we have just seen, it is the goal of nature. Since all three educators must work together, the two that we can control must follow the lead of the one which is beyond our control. Perhaps this word "nature" is too vague. Let us try to define it.

Nature, it has been said, is only habit. Really? Are there not habits formed under pressure which leave the original nature unchanged? One example is a tree which has been forced to grow sidewise. It keeps its artificial shape, but when set free any new growth is straight up. It is the same with human dispositions. While the conditions remain the same, even the most unnatural habits are retained. But change the conditions and nature reasserts herself. . . . If "nature" be restricted to habits conformable to nature, we need say no more.

We are born capable of sensation and from the first are affected in different ways by the objects around us. When we become conscious of our sensations we naturally tend to seek or to avoid the objects which produce them: at first, because they are agreeable or disagreeable to us . . . at last, because of the judgments we pass on them by reference to the idea of happiness or perfection we get from reason. These tendencies extend and strengthen with the growth of sensibility and intelligence, but under the pressure of habit they are changed to some extent by our opinions. The tendencies before this change are what I call our nature. In my view everything ought to be in conformity with these original inclinations.

No difficulty would arise if our three educators were merely different; but what can be done when they conflict? Obviously consistency is impossible if we seek to educate a man for others, instead of for himself. Since we have to combat either nature or society, we must choose between making a man or making a citizen—we cannot make both. . . .

The Spartan Pedaretes presented himself for admission to the council of the Three Hundred and was rejected; he went away rejoicing that there were three hundred Spartans better than himself. . . . That was a citizen. . . .

If you wish to know what is meant by communal education, read Plato's *Republic* . . . it is the best treatise on education ever written. [But] . . . communal education does not and cannot exist, for there is neither country nor real citizen. The very words should be struck from the language. . . .

I do not consider our ridiculous colleges as communal institutions, nor do I include in this category a fashionable education, for this education facing two ways at once achieves nothing. It is fit only to produce hypocrites, always claiming to live for others, but thinking of themselves alone. These claims, however, deceive nobody, for everyone has his share in them; they are so much wasted time. Our inner conflicts are caused by these contradictions. Drawn this way by nature and that way by man, we take a middle path that leads us nowhere. In this muddled and tense state we go through life and end up with our contradictions unsolved, never having been any good to ourselves or to anyone else.

There remains the education of nature, which amounts to domestic education in the home. But how will a man who has been educated entirely for himself get on with other people? If the twofold aims could be resolved into one, a great obstacle to happiness would be removed. To judge of this you must see the man full-grown; you must have noted his tendencies, watched his progress, followed his steps; in sum you must really know a natural man. . . .

What can be done to produce this exceptional man? As a matter of fact, all we have to do is to prevent anything being done. When it is only a matter of sailing against the wind it is enough to tack, but when the sea runs high and you just want to stand where you are, you must throw out your anchor. . . .

In the social order where all stations in life are fixed, everyone needs to be educated for his own station. The man who leaves the place for which he has been trained is useless in any other. In Egypt, where the son was obliged to follow in his father's footsteps, education had at least a sure aim. In our country where social ranks are fixed, but the men in them are constantly changing, nobody knows whether he is doing his son a good or bad turn when he educates him for his own rank.

In the natural order, on the other hand, where all men are equal, manhood is the common vocation. A well-educated man cannot fail to do well in that vocation. That my student is intended for the army, the church or the bar, does not greatly concern me. Before the vocation determined by his parents comes the call of nature to the life of mankind. Life is the business I would have him learn. When he leaves my hands, I admit he will not be a magistrate, or a soldier, or a priest. First and foremost, he will be a man. All that a man must be he will be when the need arises, and as capably as anyone else. Whatever the changes of fortune he will always be able to find a place for himself. . . . To my mind those of us who can best endure the good and evil of life are the best educated; therefore true education consists less in precept than in practice. . . .

It is not enough to merely preserve a child's life; he must be taught to preserve his own life when he is a man, to bear the buffets of fortune, to stand up against wealth and poverty, to live at need among the snows of Iceland or on the scorching rocks of Malta. In vain you guard against death—he must die. And even if you do not kill him with your precautions, they are mistaken in any case. Teach him to live life rather than avoid death: life is not breath, but action, the use of the senses, the mind, the capabilities, every part of ourselves which makes us conscious of our being. Life is less a matter of length of days and more a matter of a keen feeling for life. A man may be buried at a hundred and may never have lived at all. He would have done better had he died young.

Our wisdom is slavish prejudice, our customs are controls, constraits, compulsions. Civilized man is born and dies a slave. The infant is bound up in swaddling clothes, the corpse is nailed down in his coffin. All his life long man is imprisoned by our institutions. . . . Even the head is confined by a cap. One would think they were afraid the child should look as if it were alive.

Thus the internal impulses which should lead to growth find an insurmountable obstacle in the way of the necessary movements. The child exhausts his strength in vain struggles, or he gains strength very slowing. He was freer and less constrained in the womb. He has gained nothing by birth. . . .

This irrational practice comes from a departure from nature. Mothers despise their first duty and are no longer willing to suckle their own children; they hand them over to hired nurses. These women, finding themselves mothers of strange children, lack the attraction of natural affection and are only concerned with saving themselves work. A child that has been left free needs constant watching. . . . Do these fine mothers who get rid of their children and have a gay time in the city understand the sort of treatment the swaddled baby is getting in the village?. . .

The claim is made that when children are left free they will acquire bad postures and misshapen limbs from their movements. . . . Children do not possess the strength that would make their movements dangerous to themselves, and the pain of a bad posture quickly warns them of the need for change. . . .

Our bookish eagerness to instruct is always causing us to teach children what they can learn better for themselves, and to forget the things they need to be taught. Is there anything more asinine than the pains we take to teach them to walk when there has never yet been a child who failed to walk by reason of his nurse's neglect? Think rather of the many persons who walk badly all their lives long, because they have been taught to walk badly. Emile. . . will run and frolick and tumble a hundred times a day. The oftener he falls the better. He will soon learn to pick himself up. The blessedness of freedom compensates for many bruises. . . .

But when mothers are willing to nurse their own children, then a general reform of morals will take place. Natural feeling will revive in every heart; there will be a surplus of citizens for the state; this first step by itself will restore mutual affection. . . . No mother, no child. Their duties are reciprocal, and when ill done by the one they will be neglected by the other. The child's love for his mother should precede any sense of obligation. If the call of the blood is not strengthened by training and habit, it fades out in the early years and the heart, one might say, dies still-born. We have taken steps away from nature. . . .

A whole assembly of reflections introduce themselves when one begins to consider the structure of language and the first utterances of children. First of all, they have their own kind of grammar, with a syntax that has rules more general than ours. If you pay careful attention you will be surprised by the precision with which they follow particular analogies which are only inadmissable because they are contrary to usage. It is an intolerable piece of pedantry to correct all these little faults. Fear not, the children will correct them for themselves in good time. Always speak correctly in their presence and you can best assured that without any criticism on your part their language will be unconsciously refined on the model of yours. . . .

The child who is learning to speak should hear only words he can understand, and use only words he can pronounce. Do not trouble to speculate about what he is saying when he begins to lisp. To expect to be always listened to is a form of domination which a child has no right to enjoy. It is enough to make adequate provision for his needs; it is up to him to make you understand anything beyond that. . . .

Early let the child feel the weighty yoke which nature places on man, the yoke of the necessity in things as opposed to human caprice. If there is anything he should not do, do not forbid him, but prevent him without explanation or reasoning. Whatever you give, bestow at the first word without pleadings or prayers, and above all without conditions. Give with pleasure, refuse with regret, but let your refusals be irrevocable. Your "No" once pronounced must be a wall of brass which the child will stop trying to batter down once he has exhausted his strength against it five or six times.

2. KANT: The Dignity of the Moral Will

To call Immanuel Kant (1724–1804) a romantic would be grotesque, if for no other reason than that he comes close to presenting reason and emotion, reason and inclination as opposed to each other. And yet the age is unthinkable without him. In his stress on reason he is the apotheosis and extreme point of the Enlightenment; but here the Enlightenment transcends itself and verges on something different.

Kant stressed the many-sidedness of reason, and thereby stressed the many-sidedness of the reasoning being, man. With pure reason he seeks to ascertain what *is* in the physical, sensuously appearing world;* with practical reason he ascertains what *ought* to be in his own behavior; with esthetic judgment he ascertains what is beautiful and therein detects what in nature and art is analogous to the purposiveness and end-directedness of his own moral behavior; he ascertains the "just right," the bond that marks a harmony between the physical and moral worlds.

It is said that when Kant, a closet-scholar who regulated his life like clockwork, first read Rousseau, he was so fascinated that he could not put his copy down and his schedule was disrupted. How unlike Rousseau, who had no schedule to disrupt. But this only goes to show what the romantics—be it noted—were quite aware of: Thought has a life of its own, independent of the particular temperament of the individual thinker; it is directly worldly in its reference and from it derives its structure; it is not the mere contents of an isolated ego.

What most fascinated the German philosopher in Rousseau was the idea of freedom as autonomy and the claim that the good will has a general law as its object; when Kant speaks of "autonomy," it should be understood that he means moral freedom. Rousseau has written in his *Social Contract*, Book I, Chapter 8: "It is *slavery* to be under the impulse of mere appetite, and *freedom* to obey a law which we prescribe for ourselves." Kant agreed strongly with Rousseau that the Encyclopaedists' incessant equation of goodness with the amelioration of social ills is just chatter unless the principle which motivates this amelioration is first morally determined. Goodness is a quality of the inner man, his will, his heart, his motivation, however secret; it is not a show. The *more* is not the moral. Rousseau brings morality back into social theory as neither Locke nor Montesquieu had done; Kant applauds him for it:

> Rousseau was not so wrong in preferring the condition of the savage, if we neglect the last step our species still has to take. We are cultivated to a high degree by art and science. We are civilized to excess by all kinds of social niceties and refinements. But to consider ourselves truly ethical, much is still lacking. . . . So long as . . . states employ all their power for vain and violent expansion and thus constantly block the slow efforts of their citizens toward inner development . . . we can expect nothing of this sort. . . . All good not based on morally good intention is nothing but vain illusion and splendid misery.†

* For more commentary on this point see the introduction to Fichte, p. 117.

† *Idea of a Universal History in the Interest of World Citizenship*, *Werke*, IV, 161.

In a sense, Kant tried to beat the rationalists at their own game. If theoretical reason in one of its roles is limited—for example, the constitutive function of pure reason is limited to the range of sense experience—then it is reason in another of its roles, the critical, which discovers that limit. If theoretical reason is limited to its area, that leaves room for reason of another sort in another area, for instance, the "practical reason" of ethics. Kant was saying that the rationalists simply did not know how finely and flexibly rational a man can be, particularly with respect to the moral organization of his life. Their conception of practical reason was crude, superficial—unreasonable; and thus they actually demeaned what they intended to enhance—man.

Kant was saying that man is unique in nature, without being out of nature; that all things act according to a law, but that man can act, in addition, according to the *idea* of a law. The idea of sheer rational lawfulness, universal and morally necessary, can motivate his actions, and when it does his will is absolutely good; it is an intrinsic, irreplaceable source of worth for which there is no price, no equivalent. This is the actual dignity of man: to attain the autonomy or self-sufficiency of willing his acts to be in conformity with a law of practical reason he imposes upon himself, and to do so despite any inclination to the contrary. Autonomy is just the obedience of the rational will to its own law. The law, a categorical imperative, is briefly: So act that you can will the reason for your act to be a reason for all men to act. To act in this manner is to achieve a dignity which is unshakable, since the goodness of the act and the dignity involved in it are independent of the fortuitous consequences of the act, independent of the fickle opinions of contemporaries. The "good of it" is, in part, that one need no longer worry about what the "good of it" is.

The selection is taken from the first two sections of *The Foundation of the Metaphysics of Morality*.*

I

Nothing in the whole world, or even outside of the world, can possibly be regarded as good without limitation except a *good will*. No doubt it is a good and desirable thing to have intelligence, sagacity, judgment, and other intellectual gifts, by whatever name they may be called; it is also good and desirable in many respects to possess by nature such qualities as courage, resolution, and perseverance; but all these gifts of nature may be in the highest degree pernicious and hurtful, if the will which directs them, or what is called the *character*, is not itself good. The same thing applies to *gifts of fortune*. Power,

* Translated by John Watson, 1901.

wealth, honour, even good health, and that general well-being and contentment with one's lot which we call *happiness*, give rise to pride and not infrequently to insolence, if a man's will is not good; nor can a reflective and impartial spectator ever look with satisfaction upon the unbroken prosperity of a man who is destitute of the orna- ment of a pure and good will. A good will would therefore seem to be the indispensable condition without which no one is even worthy to be happy.

A man's will is good, not because the consequences which flow from it are good, nor because it is capable of attaining the ends which it seeks, but it is good in itself, or because it wills the good. By a good will is not meant mere well-wishing; it consists in a resolute employment of all the means within one's reach, and its intrinsic value is in no way increased by success or lessened by failure.

This idea of the absolute value of mere will seems so extraordi- nary that, although it is endorsed even by the popular judgment, we must subject it to careful scrutiny.

If nature had meant to provide simply for the maintenance, the well-being, in a word the happiness, of beings which have reason and will, it must be confessed that, in making use of their reason, it has hit upon a very poor way of attaining its end. As a matter of fact the very worst way a man of refinement and culture can take to secure enjoyment and happiness is to make use of his reason for that purpose. Hence there is apt to arise in his mind a certain degree of *misology*, or hatred of reason. Finding that the arts which minister to luxury, and even the sciences, instead of bringing him happiness, only lay a heavier yoke on his neck, he at length comes to envy, rather than to despise, men of less refinement, who follow more closely the promptings of their natural impulses, and pay little heed to what reason tells them to do or to leave undone. It must at least be admitted, that one may deny reason to have much or indeed any value in the production of happiness and contentment, without tak- ing a morose or ungrateful view of the goodness with which the world is governed. Such a judgment really means that life has another and a much nobler end than happiness, and that the true vocation of reason is to secure that end.

The true object of reason then, in so far as it is practical, or capa- ble of influencing the will, must be to produce a will which is *good in itself,* and not merely good *as a means* to something else. This will is not the only or the whole good, but it is the highest good, and the condition of all other good, even of the desire for happiness itself. It is therefore not inconsistent with the wisdom of nature that the cultivation of reason which is essential to the furtherance of its first and unconditioned object, the production of a good will, should, in this life at least, in many ways limit, or even make impossible, the attainment of happiness, which is its second and conditioned object.

To bring to clear consciousness the conception of a will which is good in itself, a conception already familiar to the popular mind, let us examine the conception of *duty*, which involves the idea of a good will as manifested under certain subjective limitations and hindrances.

I pass over actions which are admittedly violations of duty, for these, however useful they may be in the attainment of this or that end, manifestly do not proceed *from* duty. I set aside also those actions which are not actually inconsistent with duty, but which yet are done under the impulse of some natural inclination, although *not a direct inclination* to do these particular actions; for in these it is easy to determine whether the action that is consistent with duty, is done *from duty* or with some selfish object in view. It is more difficult to make a clear distinction of motives when there is a *direct* inclination to do a certain action, which is itself in conformity with duty. The preservation of one's own life, for instance, is a duty; but, as everyone has a natural inclination to preserve his life, the anxious care which most men usually devote to this object, has no intrinsic value, nor the maxim from which they act any moral import. They preserve their life *in accordance with* duty, but not *because of* duty. But, suppose adversity and hopeless sorrow to have taken away all desire for life; suppose that the wretched man would welcome death as a release, and yet takes means to prolong his life simply from a sense of duty; then his maxim has a genuine moral import.

But, secondly, an action that is done from duty gets its moral value, *not from the object* which it is intended to secure, but from the maxim by which it is determined. Accordingly, the action has the same moral value whether the object is attained or not, if only the *principle* by which the will is determined to act is independent of every object of sensuous desire. What was said above makes it clear, that it is not the object aimed at, or, in other words, the consequences which flow from an action when these are made the end and motive of the will, that can give to the action an unconditioned and moral value. In what, then, can the moral value of an action consist, if it does not lie in the will itself, as directed to the attainment of a certain object? It can lie only in the principle of the will, no matter whether the object sought can be attained by the action or not. For the will stands as it were at the parting of the ways, between its *a priori* principle, which is formal, and its *a posteriori,* material motive. As so standing it must be determined by something, and, as no action which is done from duty can be determined by a material principle, it can be determined only by the formal principle of all volition.

From the two propositions just set forth a third directly follows, which may be thus stated: *Duty is the obligation to act from reverence for law.* Now, I may have a natural *inclination* for the object that I expect to follow from my action, but I can never have *reverence* for that which is not a spontaneous activity of my will, but merely an effect of it; neither can I have reverence for any natural inclination, whether it is my own or another's. If it is my own, I can at most only approve of it; if it is manifested by another, I may regard it as conducive to my own interest, and hence I may in certain cases even be said to have a love for it. But the only thing which I can reverence or which can lay me under an obligation to act, is the law which is connected with my will, not as a consequence, but as a principle; a principle which is not dependent upon natural inclination, but overmasters it, or at least allows it to have no influence whatever in determining my course of action. Now if an action which is done out of regard for duty sets entirely aside the influence of natural inclination and along with it every object of the will, nothing else is left by which the will can be determined but objectively the *law* itself, and subjectively *pure reverence* for the law as a principle of action. Thus there arises the maxim, to obey the moral law even at the sacrifice of all my natural inclinations.

The supreme good which we call moral can therefore be nothing but the *idea of the law* in itself, in so far as it is this idea which determines the will, and not any consequences that are expected to follow. Only a *rational* being can have such an idea, and hence a man who acts from the idea of the law is already morally good, no matter whether the consequences which he expects from his action follow or not.

Now what must be the nature of a law, the idea of which is to determine the will, even apart from the effects expected to follow, and which is therefore itself entitled to be called good absolutely and without qualification? As the will must not be moved to act from any desire for the results expected to follow from obedience to a certain law, the only principle of the will which remains is that of the conformity of actions to universal law. In all cases I must act in such a way *that I can at the same time will that my maxim should become a universal law.* This is what is meant by conformity to law pure and simple; and this is the principle which serves, and must serve, to determine the will, if the idea of duty is not to be regarded as empty and chimerical. As a matter of fact the judgments which we are wont to pass upon conduct perfectly agree with this principle, and in making them we always have it before our eyes.

May I, for instance, under the pressure of circumstances, make a promise which I have no intention of keeping? The question is not whether it is prudent to make a false promise, but whether it is morally right. To enable me to answer this question shortly and conclusively, the best way is for me to ask myself whether it would satisfy me that the maxim to extricate myself from embarrassment by giving a false promise should have the force of a universal law, applying to others as well as to myself. And I see at once, that, while I can certainly will the lie, I cannot will that lying should be a universal law. If lying were universal, there would, properly speaking, be no promises whatever. I might say that I intended to do a certain thing at some future time, but nobody would believe me, or if he did at the moment trust to my promise, he would afterwards pay me back in my own coin. My maxim thus proves itself to be self-destructive, so soon as it is taken as a universal law.

Duty, then, consists in the obligation to act from *pure* reverence for the moral law. To this motive all others must give way, for it is the condition of a will which is good *in itself*, and which has a value with which nothing else is comparable.

There is, however, in man a strong feeling of antagonism to the commands of duty, although his reason tells him that those commands are worthy of the highest reverence. For man not only possesses reason, but he has certain natural wants and inclinations, the complete satisfaction of which he calls happiness. These natural inclinations clamorously demand to have their seemingly reasonable claims respected; but reason issues its commands inflexibly, refusing to promise anything to the natural desires, and treating their claims with a sort of neglect and contempt. From this there arises a *natural dialectic,* that is, a disposition to explain away the strict laws of duty, to cast doubt upon their validity, or at least, upon their purity and stringency, and in this way to make them yield to the demands of the natural inclinations.

Thus men are forced to go beyond the narrow circle of ideas within which their reason ordinarily moves, and to take a step into the field of *moral philosophy*, not indeed from any perception of speculative difficulties, but simply on practical grounds. The practical reason of men cannot be long exercised any more than the theoretical, without falling insensibly into a dialectic, which compels it to call in the aid of philosophy; and in the one case as in the other, rest can be found only in a thorough criticism of human reason.

II

So far, we have drawn our conception of duty from the manner in which men employ it in the ordinary exercise of their practical reason. The conception of duty, however, we must not suppose to be therefore derived from experience. On the contrary, we hear frequent complaints, the justice of which we cannot but admit, that no one can point to a single instance in which an action has undoubtedly been done purely from a regard for duty; that there are certainly many actions which are not *opposed* to duty, but none which are indisputably done *from* duty and therefore have a moral value. Nothing indeed can secure us against the complete loss of our ideas of duty, and maintain in the soul a well-grounded respect for the moral law, but the clear conviction, that reason issues its commands on its own authority, without caring in the least whether the actions of men have, as a matter of fact, been done purely from ideas of duty. For reason commands inflexibly that certain actions should be done, which perhaps never have been done; actions, the very possibility of which may seem doubtful to one who bases everything upon experience. Perfect disinterestedness in friendship, for instance, is demanded of every man, although there may never have been a sincere friend; for pure friendship is bound up with the idea of duty as duty, and belongs to the very idea of a reason which determines the will on *a priori* grounds, prior to all experience.

It is, moreover, beyond dispute that unless we are to deny to morality all truth and all reference to a possible object, the moral law has so wide an application that it is binding, not merely upon man, but upon all *rational beings,* and not merely under certain contingent conditions, and with certain limitations, but absolutely and necessarily. And it is plain that no experience could ever lead us to suppose that laws of this apodictic character are even possible.

There is, therefore, no genuine supreme principle of morality, which is not independent of all experience, and based entirely upon pure reason. If, then, we are to have a philosophy of morality at all, as distinguished from a popular moral philosophy, we may take it for granted without further investigation that moral conceptions, together with the principles which flow from them, are given *a priori* and must be presented in their generality (*in abstracto*).

Such a metaphysic of morality, which must be entirely free from all admixture of empirical psychology, theology, physics, and hyperphysics, and above all from all occult or, as we may call them, hypophysical qualities, is not only indispensable as a foundation for a sound theory of duties, but it is also of the highest importance in the practical realization of moral precepts. For the pure idea of duty, unmixed with any foreign ingredient of sensuous desire, in a word, the idea of the moral law, influences the heart of man much more powerfully through his reason, which in this way only becomes conscious that it can of itself be practical, than do all the motives which have their source in experience. Conscious of its own dignity, the moral law treats all sensuous desires with contempt, and is able to master them one by one.

From what has been said it is evident that all moral conceptions have their seat and origin in reason entirely *a priori*, and are apprehended by the ordinary reason of men as well as by reason in its purely speculative activity. We have also seen that it is of the greatest importance, not only in the construction by speculative reason of a theory of morality, but also with a view to the practical conduct of life, to derive the conceptions and laws of morality from pure reason, to present them pure and unmixed, and to mark out the sphere of this whole practical or pure knowledge of reason. Nor is it permissible, in seeking to determine the whole faculty of pure practical reason, to make its principles dependent upon the peculiar nature of human reason, as we were allowed to do, and sometimes were even forced to do, in speculative philosophy, for moral laws must apply to every rational being, and must therefore be derived from the very conception of a rational being as such.

To show the need of advancing not only from the common moral judgments of men to the philosophical, but from a popular philosophy, which merely gropes its way by the help of examples, to a metaphysic of morality, we must begin at the point where the practical faculty of reason supplies general rules of action, and exhibit clearly the steps by which it attains to the conception of duty.

Everything in nature acts in conformity with law. Only a rational being has the faculty of acting in conformity with the *idea* of law, or from principles; only a rational being, in other words, has a will. And as without reason actions cannot proceed from laws, will is simply practical reason.

If the will is infallibly determined by reason, the actions of a rational being are subjectively as well as objectively necessary; that is, will must be regarded as a faculty of choosing *that only* which reason, independently of natural inclination, declares to be practically necessary or good. . . .

Will is conceived of as a faculty of determining itself to action *in accordance with the idea of certain laws*. Such a faculty can belong only to a rational being. Now that which serves as an objective principle for the self-determination of the will is an *end*, and if this end is given purely by reason, it must hold for all rational beings. On the other hand, that which is merely the condition of the possibility of an action the effect of which is the end, is called the *means*. The subjective ground of desire is natural inclination, the objective ground of volition is a motive; hence there is a distinction between subjective ends, which depend upon natural inclination, and objective ends, which are connected with motives that hold for every rational being. Practical principles that abstract from all subjective ends are *formal*; those that presuppose subjective ends, and therefore natural inclinations, are *material*. The ends which a rational being arbitrarily sets before himself as material ends to be produced by his actions, are all merely relative; for that which gives to them their value is simply their relation to the peculiar susceptibility of the subject. They can therefore yield no universal and necessary principles, or practical laws, applicable to all rational beings, and binding upon every will. Upon such relative ends, therefore, only hypothetical imperatives can be based.

Suppose, however, that there is something the existence of which has in itself an absolute value, something which, *as an end in itself*, can be a ground of definite laws; then, there would lie in that, and only in that, the ground of a possible categorical imperative or practical law.

Now, I say, that man, and indeed every rational being as such, *exists* as an end in himself, *not merely as a means* to be made use of by this or that will, and therefore man in all his actions, whether these are directed towards himself or towards other rational beings, must always be regarded as an end. No object of natural desire has more than a conditioned value; for if the natural desires, and the wants to which they give rise, did not exist, the object to which they are directed would have no value at all. So far are the natural desires and wants from having an absolute value, so far are they from being sought simply for themselves, that every rational being must wish to be entirely free from their influence. The value of every object which human action is the means of obtaining, is, therefore, always conditioned. And even beings whose existence depends upon nature, not upon our will, if they are without reason have only the relative value of means, and are therefore called *things*. Rational beings, on the other hand, are called *persons*, because their very nature shows them to be ends in themselves, that is, something which cannot be made use of simply as a means. A person being thus an object of respect, a certain limit is placed upon arbitrary will. Persons are not purely subjective ends, whose existence has a value *for us* as the effect of our actions, but they are *objective ends*, or beings whose existence is an end in itself, for which no other end can be substituted. If all value were conditioned, and therefore contingent, it would be impossible to show that there is any supreme practical principle whatever.

If, then, there is a supreme practical principle, a principle which in relation to the human will is a categorical imperative, it must be an *objective* principle of the will, and must be able to serve as a universal practical law. For, such a principle must be derived from the idea of that which is necessarily an end for everyone because it is an *end in itself*. Its foundation is this, that *rational nature* exists as an end in itself. Man necessarily conceives of his own existence in this way, and so far this is a <u>subjective</u> principle of human action. But in this way also every other rational being conceives of his own existence, and for the very same reason; hence the principle is also *objective*, and from it, as the highest practical ground, all laws of the will must be capable of being derived. The practical imperative will therefore be this: *Act so as to use humanity, whether in your own person or in the person of another, always as an end, never as merely a means.*

The principle that humanity and every rational nature is an end in itself is not borrowed from experience. For, in the first place, because of its universality it applies to all rational beings, and no experience can apply so widely. In the second place, it does not regard humanity subjectively, as an end of man, that is, as an object which the subject of himself actually makes his end, but as an objective end, which ought to be regarded as a law that constitutes the supreme limiting condition of all subjective ends, and which must therefore have its source in pure reason. The objective ground of all practical laws consists in the *rule* and the form of universality, which makes them capable of serving as laws, but their *subjective* ground consists in the *end* to which they are directed. Now, by the second principle, every rational being, as an end in himself, is the subject of all ends. From this follows the third practical principle of the will, which is the supreme condition of its harmony with universal practical reason, namely, the idea of *the will of every rational being as a will which lays down universal laws of action.*

This formula implies that a will which is itself the supreme lawgiver cannot possibly act from interest of any sort in the law, although no doubt a will may stand under the law, and may yet be attached to it by the bond of interest.

At the point we have now reached, it does not seem surprising that all previous attempts to find out the principle of morality should have ended in failure. It was seen that man is bound under law by duty, but it did not strike anyone that the *universal* system of laws to which he is subject are laws which he *imposes upon himself*, and that he is only under obligation to act in conformity with his own will, a will which by the purpose of nature prescribes universal laws. Now so long as man is thought to be merely subject to law, no matter what the law may be, he must be regarded as stimulated or constrained to obey the law from interest of some kind; for as the law does not proceed from *his own* will, there must be *something external* to his will which compels him to act in conformity with it. This perfectly necessary conclusion frustrated every attempt to find a supreme principle of duty. Duty was never established, but merely the necessity of acting from some form of interest, private or public. The imperative was therefore necessarily always conditioned, and could not possibly have the force of a moral command. The supreme principle of morality I shall therefore call the principle of the *autonomy* of the will, to distinguish it from all other principles, which I call principles of *heteronomy*.

The conception that every rational being in all the maxims of his will must regard himself as prescribing universal laws, by reference to which himself and all his actions are to be judged, leads to a cognate and very fruitful conception, that of a *kingdom of ends*.

By *kingdom*, I mean the systematic combination of different rational beings through the medium of common laws. Now, laws determine certain ends as universal, and hence, if abstraction is made from the individual differences of rational beings, and from all that is peculiar to their priviate ends, we get the idea of a complete totality of ends conbined in a system; in other words, we are able to conceive of a kingdom of ends, which conforms to the principles formulated above.

All rational beings stand under the law that each should treat himself and others, *never simply as means*, but always as *at the same time as ends in themselves*. Thus there arises a systematic combination of rational beings through the medium of common objective laws. This may well be called a kingdom of ends, because the object of those laws is just to relate all rational beings to one another as ends and means. Of course this kingdom of ends is merely an ideal. . . . In the realm of ends everything has either a price or *dignity*. Whatever has a price can be replaced by something else which is *equivalent*; whatever is above all price, and therefore has no equivalent, has dignity.

3. SCHILLER: The Beautiful Is Educational

A study of Friedrich von Schiller (1759–1805), German poet, dramatist, Kantian scholar, gives an initial balance of vision to our examination of the romantics and later nineteenth-century thinkers. He is both a step toward pure romanticism (if such exists) and a cautious step to the side. His reconnoitering movement is a reminder that at every moment there was more to the age than a one-track emotional extravagance.

The step toward romanticism is Schiller's contention that only when Kant's practical reason becomes an emotional and volitional force can it become a decisive factor in human history. He objects to Kant's rigid distinction between moral duty on the one hand and sentiment and inclination on the other. For Schiller, the wedding of the possible (the ideal) and the necessary is to take place through the esthetic education of man; only in the appreciation of beauty is the moral ideal actually inspiring, that is, behaviorally effective. This is a development of the hint contained in Kant's most nearly romantic work, *Critique of Judgment*: The beautiful is a symbol of the moral ideal.

The step to the side *vis-à-vis* romanticism—the caution and respect for perspective—is Schiller's realism. By this slippery word I simply mean his belief that there is a brute element in experience, a "happened upon," which is real in its own way and which is not already structured by mind—is not ideal. Unlike most romantics, then, Schiller is not a metaphysical monist and idealist; indeed, he has been called a classicist. His realism is a dualism which corresponds in a way to Plato's: the ideal forms on the one hand and brute matter on the other—mud, hair, and filth. In the latter category Schiller would assign untrained emotions. Hence along with his realism and dualism goes his keen sense of the difficulty involved in attaining a balance between the emotional and rational factors in human experience (an absolute dichotomy need not be intended), a keen sense of the difficulties of freedom. With too much emotion there is libertinism, soon fear of all freedom, then acceptance of despotic protection; with too little emotion there is impotence. What is required, says Schiller, is a new education which is "a task for more than one century." As we see in *The Aesthetic Education of Man* (1795),* Schiller inserts ominous remarks about the future, which recalls Rousseau and which is in marked contrast to claims of human perfectibility and implicit divinity made by some romantics of the more extreme sort (Lorenz Oken [1779–1851], for example).

LETTER II

I might perhaps make a better use of the opening you afford me if I were to direct your mind to a loftier theme than that of art. It would appear to be unseasonable to go in search of a code for the aesthetic world, when the moral world offers matter of so much higher interest, and when the spirit of philosophical inquiry is so stringently challenged by the circumstances of our times to occupy itself with the most perfect of all works of art—the establishment and structure of a true political freedom.

Nevertheless, I think I can not only excuse, but even justify by solid grounds, my step in resisting this attractive purpose and in preferring beauty to freedom. I hope that I shall succeed in convincing

* Based on an unsigned translation, in *Works of Schiller*, ed. N. H. Dole (Boston: Wyman Fogg Company, 1902).

you that this matter of art is less foreign to the needs than to the tastes of our age; nay, that, to arrive at a solution even in the political problem, the road of aesthetics must be pursued, because it is through beauty that we arrive at freedom. . . .

LETTER III

. . . Now the term natural condition can be applied to every political body which owes its establishment originally to forces and not to laws, and such a state contradicts the moral nature of man, because lawfulness can alone have authority over this. At the same time this natural condition is quite sufficient for the physical man, who only gives himself laws in order to get rid of brute force. Moreover, the physical man is a *reality*, and the moral man *problematical*. Therefore when the reason suppresses the natural condition, as she must if she wishes to substitute her own, she weighs the real physical man against the problematical moral man, she weighs the existence of society against a possible, though morally necessary, ideal of society. She takes from man something which he really possesses, and without which he possesses nothing, and refers him as a substitute to something that he ought to possess and might possess; and if reason had relied too exclusively on him she might, in order to secure him a state of humanity in which he is wanting and can want without injury to his life, have robbed him even of the means of animal existence, which is the first necessary *condition* of his being a man. Before he had opportunity to hold firm to the law with his will, reason would have withdrawn from his feet the ladder of nature.

The great point is, therefore, to reconcile these two considerations, to prevent physical society from ceasing for a moment *in time*, while the moral society is being formed in the *idea*; in other words, to prevent its existence from being placed in jeopardy for the sake of the moral dignity of man. When the mechanic has to mend a watch he lets the wheels run out; but the living watchworks of the state have to be repaired while they act, and a wheel has to be exchanged for another during its revolutions. Accordingly props must be sought for to support society and keep it going while it is made independent of the natural conditon from which it is sought to emancipate it.

This prop is not found in the natural character of man, who, being selfish and violent, directs his energies rather to the destruction than to the preservation of society. Nor is it found in his moral character, which has yet to be formed, and which can never be worked upon or calculated on by the lawgiver, because it is free and *never appears*.* It would seem, therefore, that another measure must be adopted. It would seem that the physical character of the arbitrary must be separated from moral freedom; that it is incumbent to make the former harmonise with the laws and the latter dependent on impressions; it would be expedient to remove the former still farther from matter and to bring the latter somewhat more near to it; in short, to produce a third character related to both the others—the physical and the moral—paving the way to a transition from the sway of mere force to that of law, without preventing the proper development of the moral character, but serving rather as a pledge in the sensuous sphere of a morality in the unseen. . . .

Can this effect of harmony be attained by the state? That is not possible, for the state, as at present constituted, has given occasion to evil, and the state as conceived in the idea, instead of being able to establish this more perfect humanity, ought to be based upon it. Thus the researches in which I have indulged would have brought me back to the same point from which they had called me off for a time. The present age, far from offering us this form of humanity, which we have acknowledged as a necessary condition of an improvement of the state, shows us rather the diametrically opposite form. If, therefore the principles I have laid down are correct, and if experience confirms the picture I have traced of the present time, it would be necessary to qualify as unseasonable every attempt to effect a similar change in the state, and all hope as chimerical that would be based on such an attempt, until the division of the inner man ceases, and nature has been sufficiently developed to become herself the instrument of this great change and secure the reality of the political creation of reason.

In the physical creation, nature shows us the road that we have to follow in the moral creation. Only when the struggle of elementary forces has ceased in inferior organisations does nature rise to the noble form of the physical man. In like manner, the conflict of the elements of the moral man and that of blind instincts must have ceased, and a coarse antagonism in himself, before the attempt can be hazarded. On the other hand, the independence of man's charac-

---

* The moral self for Kant is a "thing in itself"—a noumenon, not a phenomenon or appearance. See the introductions to Fichte and Schelling. (Ed.)

ter must be secured, and his submission to despotic forms must have given place to a suitable liberty, before the variety in his constitution can be made subordinate to the unity of the ideal. When the man of nature still makes such an anarchical abuse of his will, his liberty ought hardly to be disclosed to him. And when the man fashioned by culture makes so little use of his freedom, his free will ought not to be taken from him. The concession of liberal principles becomes a treason to social order when it is associated with a force still in fermentation, and increases the already exuberant energy of its nature. Again, the law of conformity under one level becomes tyranny to the individual when it is allied to a weakness already holding sway and to natural obstacles, and when it comes to extinguish the last spark of spontaneity and of originality.

The tone of the age must therefore rise from its profound moral degradation; on the one hand it must emancipate itself from the blind service of nature, and on the other it must revert to its simplicity, its truth, and its fruitful sap; a sufficient task for more than a century. However, I admit readily, more than one special effort may meet with success, but no improvement of the whole will result from it, and contradictions in action will be a continual protest against the unity of maxims. It will be quite possible, then, that in remote corners of the world humanity may be honoured in the person of the Negro, while in Europe it may be degraded in the person of the thinker. The old principles will remain, but they will adopt the dress of the age, and philosophy will lend its name to an oppression that was formerly authorised by the Church. In one place, alarmed at the liberty which in its opening efforts always shows itself an enemy, it will cast itself into the arms of a convenient servitude. In another place, reduced to despair by a pedantic tutelage, it will be driven into the savage license of the state of nature. Usurpation will invoke the weakness of human nature, and insurrection will invoke its dignity, till at length the great sovereign of all human things, blind force, shall come in and decide, like a vulgar pugilist, this pretended contest of principles.

LETTER VIII

Must philosophy therefore retire from this field, disappointed in its hopes? Whilst in all other directions the dominion of forms is extended, must this the most precious of all gifts be abandoned to a formless chance? Must the contest of blind forces last eternally in the political world, and is social law never to triumph over a hating egotism?

Not in the least. It is true that reason herself will never attempt directly a struggle with this brutal force which resists her arms, and she will be as far as the son of Saturn in the Iliad from descending into the dismal field of battle, to fight them in person. But she chooses the most deserving among the combatants, clothes him with divine arms as Jupiter gave them to his son-in-law, and by her triumphing force she finally decides the victory.

Reason has done all that she could in finding the law and promulgating it; it is for the energy of the will and the ardour of feeling to carry it out. To issue victoriously from her contest with force, truth herself must first become a *force*, and turn one of the instincts of man into her champion in the empire of phenomena. For instincts are the only motive forces in the material world. If hitherto truth has so little manifested her victorious power, this has not depended on the understanding, which could not have unveiled it, but on the heart which remained closed to it and on instinct which did not act with it.

Whence, in fact, proceeds this general sway of prejudices, this night of the understanding in the midst of the light disseminated by philosophy and experience? The age is enlightened, that is to say, that knowledge, obtained and vulgarised, suffices to set right at least our practical principles. The spirit of free inquiry has dissipated the erroneous opinions which long barred the access to truth, and has undermined the ground on which fanaticism and deception had erected their throne. Reason has purified itself from the illusions of the senses and from a mendacious sophistry, and philosophy herself raises her voice and exhorts us to return to the bosom of nature, to which she had first made us unfaithful. Whence then is it that we remain still barbarians?

There must be something in the spirit of man—as it is not in the objects themselves—which prevents us from receiving the truth, notwithstanding the brilliant light she diffuses, and from accepting her, whatever may be her strength for producing conviction. This something was perceived and expressed by an ancient sage in this very significant maxim: *Sapere aude*.*

Dare to be wise! A spirited courage is required to triumph over the

* Dare to be wise.

impediments that the indolence of nature as well as the cowardice of the heart oppose to our instruction. It was not without reason that the ancient mythos made Minerva issue fully armed from the head of Jupiter, for it is with warfare that this instruction commences. From its very outset it has to sustain a hard fight against the senses, which do not like to be roused from their easy slumber. The greater part of men are much too exhausted and enervated by their struggle with want to be able to engage in a new and severe contest with error. Satisfied if they themselves can escape from the hard labour of thought, they willingly abandon to others the guardianship of their thoughts. And if it happens that nobler necessities agitate their soul, they cling with a greedy faith to the formula that the state and the Church hold in reserve for such cases. If these unhappy men deserve our compassion, those others deserve our just contempt, who, though set free from those necessities by more fortunate circumstances, yet willingly bend to their yoke. These latter persons prefer this twilight of obscure ideas, where the feelings have more intensity, and the imagination can at will create convenient chimeras, to the rays of truth which put to flight the pleasant illusions of their dreams. They have founded the whole structure of their happiness on these very illusions, which ought to be combated and dissipated by the light of knowledge, and they would think they were paying too dearly for a truth which begins by robbing them of all that has value in their sight. It would be necessary that they should be already sages to love wisdom: a truth that was felt at once by him to whom philosophy owes its name.*

It is therefore not going far enough to say that the light of the understanding only deserves respect when it reacts on the character; to a certain extent it is from the character that this light proceeds; for the road that terminates in the head must pass through the heart. Accordingly, the most pressing need of the present time is to educate the sensibility, because it is the means, not only to render efficacious in practice the improvement of ideas, but to call this improvement into existence.

LETTER IX

But perhaps there is a vicious circle in our previous reasoning! Theoretical culture must, it seems, bring along with it practical cul-

* The Greek word means, as is known, love of wisdom.

ture, and yet the latter must be the condition of the former. All improvement in the political sphere must proceed from the ennobling of the character. But, subject to the influence of a social constitution still barbarous, how can character become ennobled? It would then be necessary to seek for this end an instrument that the state does not furnish, and to open sources that would have preserved themselves pure in the midst of political corruption.

I have now reached the point to which all the considerations tended that have engaged me up to the present time. This instrument is the art of the beautiful; these sources are open to us in its immortal models.

Art, like science, is emancipated from all that is positive, and all that is humanly conventional; both are completely independent of the arbitrary will of man. The political legislator may place their empire under an interdict, but he cannot reign there. He can proscribe the friend of truth, but truth subsists; he can degrade the artist, but he cannot change art. No doubt, nothing is more common than to see science and art bend before the spirit of the age, and creative taste receive its law from critical taste. When the character becomes stiff and hardens itself, we see science severely keeping her limits, and art subject to the harsh restraint of rules; when the character is relaxed and softened, science endeavours to please and art to rejoice. For whole ages philosophers as well as artists show themselves occupied in letting down truth and beauty to the depths of vulgar humanity. They themselves are swallowed up in it; but, thanks to their essential vigour and indestructible life, the true and the beautiful make a victorious fight, and issue triumphant from the abyss. . . .

But how will the artist avoid the corruption of his time which encloses him on all hands? By despising its opinion. Let him raise his eyes to his own dignity, and to law; let him not lower them to necessity and fortune. Equally exempt from a vain activity which would imprint its trace on the fugitive moment, and from the dreams of an impatient enthusiasm which applies the measure of the absolute to the paltry productions of time, let the artist abandon the real to the understanding, for that is its proper field. But let the artist endeavour to give birth to the ideal by the union of the possible and of the necessary. Let him stamp illusion and truth with the image of this ideal; let him apply it to the play of his imagination and his most serious actions, in short, to all sensuous and spiritual forms; then let him quietly launch his work into infinite time. . . .

4. HERDER: The Part Reflects the Whole

If one wished to play the game of picking the first romantic, he could do worse than to choose Johann Herder (1744–1803), German philosopher, poet and critic. (Of course, Ovid would not be such a bad choice either.) Although not given their paradigmatic statement, nearly all the themes of romanticism are introduced in Herder's work. There is the romantic sense of history: The past is studied neither as a static entity nor merely for its own sake, but for that of the present and future. One finds idealism, organicism, monism, pantheism: An "ideal influence" is the single bond of creation; all the galaxies swimming in space are "bright drops out of the ocean of Deity"; the dewdrop on a rose (the microcosm) displays the law of the whole (the macrocosm). Opposites are conceived as interdependent—"unity only through variety and union only through opposition"—from which derives Herder's contention that life is dependent upon death. Or rather, life is dependent upon *apparent* death, since real death would be total inactivity, which is impossible in a world of total and continuous change. His argument for life's dependence is this: To continue to be in a world of change, one must continue to change; but to be mature, one must have been immature in the past, and one must decline from maturity in the future, since that is the only direction change can take. Individual life arises only because it can sink back into the generating whole, which is ever young. We love our lives best when we love our timely deaths. Obviously, there is a tendency here to be optimistic about progress.

Herder was a dissident student of Kant and a seminal teacher of the thinkers of the age; his influence of Goethe in the Strasbourg era was profound. *God: Some Conversations*, from which the selection* is taken, was written while he was still occupied with his historical and philoslophical magnum opus, *Ideas.*

. . . What I should like to call your attention to are the simple laws by which all living forces of nature produce their thousandfold organizations; for everything which the highest Wisdom does must be in the highest degree simple. The laws, then, seem to me to consist in three words which again are fundamentally only one living conception:

* The selection is from "The Fifth Conversation." My thanks to the Hafner Publishing Company of New York City for their very kind permission to use this translation by Frederick H. Burkhardt.

1. Persistence: that is, the inner persistence of every being.
2. The union of likes and repulsion of opposites.
3. Assimilation to self, and reproduction of one's nature in another.

If, to use your expression, Theano, you would also like to hear me stammer about this, then my speech is at your service. We at least, Philolaus, shall thereby crown our discussion of Spinoza, for you know that he himself constructed his moral philosophy on these conceptions.

First, then: Every being is what it is, and has neither any conception of nothingness, nor any desire for it. The whole perfection of a thing is its reality. The awareness of this reality is the inherent reward of its existence, its inner joy. In the so-called moral world, which is also a natural world, Spinoza sought to refer all the passions and strivings of man back to this inner love for existence and for persistence therein. In the physical world, there have been various names, in part unworthy, given to the phenomena which follow from this law of nature. Now it is called the "force of inertia," since everything remains what it is and does not change without a cause; and then again it is called, though from another point of view, the "force of gravity," according to which everything has its center of gravity upon which it rests. Like their opposite, motion, inertia and gravity are only appearances, since space and body themselves are only appearances. The true essential in everything is persistence, continuation of its existence, which it neither can nor wants to disturb. That everything thus strives after a condition of persistence, its structure itself shows, and you, Theano, as a sketcher of nature, will be able to explain much in the form of things if you pay attention to this. Let us take the easiest example from the system of those things which combine the greatest homogeneity with the greatest mobility and which can thus, as it were, elect a form. We call this class, fluid things. Very well, then, Philolaus, what form is assumed by all fluid things whose parts tend to work unhindered toward homogeneity with one another?

PHILOLAUS: The form of a drop.

THEOPHRON: And why a drop? Should we perhaps assume a drop-forming principle in nature which arbitrarily prefers this form?

PHILOLAUS: By no means! The drop is a sphere. In a sphere all the parts homogeneously surround a central point in harmony and order. The sphere rests upon itself; its center of gravity is in the middle. Its form is thus the most beautiful state of persistence of homogeneous entities which enter into connection around this middle point and counterbalance one another with equal forces. Thus a world comes into being in the drop according to necessary laws of harmony and order.

THEOPHRON: Consequently, dear Philolaus, in the law by which the drop is formed, you have at the same time the law by which our earth, the sun, and all heavenly systems are formed. For our earth, too, once emerged from the fluid state and was collected in a drop. So the sun and that whole system in which it rules with attracting power is a greater drop. Everything tends to gravitate toward a center and is only maintained in its revolution by other forces. Thus the revolution of all planets must more or less approximate a circle. The sun in its system, together with a million other suns, again forms a circle or an ellipse in which they all move about a common middle- or focal-point, as is shown by the Milky Way and by those systems of suns, the Nebulae. All are bright drops out of the ocean of the Deity, which sought their state of persistence according to inherent eternal laws of harmony and order in their structure and motion, and found it. Not otherwise than in the form of the sphere and in revolution, the product of opposite forces, could they find it; not through arbitrariness, but in accordance with inherent laws of homogeneously working forces in fluidity, in spherical form, in elliptical revolution. The little tear, Theano, which you find of a morning in the calyx of a rose, shows you the law by which earth, suns, and all solar, yes, even world-systems took form. For if we permit our fancy the vast flight of conceiving the entire universe, the result is not a colossus but a sphere which rests upon itself.

THEANO: Thank you, Theophron, for the immeasurably expansive view which rests on such a simple self-supporting law of nature. But come back to our earth, or at least to our solar system, for I do not like to fly so high. You spoke of a second law of nature, that likes attract, and opposites repel each other. Won't you give examples of this?

THEOPHRON: I shall keep to my fluid drop. You know, do you not, Theano, the stone of hate and love in the natural world?

THEANO: You mean the magnetic stone?

THEOPHRON: None other, and although the theory of it is still very obscure, the experiences with it are by comparison the more plain. You know, then, its two poles and their friendly or inimical activity?

THEANO: I know them, and I also know that there is a point of greatest love and a point of complete indifference on its axis.

THEOPHRON: Then you know all that I need for my example. Consider the magnet as a round drop in which the magnetic force is distributed so homogeneously and evenly, that its opposite ends form the north and soul poles. You know that one cannot come into being without the other.

THEANO: I know that, and also that if one changes one, one changes both.

THEOPHRON: Then you have in the magnet the most beautiful image of what hate and love in nature are, and I am sure that the identical thing will be found in many, and perhaps in all fluids.

PHILOLAUS: And that identical thing is—?

THEOPHRON: That wherever a system of homogeneous forces acquires an axis, they so dispose themselves about it and about their middle point, that every like force flows to the like pole; and from it they are ordered according to geometrical laws through all the grades of progression to a culmination, and then through the point of indifference to the opposite pole. Every sphere would in this way be a union of two hemispheres with opposite poles, as every ellipse with its two foci. And the laws of this construction would according to fixed laws lie in the active forces of the system which is thus formed. Just as there cannot be a north pole without a south pole in a sphere, so too in a regularly formed system of forces there can be no structure in which the friendly and the inimical are not likewise separated; and hence it forms a whole precisely through the counterbalance which the two effect with one another according to increasing and diminishing grades of the union. There could probably be no system of electrical forces in the world, if there were not two electricities in opposition to one another, which have, moreover, actually been found by experience. It is the same with heat and cold, and probably the same with every system of forces which can maintain unity only through variety, and union only through opposition. Empirical natural science, which is still so young, will one day advance so far in all this, that it will finally banish from the world all blind arbitrariness, in which everything would fall apart and all the laws of nature would cease. For you must concede to me, my friends, that if the magnet, electrical force, light, heat and cold, attraction, gravity and so on, function arbitrarily, if the triangle is no triangle, and the circle no circle, then we could declare all the observations of physics and mathematics to be nonsense, and wait for arbitrary revelations. But if it is certain that we have already found mathematically exact laws of nature in so many forces, who will dare to set the limits where they are no longer to be found, and where the blind will of God begins? In Creation, everything is connection and order. Thus if only a single natural law exists anywhere in it, natural laws must prevail everywhere, or else creation would fall apart like a chaos.

THEANO: But, my friend, you are getting away from the law of hate and love, whereby, according to your system, the one cannot be without the other.

THEOPHRON: Because everything exists in the world that can exist, opposites must also exist, and a law of the highest Wisdom must everywhere form a system out of this opposition, out of this north and south pole. In every region of nature there is the table of the thirty-two winds, in every ray of sunlight the whole color prism, and it is only a question of which wind blows now and then, which color appears here and there. As soon as the solid emerges from the fluid, everything is crystallized and formed in accordance with the inner laws which lie in our system of active forces. Everything attracts, repels, or remains indifferent to everything else, and the axis of these active forces is continuous throughout all gradations. The chemist institutes nothing but marriages and divorces; nature does so in a much richer, deeper way. Everything seeks and finds its mutual love, and natural science itself could not help adopting the expression, "elective attraction" for the combinations of bodies. Opposites repel one another and are brought together in the point of indifference. Often the forces interchange rapidly, whole systems behaving differently, as do the individual forces of the system among themselves. Hate can become love, love hate—all for one and the same reason, that every system seeks to persist in itself and orders its forces to that end. Thus you see how cautious one must be with analogies between external phenomena, since merely because we find several similar laws in them, one is not immediately justified in considering magnetism, for example, to be the same as electricity. The systems of forces can be very different from one another and yet function in accordance with the same laws, because finally everything in nature must be interconnected, and there can be but one principal law, according to which even the most different forces are ordered.

THEANO: Your law of persistence, of hatred and love, in my opinion, comes very close to this principal law; for it appears everywhere regardless of all the innumerable differences and opposed phenomena in nature. I should like to be a higher spirit for a few minutes, that I might observe this great workshop from the inside.

THEOPHRON: Do not wish that, Theano! The spectator from the outside has perhaps a better, or at least a more agreeable, view than an observer from inside who could never survey the whole either. The spectator in front of the stage is more comfortable than he who peeps from the wings. The search for truth has the greater charm; the possession of it may make one satiated and indolent. To pursue nature, first to conjecture her lofty laws, then to observe, test and confirm them, then to find them verified a thousandfold and to apply them anew, finally, to perceive everywhere the same wisest law, the same divine necessity, to come to love it and make it one's own—all this gives human life its value. For, good Theano, are we merely spectators? Are we not ourselves actors, participants in nature, and her followers? Do not hate and love reign also in the kingdom of man? And are not both equally necessary for the formation of the whole? He who cannot hate, cannot love either, only he must learn to hate rightly and love rightly. There is also a point of indifference amongst men, but praise God! in the whole magnetic axis, this is but one single point.

PHILOLAUS: Now I must remind you, Theophron, that you still owe us your third part of the great law of nature, namely: "How beings assimilate one to another and form a continuous series in the reproduction of their kind."

THEANO: I need not leave at this point, need I, Theophron?

THEOPHRON: In the name of all the Graces no, Theano! For we are discussing the most hallowed and certainly divine law. All things that love one another, become assimilated the one to the other. As two colors flow together so that a third intermediate one is produced, so in a wonderful manner, human souls, yes, even facial expressions and features, the subtlest shades of thought and action, become like one another through mutual intercourse. Insanity, illness, fanaticism, fear and all passions, are infectious evils not because of that which is evil or nothingness in them, but because of the strength of their active forces. How then should not the activity of regular forces, that is order, harmony and beauty extend and impart itself to others with much more vital power? We saw that organizations come into being only because stronger forces attract weaker ones into their province, and cast them into a form according to the implanted laws of a necessary goodness and truth. All goodness imparts itself. It has the nature of God, who could do nothing else but impart Himself; it has also His infallible efficacy. The laws of beauty for example, urge themselves upon us, they shine upon us, they pass over into us imperceptibly, and this is precisely the secret of the universally connected, active, self-existent creation. The friendly intercourse of human souls makes them similar to one another without compulsion, without words. As Leibnitz assumed an ideal influence of the monads upon one another, so I should like to make this ideal influence the secret bond of creation, which we observe irrepressible and indestructible in thinking and acting beings. Let no one despair of the efficacy of its existence. The more order there is in it, and the more it acts conformably to the laws of nature, the more infallible is its activity. Like God, it works omnipotently, and cannot do otherwise than bring order into a chaos around it, and dispel darkness so that there will be light. It makes similar to its beautiful form all that is in agreement with it, yes, more or less, even that which is in opposition to it.

THEANO: A comforting, beautiful truth, Theophron! It already bears the seal of truth in speaking to our heart and by recalling to me a thousand experiences of my life. There is an unnamable force in the existence of a person, in the way in which his active, calm example works. Everything good in me became mine in this manner. Your way of thinking, Theophron, pleases me because it makes present in all that is about me the all-active One who, according to essential laws of harmony and beauty, acts upon us through the existence of His creatures themselves. Now I feel that everything living in His realm should become like God, yes, if I may say so, must become like Him. His nature, His thoughts and activities force themselves upon us as immutable laws, even against our will in thousand upon thousand proofs of His order, goodness and beauty. He who does not wish to follow, must follow; for everything compels him; he cannot escape the all-powerful chain. Happy he who follows willingly! He possesses the sweet, illusory reward that he is forming himself, although God unremittingly forms him. In that he obeys intelligently and serves with love, all creatures and events stamp him with the imprint of the Deity. He becomes intelligent, good, orderly, happy. He becomes like God.—But let us return to the physical economy of things. Is there not compulsion in the fact that one force overthrows another, attracts it to itself and unites it with its nature? When I observe that all the life of creatures depends upon the destruction of other species, that man lives on animals, animals on one another, or only on plants and fruits, then, to be sure, I see organic wholes which form themselves, but which at the same time destroy others. That is to say, I see murder and death in creation. Is not a blade of grass a flower, the fruit of a tree, and finally an animal which becomes the food of another, just as beautiful an organization as that which destructively converts it into itself? Theophron, drive away this cloud for me, which is drawn like a veil over my view of the sun beaming from every created thing!

THEOPHRON: It will flee, Theano, when you observe that without this apparent death in creation all would be real death, that is, an inactive quiescence, an empty realm of shadows in which all true, active existence would die. Just now you spoke like a disciple of Plato. Have you not found in your teacher, that in the changing, all is change, that on the wing of time, all is process, haste and migration? Stop but one wheel in creation, and all wheels stand still. Permit one point of what we call matter to be dead and inactive, then death is everywhere. Philolaus, you are not under the unphilosophical illusion that there is, for example, an absolutely solid body in nature, are you?

PHILOLAUS: How could I be? All motion would thereby be frustrated, and, however small it might be, it would stop the wheels of all creation.

THEOPHRON: Very well then! If there can be no absolute rest, no complete impenetrability, solidity, inertia, which would be an all-vitiating nothingness and hence a contradiction, then, my friends, we must venture in our thoughts upon Plato's stream, where everything mutable is a wave, where everything temporal is a dream. You are frightened, Theano? Do not fear! It is the wave of a river which is all existence itself, the dream of a self-dependent, essential truth. The Eternal who wanted to become revealed in temporal phenomena, the Indivisible who wanted to become visible in spatial structure, could not do otherwise than give to each form the shortest and at the same time the longest existence which its appearance demanded in accordance with the image of space and time. All that appears must disappear. It disappears as soon as it can, but it also stays as long as it can. Here, as everywhere, the two extremes fall together, and are, as a matter of fact, one and the same. Every finite being, as a phenomenon, brings the seed of destruction with it. With unremitting pace it hastens to its apogee so that it may hasten down and become, to our senses, the most minute. You observe that this is implied even in the structure of the line which I draw for you here.

THEANO: Sad observation!

THEOPHRON: Observe the flower, how it hastens to its bloom. It draws sap, air, light and all elements to itself, and fashions them so that it grows, prepares vital fluid, and puts forth a blossom. The blossom exists and disappears. It has applied all its force, its love and life to become a mother, to leave images of itself behind, and to multiply its potent existence by propagation. But now its appearance too is ended. It has consumed it in the indefatigable service of nature, and one can say that it worked toward its destruction from the beginning of its life. But what is destroyed in it save an appearance which could no longer maintain itself, which, when it had attained the apogee of the line, in which the form and degree of its beauty consisted, hastened down again? It did not do this, now that it was dead, as if to make place for younger, living appearances. That would be a sad picture. But rather, during its life, with all the joy of existence, it brought the latter into being, and left in it a seed of the wisest, most beautiful form for the ever-blooming garden of time in which it too had bloomed. For it itself did not die with this appearance. The force of its root continues. It will wake again out of its winter sleep and arise in new beauty of spring and youth with the daughters of those beings which are now its friends and sisters, standing beside it virginal and fair. There is thus no death in creation. It is a hastening away of that which cannot remain; it is the working of an eternally young, indefatigable, enduring force, which in accordance with its nature cannot be inactive, motionless, or unoccupied for a moment. It works incessantly in the richest, most beautiful way toward its own and as many other existences as it can produce and impart. In a world in which everything changes, every force is in eternal activity, and hence in eternal metamorphosis of its organs. For this transformation itself is the expression of its indestructible activity, replete with wisdom, goodness and beauty. As long as the flower lived, it worked toward its own bloom, and toward the reproduction of its existence. Through its own organic powers it became a creator, the highest thing a creature can become. When it died, it withdrew a spent appearance from the world. The inner living force which produced and maintained it drew back into itself, in order to reveal itself once more to the world in rejuvenated beauty. Can you imagine a more beautiful law of wisdom and goodness in what is called change, Theano, than that everything presses on in the greatest haste to new life, to new youth and beauty, and therefore changes every moment?

THEANO: I see a beautiful glimmer, Theophron, but I do not yet see the dawn.

THEOPHRON: Then think of all the forces of nature in this incessant work, in this haste to change on the wing of time. Not the smallest of a leaf can be inactive for a moment, or there would be death in creation. It attracts, it repels, it respires. For that reason, Theano, the leaf is formed with its two sides so different. The forces dwelling in it are eternally changing their organic dress. Life, thus, is movement, activity, the activity of an inner force, united with the deepest enjoyment of and striving for persistence. And since nothing can remain unchanged in the realm of change, and yet everything wants to and must maintain its existence, everything is in this state of incessant motion, this eternal palingenesis so that it will last eternally and appear eternally young.

THEANO: But is this change also progress?

THEOPHRON: Supposing it were not! It would still be the only means of escaping death, and an eternal death. That is, it would maintain our living force in continual activity, in an inwardly felt existence. It would then be as desirable a benefit as an eternal life is more desirable than an eternal death. But then, Theano, can you very well conceive of an unceasing life, a continually operative force without continual operation, that is, an advance without advancement?

THEANO: It seems a contradiction.

THEOPHRON: And it is one! Every force which takes on appearances in space and time must indeed keep the limits which space and time give it. But with every activity it makes its subsequent activity easier. And, since it cannot do this otherwise than by implanted, internal laws of harmony, wisdom and goodness which, as you have yourself remarked, are benevolently forced upon every creature, impressed upon it, and which assist it in every one of its activities, therefore you see everywhere a progress out of chaos into order, an inner increase and enhanced beauty of forces in ever-widening limits according to ever more observed laws of harmony and order. Every blind force is infused with light, every lawless power with reason and goodness. None of its operations, no activity in creation was in vain. Thus there must be progress, advance in the realm of God, since there can be no standstill, and still less a regress. Moreover, our eye need not be repelled by the forms of death, for if there is no death in creation, then there is no form of death. Whatever this be called, decay, ailment, trituration, it is the transition to new young organization, the old outworn silkworm spinning its cocoon so that it will appear as a new creature. Are you content, Theano?

THEANO: I am, and I resign myself to the wisest, highest goodness which brought me here and gave me undeservedly, but certainly not for nothing, so many powers, and which surrounds me with a thousand forces full of love and goodness with which to order my reason, my heart, my actions according to one eternal law of necessary self-grounded wisdom and goodness.—But Philolaus, you are silent and let me speak, who should and wants to be silent. You even forget your notebook.

PHILOLAUS: I shall catch up and put down at once a list of conclusions which seem to me to follow incontestably from Theophron's system of a truth and goodness necessary in itself. I left off at the second principle. Thus, to continue:*

III. All the forces of nature function organically. Every organization is nothing else than a system of living forces, which serve a principal force in accordance with eternal laws of wisdom, goodness and beauty.

IV. The laws according to which the one rules and the others serve, are: Inherent persistence of every being; union of likes and separation of opposites; finally, assimilation to self and reproduction of one's nature in another. They are activities through which the Deity has revealed Himself, and no other, nor higher ones are conceivable.

V. There is no death in creation, but metamorphosis. Metamorphosis in accordance with the wisest, best law of necessity by which every force in the realm of change seeks to maintain itself ever-new and ever-active, and thus through attraction and repulsion, through friendship and enmity, incessantly changes its organic garb.

VI. There is no rest in creation, for an inactive rest would be

---

* The first two are: I. The highest Existence knew of nothing higher than existence to give his creatures; II. The Deity in whom there is but one essential force which we call power, wisdom and goodness, could produce nothing else than a living impression of the same, which is itself therefore, power, wisdom and goodness, and which must inseparably form the essence of every existence appearing in the world. (Ed.)

death. Every living force is active and continues active. Thus, with every continuation of activity, it progresses and perfects itself according to inner eternal laws of wisdom and goodness, which are urged upon it and inherent in it.

VII. The more it augments itself, the more it works upon others, enlarges its limits, organizes and impresses them with the image of the goodness and beauty that dwells in it. Thus in the whole of nature one necessary law rules, to the effect that order emerges from chaos, that active forces emerge from dormant capacities. The activity of this law is not to be restrained.

VIII. Thus nothing evil which could have reality exists in the realm of God. All that is evil is a nonentity. But we call evil that which is limitation, or opposition, or transition, and none of the three deserves this name. Theophron, I thirst to discuss this point with you. I have in mind a Theodicy of wise necessity.

IX. But, as limits appertain to the measure of every existence in space and time, and, as in the realm of God where everything exists, opposites must also exist, so it appertains to the highest goodness of this realm that opposites themselves help and need each other; because only through the union of the two does a world come into being in every substance, that is to say, an existing, whole being, complete in goodness as well as in beauty.

X. The errors of men also are good to an intelligent mind, for they must soon show themselves as errors to him, and thus help him, by way of contrast, to more light, to purer goodness and truth. Nor is this all arbitrary, but according to eternal laws of reason, order and goodness.

Are you content with my conclusions, Theophron?

THEOPHRON: Entirely! Your keen mind always hastens on ahead of me, Philolaus, like a noble steed for which we only need to open the race-course, and it flies to the goal. I thank the shade of Spinoza for having provided me with such pleasant hours of conversation with you; for opportunities to discuss matters of this sort are rare with me, and yet they singularly elevate the mind and educate it to clear, keen, unique, necessary truth. In addition, these conversations with you afford me a second enjoyment, namely they bring back to me my youthful ideas, with which I spent and surely more than dreamed away many sweet hours at the feet of Leibniz, Shaftesbury and Plato.

THEANO: The better would it please me, Theophron, if you would write down something consecutive on this matter. A conversation fades away, and even a written conversation on matters of this sort always seems to lack something. One is drawn on and is at the end before one realizes it. One always feels, however, an inclination to retrace one's steps.

THEOPHRON: Then retrace the steps, Theano, until the conversation itself, as it were, flows from the soul. Among its many defects, it yet has the merit of keeping us from learning by heart, and true philosophy must never be learned by heart.

THEANO: I wish my brother knew that rule. For some time he has been held captive by a philosophy which confuses both his head and mine as soon as he discusses it. I wish, Theophron, that you would take leave of Spinoza, Descartes, Leibniz and whomever else it may be, and write down only your own thoughts.

THEOPHRON: I am glad to tread in footsteps which already lie before me, Theano. I still lack a great deal to be able to conceive a work on which necessary, eternal Truth would set her seal.

5. SCHLEGEL: The Insight of the Esthetic

If the romantic movement could be said to have a spokesman, then it would be one of the brothers Schlegel, August Wilhelm (1767–1845) and Friedrich (1772–1829). And if the movement could be said to have possessed an official publication for the dissemination of a cultural program, then it would have been the *Athenaeum*, an esthetico-critical journal edited jointly by the brothers and first published in 1798 in Germany. Neither was a great creative artist or a great philosopher in the narrower sense; they nevertheless enjoyed a tremendous appreciation of the history of civilization, and possessed an ardent desire to have it perpetuated on a new level. They are "culture heroes," as the Germans put it.

Their work affords a bird's-eye view of the place of romanticism in the history of the West, at least as the romantics saw it. They regarded romanticism as a synthesis of civilization, a new level of organization in the evolving whole, as necessary to their time as the Thomistic synthesis was to its; except that romanticism had so much more to include: the later Middle Ages, the mountain of Shakespeare's work, a purified new science, the culture of the East newly made available for research, etc.

Wilhelm Schlegel's plea for open-mindedness is really remarkable; he was convinced that we must subject ourselves to the discipline of the

past, be admitted to its world and feel at home there before we can
successfully transcend it in a new whole.

> Translations in prose, or even in verse, in which they are but
> dressed up again in the modern taste, can afford no true idea of the
> Grecian drama. . . . Although our language is extremely flexible,
> and in many respects resembling the Greek, it is after all, a battle
> with unequal weapons; and stiffness and harshness not infrequently
> take the place of the easy sweetness of the Greek. . . . So long
> as we have to struggle with difficulties it is impossible to have any
> true enjoyment of a work of art. To feel the ancients as we ought,
> we must become in some degree one of themselves, and breathe as it
> were the Grecian air.*

Their work contains the essential and synoptic or, if you will, the
classical romantic statement. It was, above all, the sentiment of the age
that needed to be defined; for the romantics were convinced that the
whole man could be revived and set free in a rejuvenated civilization only
if he could become emotionally involved in cultural life. But Friedrich
Schlegel noted the problem: "Sensitiveness of soul is the most glorious,
yet dangerous gift of heaven." He carefully distinguished sentiment from
sentimentality. He does not intend "the common disreputable meaning
of sentimental in which the term connotes almost everything that in
stupid fashion is touching and weepy and brimful of those familiar
noble emotions in the presence of which spineless people are prone to
feel so inexpressibly contented and important."

Friedrich's remarks on "the unknown self" are prophetic. Striving
and effort seem not to achieve the "art of life," and yet someday, at a
twinkling,

> when the abundance of knowledge and of love, like some new-found
> power, shall start suddenly and incomprehensibly into existence, and
> the first thrill of delight be passed, man will doubt to whom he
> should pay his debt of gratitude. He would not dare to appropriate
> to himself what his most passionate exertions have failed to effect
> . . . but he cannot attribute to any extraneous power that of which
> he is so intimately conscious as his own peculiar possession. He has
> gained a new portion of his unknown self: he thanks the unknown
> god! The new-found harmony is not gained by his deserts, but is
> his own act.†

* *Lectures on Dramatic Art and Literature*, translated by John Black (London: George Bell & Sons, 1904), p. 47. The main selection is 18:27.

† *The Aesthetic and Miscellaneous Works of F. Schlegel*, trans. by E.
Millington (London: George Bell & Sons, 1875), p. 424.

All during our apparently vain efforts, subconscious allies are set loose behind the scenes, as William James was later to put it, and when they have reached a critical intensity they erupt into awareness. Of course, if our efforts are misdirected from the beginning, then what are let loose behind the scenes are not allies, but agents destructive to the personality; but this darker side of the subconscious was not so clearly seen by Friedrich Schlegel.

A portion of Wilhelm Schlegel's first lecture on "Dramatic Art and Literature" (1808) exemplifies the historical sense of romanticism. Wilhelm's concern focuses on the problems generated by the inclusion of the spirit of Christianity in the historical synthesis; this spirit is the yearning for the open-ended, the infinite. Not only do the galaxies swim out beyond our ken, but the mind which attempts to grasp this can reflect infinitely on the attempt in which it is engaged; this reflection includes the criticism of its own concepts.

Now, more important even than the search for truth is the search for meaning, Wilhelm suggests; form and meaning, on their outward boundary, are not yet determined. Hence the problem of the modern age, as he sees it, is to modernize our heritage so that form and matter constitute a productive rather than destructive tension. Tension there must be. The problem is to discover a finite symbol of the infinite; and with this he carries us into the philosophical systems of Schelling and Hegel.*

. . . We see numbers of men, and even whole nations, so fettered by the conventions of education and habits of life, that, even in the appreciation of the fine arts, they cannot shake them off. Nothing to them appears natural, appropriate, or beautiful, which is alien to their own language, manners, and social relations. With this exclusive mode of seeing and feeling, it is no doubt possible to attain, by means of cultivation, to great nicety of discrimination within the narrow circle to which it limits and circumscribes them. But no man can be a true critic or connoisseur without universality of mind, without that flexibility which enables him, by renouncing all personal predilections and blind habits, to adapt himself to the peculiarities of other ages and nations—to feel them, as it were, from their proper central point, and, what ennobles human nature, to recognise and duly appreciate whatever is beautiful and grand under the external accessories which were necessary to its embodying, even though occasionally they may seem to disguise and distort it. There is no monopoly of poetry for particular ages and nations; and consequently that despotism in taste, which would seek to invest with universal

* W. Schlegel, *Lectures on Dramatic Art and Literature*, trans. John Black (London: George Bell & Sons, 1904).

authority the rules which at first, perhaps, were but arbitrarily advanced, is but a vain and empty pretension. Poetry, taken in its widest acceptation, as the power of creating what is beautiful, and representing it to the eye or the ear, is a universal gift of Heaven, being shared to a certain extent even by those whom we call barbarians and savages. Internal excellence is alone decisive, and where this exists, we must not allow ourselves to be repelled by the external appearance. Everything must be traced up to the root of human nature: if it has sprung from thence, it has an undoubted worth of its own; but if without possessing a living germ, it is merely externally attached thereto, it will never thrive nor acquire a proper growth. Many productions which appear at first sight dazzling phenomena in the province of the fine arts, and which as a whole have been honoured with the appellation of works of a golden age, resemble the mimic gardens of children: impatient to witness the work of their hands, they break off here and there branches and flowers, and plant them in the earth; everything at first assumes a noble appearance: the childish gardener struts proudly up and down among his showy beds, till the rootless plants begin to droop, and hang their withered leaves and blossoms, and nothing soon remains but the bare twigs, while the dark forest, on which no art of care was ever bestowed, and which towered up towards heaven long before human remembrance, bears every blast unshaken, and fills the solitary beholder with religious awe.

Let us now apply the idea which we have been developing, of the universality of true criticism, to the history of poetry and the fine arts. This, like the so-called universal history, we generally limit (even though beyond this range there may be much that is both remarkable and worth knowing) to whatever has had a nearer or more remote influence on the present civilisation of Europe: consequently, to the works of the Greeks and Romans, and of those of the modern European nations, who first and chiefly distinguished themselves in art and literature. It is well known that, three centuries and a half ago, the study of ancient literature received a new life, by the diffusion of the Grecian language (for the Latin never became extinct); the classical authors were brought to light, and rendered universally accessible by means of the press; and the monuments of ancient art were diligently disinterred and preserved. All this powerfully excited the human mind, and formed a decided epoch in the history of human civilisation; its manifold effects have extended to our times, and will yet extend to an incalculable series of ages. But the study of the ancients was forthwith most fatally perverted. The learned, who were chiefly in the possession of this knowledge, and who were incapable of distinguishing themselves by works of their own, claimed for the ancients an unlimited authority, and with great appearance of reason, since they are models in their kind. Maintaining that nothing could be hoped for the human mind but from an imitation of antiquity, in the works of the moderns they only valued what resembled, or seemed to bear a resemblance to, those of the ancients. Everything else they rejected as barbarous and unnatural. With the great poets and artists it was quite otherwise. However strong their enthusiasm for the ancients, and however determined their purpose of entering into competition with them, they were compelled by their independence and originality of mind to strike out a path of their own, and to impress upon their productions the stamp of their own genius. Such was the case with Dante among the Italians, the father of modern poetry; acknowledging Virgil for his master, he has produced a work which, of all others, most differs from the Aeneid, and in our opinion far excels its pretended model in power, truth, compass, and profundity. It was the same afterwards with Ariosto, who has most unaccountably been compared to Homer, for nothing can be more unlike. So in art with Michael Angelo and Raphael, who had no doubt deeply studied the antique. When we ground our judgment of modern painters merely on their greater or less resemblance to the ancients, we must necessarily be unjust towards them, as Winkelmann undoubtedly has in the case of Raphael. As the poets for the most part had their share of scholarship, it gave rise to a curious struggle between their natural inclination and their imaginary duty. When they sacrificed to the latter, they were praised by the learned; but by yielding to the former, they became the favourites of the people. What preserves the heroic poems of a Tasso and a Camoëns to this day alive in the hearts and on the lips of their countrymen, is by no means their imperfect resemblance to Virgil, or even to Homer, but in Tasso the tender feeling of chivalrous love and honour, and in Camoëns the glowing inspiration of heroic patriotism.

Those very ages, nations, and ranks, who felt least the want of a poetry of their own, were the most assiduous in their imitation of the ancients; accordingly, its results are but dull school exercises, which at best excite a frigid admiration. But in the fine arts, mere imitation is always fruitless; even what we borrow from others, to assume a true poetical shape, must, as it were, be born again within us. Of what avail is all foreign imitation? Art cannot exist without nature, and man can give nothing to his fellow-men but himself.

Genuine successors and true rivals of the ancients, who, by virtue of congenial talents and cultivation have walked in their path and worked in their spirit, have ever been as rare as their mechanical spiritless copyists are common. Seduced by the form, the great body of critics have been but too indulgent to these servile imitators. These were held up as correct modern classics, while the truly great living and popular poets, whose reputation was a part of their nations' glory, and to whose sublimity it was impossible to be altogether blind, were at best but tolerated as rude and wild natural geniuses. But the unqualified separation of genius and taste on which such a judgment proceeds, is altogether untenable. Genius is the almost unconscious choice of the highest degree of excellence, and, consequently, it is taste in its highest activity.

In this state, nearly, matters continued till a period not far back, when several inquiring minds, chiefly Germans, endeavoured to clear up the misconception, and to give the ancients their due, without being insensible to the merits of the moderns, although of a totally different kind. The apparent contradiction did not intimidate them. The groundwork of human nature is no doubt everywhere the same; but in all our investigations, we may observe that, throughout the whole range of nature, there is no elementary power so simple, but that it is capable of dividing and diverging into opposite directions. The whole play of vital motion hinges on harmony and contrast. Why, then, should not this phenomenon recur on a grander scale in the history of man? In this idea we have perhaps discovered the true key to the ancient and modern history of poetry and the fine arts. Those who adopted it, gave to the peculiar spirit of *modern* art, as contrasted with the *antique* or *classical*, the name of *romantic*. The term is certainly not inappropriate; the word is derived from *romance*—the name originally given to the languages which were formed from the mixture of the Latin and the old Teutonic dialects, in the same manner as modern civilisation is the fruit of the heterogeneous union of the peculiarities of the northern nations and the fragments of antiquity; whereas the civilisation of the ancients was much more of a piece.

The distinction which we have just stated can hardly fail to appear well founded, if it can be shown, so far as our knowledge of antiquity extends, that the same contrast in the labours of the ancients and moderns runs symmetrically, I might almost say systematically, throughout every branch of art—that it is as evident in music and the plastic arts as in poetry. This is a problem which, in its full extent, still remains to be demonstrated, though, on particular portions of it, many excellent observations have been advanced already.

Among the foreign authors who wrote before this school can be said to have been formed in Germany, we may mention Rousseau, who acknowledged the contrast in music, and showed that rhythm and melody were the prevailing principles of ancient, as harmony is that of modern music. In his prejudices against harmony, however, we cannot at all concur. On the subject of the arts of design an ingenius observation was made by Hemsterhuys, that the ancient painters were perhaps too much of sculptors, and the modern sculptors too much of painters. This is the exact point of difference; for, as I shall distinctly show in the sequel, the spirit of ancient art and poetry is *plastic*, but that of the moderns *picturesque*.

By an example taken from another art, that of architecture, I shall endeavour to illustrate what I mean by this contrast. Throughout the Middle Ages there prevailed, and in the latter centuries of that era was carried to perfection, a style of architecture, which has been called Gothic, but ought really to have been termed old German. When, on the general revival of classical antiquity, the imitation of Grecian architecture became prevalent, and but too frequently without a due regard to the difference of climate and manners or to the purpose of the building, the zealots of this new taste, passing a sweeping sentence of condemnation on the Gothic, reprobated it as tasteless, gloomy, and barbarous. This was in some degree pardonable in the Italians, among whom a love for ancient architecture, cherished by hereditary remains of classical edifices, and the similarity of their climate to that of the Greeks and Romans, might, in some sort, be said to be innate. But we Northerns are not so easily to be talked out of the powerful, solemn impressions which seize upon the mind at entering a Gothic cathedral. We feel, on the contrary, a strong desire to investigate and to justify the source of this impression. A very slight attention will convince us that the Gothic architecture displays not only an extraordinary degree of mechanical skill, but also a marvellous power of invention; and, on a closer examination, we recognize its profound significance, and perceive that as well as the Grecian it constitutes in itself a complete and finished system.

To the application!—The Pantheon is not more different from

Westminster Abbey or the church of St. Stephen in Vienna, than the structure of a tragedy of Sophocles from a drama of Shakespeare. The comparison between these wonderful productions of poetry and architecture might be carried still farther. But does our admiration of the one compel us to depreciate the other? May we not admit that each is great and admirable in its kind, although the one is, and is meant to be, different from the other? The experiment is worth attempting. We will quarrel with no man for his predilection either for the Grecian or the Gothic. The world is wide, and affords room for a great diversity of objects. Narrow and blindly adopted prepossessions will never constitute a genuine critic or connoisseur, who ought, on the contrary, to possess the power of dwelling with liberal impartiality on the most discrepant views, renouncing the while all personal inclinations.

For our present object, the justification, namely, of the grand division which we lay down in the history of art, and according to which we conceive ourselves equally warranted in establishing the same division in dramatic literature, it might be sufficient merely to have stated this contrast between the ancient, or classical, and the romantic. But as there are exclusive admirers of the ancients, who never cease asserting that all deviation from them is merely the whim of a new school of critics, who, expressing themselves in language full of mystery, cautiously avoid conveying their sentiments in a tangible shape, I shall endeavour to explain the origin and spirit of the *romantic*, and then leave the world to judge if the use of the word, and of the idea which it is intended to convey, be thereby justified.

The mental culture of the Greeks was a finished education in the school of Nature. Of a beautiful and noble race, endowed with susceptible senses and a cheerful spirit under a mild sky, they lived and bloomed in the full health of existence; and, favoured by a rare combination of circumstances, accomplished all that the finite nature of man is capable of. The whole of their art and poetry is the expression of a consciousness of this harmony of all their faculties. They invented the poetry of joy.

Their religion was the deification of the powers of nature and of the earthly life: but this worship, which, among other nations, clouded the imagination with hideous shapes, and hardened the heart to cruelty, assumed, among the Greeks, a mild, a grand, and a dignified form. Superstition, too often the tyrant of the human faculties, seemed to have here contributed to their freest development. It cherished the arts by which it was adorned, and its idols became the models of ideal beauty.

But however highly the Greeks may have succeeded in the Beautiful, and even in the Moral, we cannot concede any higher character to their civilisation than that of a refined and ennobled sensuality. Of course this must be understood generally. The conjectures of a few philosophers, and the irradiations of poetical inspiration, constitute an occasional exception. Man can never altogether turn aside his thoughts from infinity, and some obscure recollections will always remind him of the home he has lost; but we are now speaking of the predominant tendency of his endeavours.

Religion is the root of human existence. Were it possible for man to renounce all religion, including that which is unconscious, independent of the will, he would become a mere surface without any internal substance. When this centre is disturbed, the whole system of the mental faculties and feelings takes a new shape.

And this is what has actually taken place in modern Europe through the introduction of Christianity. This sublime and beneficent religion has regenerated the ancient world from its state of exhaustion and debasement; it is the guiding principle in the history of modern nations, and even at this day, when many suppose they have shaken off its authority, they still find themselves much more influenced by it in their views of human affairs than they themselves are aware.

After Christianity, the character of Europe has, since the commencement of the Middle Ages, been chiefly influenced by the Germanic race of northern conquerors, who infused new life and vigour into a degenerated people. The stern nature of the North drives man back within himself; and what is lost in the free sportive development of the senses, must, in noble dispositions, be compensated by earnestness of mind. Hence the honest cordiality with which Christianity was welcomed by all the Teutonic tribes, so that among no other race of men has it penetrated more deeply into the inner man, displayed more powerful effects, or become more interwoven with all human feelings and sensibilities.

The rough but honest heroism of the northern conquerors, by its admixture with the sentiments of Christianity, gave rise to chivalry, of which the object was, by vows which should be looked upon as sacred, to guard the practice of arms from every rude and ungenerous abuse of force into which it was so likely to sink.

With the virtues of chivalry was associated a new and purer spirit of love, and inspired homage for genuine female worth, which was now revered as the acmé of human excellence, and, maintained by religion itself under the image of a virgin mother, infused into all hearts a mysterious sense of the purity of love.

As Christianity did not, like the heathen worship, rest satisfied with certain external acts, but claimed an authority over the whole inward man and the most hidden movement of the heart; the feeling of moral independence took refuge in the domain of honour, a worldly morality, as it were, which subsisting alongside of, was often at variance with that of religion, but yet in so far resembling it that it never calculated consequences, but consecrated unconditionally certain principles of action, which, like the articles of faith, were elevated far beyond the investigation of a casuistical reasoning.

Chivalry, love, and honour, together with religion itself, are the subjects of that poetry of nature which poured itself out in the Middle Ages with incredible fulness, and preceded the more artistic cultivation of the romantic spirit. This age had also its mythology, consisting of chivalrous tales and legends; but its wonders and its heroism were the very reverse of those of the ancient mythology.

Several inquirers who, in other respects, entertain the same conception of the peculiarities of the moderns, and trace them to the same source that we do, have placed the essence of the northern poetry in melancholy; and to this, when properly understood, we have nothing to object.

Among the Greeks human nature was in itself all-sufficient; it was conscious of no defects, and aspired to no higher perfection than that which it could actually attain by the exercise of its own energies. We, however, are taught by superior wisdom that man, through a grievous transgression, forfeited the place for which he was originally destined; and that the sole destination of his earthly existence is to struggle to regain his lost position, which, if left to his own strength, he can never accomplish. The old religion of the senses sought no higher possession than outward and perishable blessings; and immortality, so far as it was believed, stood shadow-like in the obscure distance, a faint dream of this sunny waking life. The very reverse of all this is the case with the Christian view: everything finite and mortal is lost in the contemplation of infinity; life has become shadow and darkness, and the first day of our real existence dawns in the world beyond the grave. Such a religion must waken the vague foreboding, which slumbers in every feeling heart, into a distinct consciousness that the happiness after which we are here striving is unattainable; that no external object can ever entirely fill our souls; and that all earthly enjoyment is but a fleeting and momentary illusion. When the soul, resting as it were under the willows of exile*, breathes out its longing for its distant home, what else but melancholy can be the key-note of its songs? Hence the poetry of the ancients was the poetry of enjoyment, and ours is that of desire: the former has its foundation in the scene which is present, while the latter hovers betwixt recollection and hope. Let me not be understood as affirming that everything flows in one unvarying strain of wailing and complaint, and that the voice of melancholy is always loudly heard. As the austerity of tragedy was not incompatible with the joyous views of the Greeks, so that romantic poetry, whose origin I have been describing, can assume every tone, even that of the liveliest joy; but still it will always, in some indescribable way, bear traces of the source from which it originated. The feeling of the moderns is, upon the whole, more inward, their fancy more incorporeal, and their thoughts more contemplative. In nature, it is true, the boundaries of objects run more into one another, and things are not so distinctly separated as we must exhibit them in order to convey distinct notions of them.

The Grecian ideal of human nature was perfect unison and proportion between all the powers—a natural harmony. The moderns, on the contrary, have arrived at the consciousness of an internal discord which renders such an ideal impossible; and hence the endeavour of their poetry is to reconcile these two worlds between which we find ourselves divided, and to blend them indissolubly together. The impressions of the senses are to be hallowed, as it were, by a mysterious connexion with higher feelings; and the soul, on the other hand, embodies its forebodings, or indescribable intuitions of infinity, in types and symbols borrowed from the visible world.

In Grecian art and poetry we find an original and unconscious unity of form and matter; in the modern, so far as it has remained true to its own spirit, we observe a keen struggle to unite the two, as being naturally in opposition to each other. The Grecian executed what it proposed in the utmost perfection; but the modern can only do justice to its endeavours after what is infinite by approximation;

* *Trauerweiden der verbannung,* literally *the weeping willows of banishment,* an allusion, as every reader must know, to the 137th Psalm. Linnaeus from this Psalm, calls the weeping willow *Salix Babylonica.* (Trans.)

and, from a certain appearance of imperfection, is in greater danger of not being duly appreciated. . . .

6. BLAKE: The Demonic in a new Mysticism

Strictly speaking, of course, only ideological programs, not cultural epochs, have spokesmen and official organs. The Englishman William Blake (1757–1827) stood outside the academic, the social, indeed outside any official establishment; with his poetry, paintings and engravings he sounded in swelling fashion several strains of the age. Both in swelling and piercing fashion he proclaimed the one with which we will be most concerned: mysticism—union with the One. His appearance must count as some kind of evidence for Hegel's claim that civilization progresses as a single, objective mind which at each moment displays a spirit of the time (*Zeitgeist*).

Like most romantic work, Blake's *The Marriage of Heaven and Hell* (1793) is two-edged, and strikes both backward and forward in time. It is both a retrieval of the mystical tradition and a hurling of it into the future. Its keynote is the salvation of the individual through inter-dependence of opposites and absorption into the One; but Blake's ecstatic inclusion of the Devil and Hell in the one molten creative mass, and his extreme stress on creativity as demonic energy, would have shocked most mystics of the past. In this he speaks for the future and anticipates Nietzsche. His mystical Christianity is almost too heretical for words. Yet he put it into words, powerful ones, which have outlived his own simple life, and which stand in marked contrast to his *Songs of Innocence*—sweet songs for young children.

THE MARRIAGE OF HEAVEN AND HELL

THE ARGUMENT

Rintrah roars and shakes his fires in the burden'd air;
Hungry clouds swag on the deep.

Once meek, and in a perilous path,
The just man kept his course along
The vale of death.

Roses are planted where thorns grow,
And on the barren heath
Sing the honey bees.

Then the perilous path was planted,
And a river and a spring
On every cliff and tomb,
And on the bleached bones
Red clay brought forth;

Till the villain left the paths of ease,
To walk in perilous paths, and drive
The just man into barren climes.

Now the sneaking serpent walks
In mild humility,
And the just man ranges in the wilds
Where lions roam.

Rintrah roars and shakes his fires in the burden'd air;
Hungry clouds swag on the deep.

&

As a new heaven is begun, and it is now thirty-three years since its advent, the Eternal Hell revives. And lo! Swedenborg is the Angel sitting at the tomb: his writings are the linen clothes folded up. Now is the dominion of Edom, and the return of Adam into Paradise. See Isaiah XXXIV and XXXV Chap.

Without Contraries is no progression. Attraction and Repulsion, Reason and Energy, Love and Hate, are necessary to Human existence.

From these contraries spring what the religious call Good and Evil. Good is the passive that obeys Reason. Evil is the active springing from Energy.

Good is Heaven. Evil is Hell.

THE VOICE OF THE DEVIL

All Bibles or sacred codes have been the causes of the following Errors:

1. That Man has two real existing principles: Viz: a body and a Soul.

2. That Energy, call'd Evil, is alone from the Body; and that Reason, call'd Good, is alone from the Soul.

3. That God will torment Man in Eternity for following his Energies.

But the following Contraries to these are True:

1. Man has no Body distinct from his Soul; for that call'd Body is a portion of Soul discern'd by the five Senses, the chief inlets of Soul in this age.

2. Energy is the only life, and is from the Body; and Reason is the bound or outward circumference of Energy.

3. Energy is Eternal Delight.

ॐ

Those who restrain desire, do so because theirs is weak enough to be restrained; and the restrained, or Reason, usurps its place and governs the unwilling.

And, being restrain'd, it by degrees becomes passive, till it is only the shadow of desire.

The history of this is written in *Paradise Lost*, and the Governor, or Reason, is call'd Messiah.

And the original Archangel, or possessor of the command of the heavenly host, is call'd the Devil or Satan, and his children are call'd Sin and Death.

But in the Book of Job, Milton's Messiah is call'd Satan.

For this history has been adopted by both parties.

It indeed appeared to Reason as if Desire was cast out; but the Devil's account is that the Messiah fell, and formed a heaven of what he stole from the Abyss.

This is shown in the Gospel, where he prays to the Father to send the comforter, or Desire, that Reason may have Ideas to build on; the Jehovah of the Bible being no other than he who dwells in flaming fire.

Know that after Christ's death, he became Jehovah.

But in Milton, the Father is Destiny, the Son a Ratio of the five senses, and the Holy Ghost Vacuum!

Note: the reason Milton wrote in fetters when he wrote of Angels and God, and at liberty when of Devils and Hell, is because he was a true Poet, and of the Devil's party without knowing it.

A MEMORABLE FANCY

As I was walking among the fires of hell, delighted with the enjoyments of Genius, which to Angels look like torment and insanity, I collected some of their Proverbs; thinking that as the sayings used in a nation mark its character, so the Proverbs of Hell show the nature of Infernal wisdom better than any description of buildings or garments.

When I came home: on the abyss of the five senses, where a flat sided steep frowns over the present world, I saw a mighty Devil folded in black clouds, hovering on the sides of the rock: with corroding fires he wrote the following sentence now perceived by the minds of men, and read by them on earth:

How do you know but ev'ry Bird that cuts the airy way,
Is an immense world of delight, clos'd by your senses five?

PROVERBS OF HELL

In seed time learn, in harvest teach, in winter enjoy.
Drive your cart and your plow over the bones of the dead.
The road of excess leads to the palace of wisdom.
Prudence is a rich, ugly old maid courted by Incapacity.
He who desires but acts not, breeds pestilence.
The cut worm forgives the plow.
Dip him in the river who loves water.
A fool sees not the same tree that a wise man sees.
He whose face gives no light shall never become a star.
Eternity is in love with the productions of time.
The busy bee has no time for sorrow.
The hours of folly are measur'd by the clock; but of wisdom, no clock can measure.
All wholesome food is caught without a net or a trap.
Bring out number, weight, and measure in a year of dearth.
No bird soars too high, if he soars with his own wings.
A dead body revenges not injuries.
The most sublime act is to set another before you.
If the fool would persist in his folly he would become wise.
Folly is the cloak of knavery.
Shame is Pride's cloak.
Prisons are built with stones of Law, Brothels with bricks of Religion.
The pride of the peacock is the glory of God.

The lust of the goat is the bounty of God.

The wrath of the lion is the wisdom of God.

The nakedness of woman is the work of God. Excess of sorrow laughs. Excess of joy weeps.

The roaring of lions, the howling of wolves, the raging of the stormy sea, and the destructive sword are portions of eternity, too great for the eye of man.

The fox condemns the trap, not himself.

Joys impregnate. Sorrows bring forth.

Let man wear the fell of the lion, woman the fleece of the sheep.

The bird a nest, the spider a web, man friendship.

The selfish, smiling fool, and the sullen, frowning fool shall be both thought wise, that they may be a rod.

What is now proved was once only imagin'd.

The rat, the mouse, the fox, the rabbit watch the roots; the lion, the tiger, the horse, the elephant watch the fruits.

The cistern contains: the fountain overflows.

One thought fills immensity.

Always be ready to speak your mind, and a base man will avoid you.

Everything possible to be believ'd is an image of truth.

The eagle never lost so much time as when he submitted to learn of the crow.

The fox provides for himself, but God provides for the lion.

Think in the morning. Act in the noon. Eat in the evening. Sleep in the night.

He who has suffer'd you to impose on him, knows you.

As the plow follows words, so God rewards prayers.

The tigers of wrath are wiser than the horses of instruction.

Expect poison from the standing water.

You never know what is enough unless you know what is more than enough.

Listen to the fool's reproach! it is a kingly title!

The eyes of fire, the nostrils of air, the mouth of water, the beard of earth.

The weak in courage is strong in cunning.

The apple tree never asks the beech how he shall grow; nor the lion, the horse how he shall take his prey.

The thankful receiver bears a plentiful harvest.

If others had not been foolish, we should be so.

The soul of sweet delight can never be defil'd.

When thou seest an Eagle, thou seest a portion of Genius; lift up thy head!

As the caterpillar chooses the fairest leaves to lay her eggs on, so the priest lays his curse on the fairest joys.

To create a little flower is the labour of ages.

Damn braces. Bless relaxes.

The best wine is the oldest, the best water the newest.

Prayers plow not! Praises reap not!

Joys laugh not! Sorrows weep not!

The head Sublime, the heart Pathos, the genitals Beauty, the hands and feet Proportion.

As the air to a bird or the sea to a fish, so is contempt to the contemptible.

The crow wish'd everything was black, the owl that everything was white.

Exuberance is Beauty.

If the lion was advised by the fox, he would be cunning.

Improvement makes straight roads; but the crooked roads without Improvement are roads of Genius.

Sooner murder an infant in its cradle than nurse unacted desires.

Where man is not, nature is barren.

Truth can never be told so as to be understood, and not be believ'd.

Enough! or Too much.

ह≈

The ancient Poets animated all sensible objects with Gods or Geniuses, calling them by the names and adorning them with the properties of woods, rivers, mountains, lakes, cities, nations, and whatever their enlarged and numerous senses could perceive.

And particularly they studied the genius of each city and country, placing it under its mental deity;

Till a system was formed, which some took advantage of, and enslaved the vulgar by attempting to realize or abstract the mental deities from their objects: thus began Priesthood,

Choosing forms of worship from poetic tales.

And at length they pronounc'd that the Gods had order'd such things.

Thus men forgot that all deities reside in the human breast.

A MEMORABLE FANCY

The Prophets Isaiah and Ezekiel dined with me, and I asked them how they dared so roundly to assert that God spoke to them; and whether they did not think at the time that they would be misunderstood, and so be the cause of imposition.

Isaiah answer'd: "I saw no God, nor heard any, in a finite organical perception; but my senses discover'd the infinite in everything, and as I was then persuaded, and remain confirm'd that the voice of honest indignation is the voice of God; I cared not for consequences, but wrote."

Then I asked: "Does a firm persuasion that a thing is so, make it so?"

He replied: "All poets believe that it does, and in ages of imagination this firm persuasion removed mountains; but many are not capable of a firm persuasion of anything."

Then Ezekiel said: "The philosophy of the East taught the first principles of human perception; some nations held one principle for the origin, and some another: we of Israel taught that the Poetic Genius (as you now call it) was the first principle and all the others merely derivative, which was the cause of our despising the Priests and Philosophers of other countries, and prophesying that all Gods would at last be proved to originate in ours and to be the tributaries of the Poetic Genius; it was this that our great poet, King David, desired so fervently and invokes so pathetically saying by this he conquers enemies and governs kingdoms; and we so loved our God that we cursed in his name all the deities of surrounding nations, and asserted that they had rebelled: from these opinions the vulgar came to think that all nations would at last be subject to the Jews.

"This," said he, "like all firm persuasions, is come to pass; for all nations believe the Jews' code and worship the Jews' God, and what greater subjection can be?"

I heard this with some wonder, and must confess my own conviction. After dinner I asked Isaiah to favour the world with his lost works; he said none of equal value was lost. Ezekiel said the same of his.

I also asked Isaiah what made him go naked and barefoot three years. He answer'd: "The same that made our friend Diogenes, the Grecian."

I then asked Ezekiel why he ate dung, and lay so long on his right and left side. He answer'd, "The desire of raising other men into a perception of the infinite: this the North American tribes practised, and is he honest who resists his genius of conscience only for the sake of present ease or gratification?"

ॐ

The ancient tradition that the world will be consumed in fire at the end of six thousand years is true, as I have heard from Hell.

For the cherub with his flaming sword is hereby commanded to leave his guard at tree of life; and when he does, the whole creation will be consumed and appear infinite and holy, whereas it now appears finite and corrupt.

This will come to pass by an improvement of sensual enjoyment.

But first the notion that man has a body distinct from his soul is to be expunged; this I shall do by printing in the infernal method, by corrosives, which in Hell are salutary and medicinal, melting apparent surfaces away, and displaying the infinite which was hid.

If the doors of perception were cleansed, everything would appear to man as it is, infinite.

For man has closed himself up, till he sees all things thro' narrow chinks of his cavern.

A MEMORABLE FANCY

I was in a Printing house in Hell, and saw the method in which knowledge is transmitted from generation to generation.

In the first chamber was a Dragon-Man, clearing away the rubbish from a cave's mouth; within, a number of Dragons were hollowing the cave.

In the second chamber was a Viper folding round the rock and the cave, and others adorning it with gold, silver, and precious stones.

In the third chamber was an Eagle with wings and feathers of air: he caused the inside of the cave to be infinite; around were numbers of Eagle-like men who built palaces in the immense cliffs.

In the fourth chamber were Lions of flaming fire, raging around and melting the metals into living fluids.

In the fifth chamber were Unnam'd forms which cast the metals into the expanse.

There they were received by Men who occupied the sixth chamber, and took the forms of books and were arranged in libraries.

ह२

The Giants who formed this world into its sensual existence, and now seem to live in it in chains, are in truth the causes of its life and the sources of all activity; but the chains are the cunning of weak and tame minds which have power to resist energy; according to the proverb, the weak in courage is strong in cunning.

Thus one portion of being is the Prolific, the other the Devouring: to the Devourer it seems as if the producer was in his chains; but it is not so; he only takes portions of existence and fancies that the whole.

But the Prolific would cease to be Prolific unless the Devourer, as a sea, received the excess of his delights.

Some will say: "Is not God alone the Prolific?" I answer: "God only Acts and Is, in existing beings or Men."

These two classes of men are always upon earth, and they should be enemies: whoever tries to reconcile them seeks to destroy existence.

Religion is an endeavour to reconcile the two.

Note: Jesus Christ did not wish to unite, but to separate them, as in the Parable of sheep and goats! and he says: "I came not to send Peace, but a Sword."

Messiah or Satan or Tempter was formerly thought to be one of the Antediluvians who are our Energies.

A MEMORABLE FANCY

An Angel came to me and said: "O pitiable foolish young man! O horrible! O dreadful state! consider the hot burning dungeon thou art preparing for thyself to all eternity, to which thou art going in such career."

I said: "Perhaps you will be willing to show me my eternal lot, and we will contemplate together upon it, and see whether your lot or mine is most desirable."

So he took me thro' a stable and thro' a church and down into the church vault, at the end of which was a mill: thro' the mill we went, and came to a cave; down the winding cavern we groped our tedious way, till a void boundless as a nether sky appear'd beneath us, and we held by the roots of trees and hung over this immensity; but I said: "If you please, we will commit ourselves to this void, and see whether providence is here also; if you will not, I will"; but he answer'd: "Do not presume, O young man, but as we here remain, behold thy lot which will soon appear when the darkness passes away."

So I remain'd with him, sitting in the twisted root of an oak; he was suspended in a fungus, which hung with the head downward into the deep.

By degrees we beheld the infinite Abyss, fiery as the smoke of a burning city; beneath us, at an immense distance, was the sun, black but shining; round it were fiery tracks on which revolv'd vast spiders, crawling after their prey, which flew or rather swum, in the infinite deep, in the most terrific shapes of animals sprung from corruption; and the air was full of them, and seem'd composed of them: these are Devils, and are called Powers of the air. I now asked my companion which was my eternal lot. He said: "Between the black and white spiders."

But now, from between the black and white spiders, a cloud and fire burst and rolled thro' the deep, black'ning all beneath so that the nether deep grew black as a sea, and rolled with a terrible noise; beneath us was nothing now to be seen but a black tempest, till looking east between the clouds and the waves, we saw a cataract of blood mixed with fire, and not many stones' throw from us appear'd and sunk again the scaly fold of a monstrous serpent; at last to the east, distant about three degrees, appear'd a fiery crest above the waves; slowly it reared like a ridge of golden rocks, till we discover'd two globes of crimson fire, from which the sea fled away in clouds of smoke; and now we saw it was the head of Leviathan; his forehead was divided into streaks of green and purple like those on a tiger's forehead: soon we saw his mouth and red gills hang just above the raging foam, tinging the black deep with beams of blood, advancing toward us with all the fury of a spiritual existence.

My friend the Angel climb'd from his station into the mill: I remain'd alone; and then this appearance was no more, but I found myself sitting on a pleasant bank beside a river by moonlight, hearing a harper, who sung to the harp; and his theme was: "The man who never alters his opinion is like standing water, and breeds reptiles of the mind."

But I arose and sought for the mill, and there I found my Angel, who, surprised, asked me how I escaped.

I answer'd: "All that we saw was owing to your metaphysics; for when you ran away, I found myself on a bank by moonlight hearing a harper. But now we have seen my eternal lot, shall I show you yours?" He laugh'd at my proposal; but I by force suddenly caught him in my arms, and flew westerly thro' the night, till we were elevated above the earth's shadow; then I flung myself with him directly into the body of the sun; here I clothed myself in white, and taking in my hand Swedenborg's volumes, sunk from the glorious clime, and passed all the planets till we came to Saturn: here I stay'd to rest, and then leap'd into the void between Saturn and the fixed stars.

"Here," said I, "is your lot, in this space—if space it may be call'd." Soon we saw the stable and the church, and I took him to the altar and open'd the Bible, and lo! it was a deep pit, into which I descended, driving the Angel before me; soon we saw seven houses of brick; one we enter'd; in it were a number of monkeys, baboons, and all of that species, chain'd by the middle, grinning and snatching at one another, but withheld by the shortness of their chains: however, I saw that they sometimes grew numerous, and then the weak were caught by the strong, and with a grinning aspect, first coupled with, and then devour'd, by plucking off first one limb and then another, till the body was left a helpless trunk this, after grinning and kissing it with seeming fondness, they devour'd too; and here and there I saw one savourily picking the flesh off his own tail; as the stench terribly annoy'd us both, we went into the mill, and I in my hand brought the skeleton of a body, which in the mill was Aristotle's *Analytics*.

So the Angel said: "Thy phantasy has imposed upon me, and thou oughtest to be ashamed." I answer'd: "We impose on one another, and it is but lost time to converse with you whose works are only Analytics."

಄

Opposition is true Friendship.

಄

I have always found that Angels have the vanity to speak of themselves as the only wise; this they do with a confident insolence sprouting from systematic reasoning.

Thus Swedenborg boasts that what he writes is new; tho' it is only the Contents or Index of already publish'd books.

A man carried a monkey about for a show, and because he was a little wiser than the monkey, grew vain, and conceiv'd himself as much wiser than seven men. It is so with Swedenborg: he shows the folly of churches, and exposes hypocrites, till he imagines that all are religious, and himself the single one on earth that ever broke a net.

Now hear a plain fact: Swedenborg has not written one new truth. Now hear another: he has written all the old falsehoods.

And now hear the reason. He conversed with Angels who are all religious, and conversed not with Devils who all hate religion, for he was incapable thro' his conceited notions.

Thus Swedenborg's writings are a recapitulation of all superficial opinions, and an analysis of the more sublime—but no further.

Have now another plain fact. Any man of mechanical talents may, from the writings of Paracelsus or Jacob Behmen, produce ten thousand volumes of equal value with Swedenborg's, and from those of Dante or Shakespeare an infinite number.

But when he has done this, let him not say that he knows better than his master, for he only holds a candle in sunshine.

A MEMORABLE FANCY

Once I saw a Devil in flame of fire, who arose before an Angel that sat on a cloud, and the Devil utter'd these words:

"The worship of God is honouring his gifts in other men, each according to his genius, and loving the greatest men best: those who envy or calumniate great men hate God, for there is no other God."

The Angel hearing this became almost blue; but mastering himself he grew yellow, and at last white, pink, and smiling, and then replied:

"Thou Idolater! is not God One? and is not he visible in Jesus Christ? and has not Jesus Christ given his sanction to the law of ten commandments? and are not all other men fools, sinners, and nothings?"

The Devil answer'd: "Bray a fool in a mortar with wheat, yet shall not his folly be beaten out of him! If Jesus Christ is the greatest man, you ought to love him in the greatest degree. Now hear how he has given his sanction to the law of ten commandments: did he not mock at the Sabbath, and so mock the Sabbath's God? murder those who were murder'd because of him? turn away the law from the woman taken in adultery? steal the labour of others to support him? bear false witness when he omitted making a defence before Pilate? covet when he pray'd for his disciples, and when he bid them shake off the dust of their feet against such as refused to lodge them? I tell you, no virtue can exist without breaking these ten commandments. Jesus was all virtue, and acted from impulse, not from rules.

When he had so spoken, I beheld the Angel, who stretched out his arms, embracing the flame of fire, and he was consumed and arose as Elijah.

Note: This Angel who is now become a Devil, is my particular friend; we often read the Bible together in its infernal or diabolical sense, which the world shall have if they behave well.

I have also the Bible of Hell, which the world shall have whether they will or no.

ello

One Law for the Lion and Ox is Oppression.

A SONG OF LIBERTY

1. The Eternal Female groan'd! It was heard over all the Earth.

2. Albion's coast is sick, silent; the American meadows faint!

3. Shadows of Prophecy shiver along by the lakes and the rivers, and mutter across the ocean: France, rend down thy dungeon!

4. Golden Spain, burst the barriers of old Rome!

5. Cast thy keys, O Rome, into the deep down falling, even to eternity down falling,

6. And weep.

7. In her trembling hands she took the new born terror, howling.

8. On these infinite mountains of light, now barr'd out by the Atlantic sea, the new born fire stood before the starry king!

9. Flag'd with grey brow'd snows and thunderous visages, the jealous wings wav'd over the deep.

10. The speary hand burned aloft, unbuckled was the shield; forth went the hand of jealousy among the flaming hair, and hurl'd the new born wonder thro' the starry night.

11. The fire, the fire is falling!

12. Look up! Look up! O citizen of London, enlarge thy countenance! O Jew, leave counting gold! Return to thy oil and wine. O African! black African! (go, winged thought, widen his forehead.)

13. The fiery limbs, the flaming hair, shot like the sinking sun into the western sea.

14. Wak'd from his eternal sleep, the hoary element roaring fled away.

15. Down rush'd, beating his wings in vain, the jealous king; his grey brow'd counsellors, thunderous warriors, curl'd veterans, among helms, and shields, and chariots, horses, elephants, banners, castles, slings, and rocks.

16. Falling, rushing, ruining! buried in the ruins, on Urthona's dens;

17. All night beneath the ruins; then, their sullen flames faded, emerge round the gloomy king.

18. With thunder and fire, leading his starry hosts thro' the waste wilderness, he promulgates his ten commands, glancing his beamy eyelids over the deep in dark dismay,

19. Where the son of fire in his eastern cloud, while the morning plumes her golden breast,

20. Spurning the clouds written with curses, stamps the stony law to dust, loosing the eternal horses from the dens of night, crying:

EMPIRE IS NO MORE! AND NOW THE LION
AND WOLF SHALL CEASE,

Chorus

Let the Priests of the Raven of dawn no longer, in deadly black, with hoarse note curse the sons of joy. Nor his accepted brethren— whom, tyrant, he calls free—lay the bound or build the roof. Nor pale religious lechery call that virginity that wishes but acts not!

For everything that lives is Holy.

II.

Evolution of the Individual:

The Essence of Romanticism

7. GOETHE: The Faustian Leap

Granting that an exaggeration is no paradigm, it is Johann Wolfgang von Goethe's (1749–1832) early-conceived *Faust*, Part I, and not, say, Novalis' magical idealism which is a paradigm and archetype of romanticism. The theme of Faust is seminal: something from youth, some life-sustaining wisdom or innocence, has been lost; without it the self is incomplete, dried out, and life is not worth the trouble; so whatever it is must be regained. The theme can be put another way: human life with all its science and learning has been cut away from its source; with this theme we find a painstaking reevaluation of religion, *i.e.*, that which, in its etymology, means to be retied, reconnected, tied back.

The Lord says to Mephistopheles, "Let it be so: To you is given the power that may seduce this soul from his true source." The regaining of youth and the regaining of source are somehow closely linked. The past can be reclaimed only by a leap into the future.

> The stern heart softens, all of its pride forgetting,
> I weep and a shudder passes through me.
> All that I have stands off from me afar,
> And all I lost is real, my guiding star.

The play begins in the cell-like study of the learned Dr. Faustus, professor of everything under the sun except his own soul.*

> *In a high-vaulted, narrow, gothic chamber,*
> *Faust is discovered restless at his desk.*

FAUST. Philosophy have I digested,
   The whole of Law and Medicine,
   From each its secrets I have wrested,
   Theology, alas, thrown in.
   Poor fool, with all this sweated lore,
   I stand no wiser than I was before.
   Master and Doctor are my titles;

---

* *Faust*, Part I, translated by Philip Wayne. Reprinted by permission of Penguin Books, Ltd.

For ten years now, without repose,
I've held my erudite recitals
And led my pupils by the nose.
And round we go, on crooked ways or straight,
And well I know that ignorance is our fate,
And this I hate.
I have, I grant, outdistanced all the others,
Doctors, pedants, clergy and lay-brothers;
All plague of doubts and scruples I can quell,
And have no fear of devil or of hell,
And in return am destitute of pleasure,
Knowing that knowledge tricks us beyond measure,
That man's conversion is beyond my reach,
Knowing the emptiness of what I teach.
Meanwhile I live in penury,
No worldly honour falls to me.
No dog would linger on like this,
And so I turn to the abyss
Of necromancy, try if art
Can voice or power of spirits start,
To do me service and reveal
The things of Nature's secret seal,
And save me from the weary dance
Of holding forth in ignorance.
Then shall I see, with vision clear,
How secret elements cohere,
And what the universe engirds,
And give up huckstering with words.
  O silver majesty of night,
Moon, look no more upon my plight,
You whom my eyes at midnight oft
Have gazed upon, when slow and soft
You crossed my papers and my books
With friendly, melancholy looks.
Would that my soul could tranquil stray
On many a moonlit mountain way,
By cavernous haunts with ghostly shadows,
Or thread the silver of the meadows,
Released from learning's smoky stew
To lave me in the moonlit dew.

But, ah, this prison has my soul,
Damnable, bricked-in, cabined hole,
Where even the heaven's dear light must pass
Saddened through the painted glass.
Hemmed in with stacks of books am I,
Where works the worm with dusty mange,
While to the vaulted roof on high
The smoky ranks of papers range;
Retorts and jars my crib encumber,
And crowded instruments and, worse,
Loads of hereditary lumber—
And this, ay this, is called my universe.

And shall I wonder why my heart
Is lamed and frightened in my breast,
Why all the springs of life that start
Are strangely smothered and oppressed?
Instead of all that life can hold
Of Nature's free, god-given breath,
I take to me the smoke and mould
Of skeletons and dust and death.
Up and away! A distant land
Awaits me in this secret book
From Nostradamus' very hand,
Nor for a better guide I look.
Now shall I read the starry pole,
In Nature's wisdom shall I seek
And know, with rising power of soul,
How spirit doth to spirit speak.
No dusty logic can divine
The meaning of a sacred sign.
Mysterious spirits, hovering near,
Answer me, if now ye hear!

(*He opens the book and lights upon the Sign of the Macrocosm.*)

Ah, strangely comes an onset of delight,
Invading all my senses as I gaze:
Young, sacred bliss-of-life springs at the sight,
And fires my blood in all its branching ways.
Was it a god who made this mystic scroll,
To touch my spirit's tumult with its healing,

And fill my wretched heart with joyous feeling,
And bring the secret world before my soul,
The hidden drive of Nature's force revealing?
Myself a god?—With lightened vision's leap
I read the riddle of the symbols, hear
The looms of Nature's might, that never sleep,
And know at last things spoken of the seer:
" 'Tis not the spirit world is sealed;
Thy heart is dead, thy senses' curtain drawn.
But, scholar, bathe, rejoicing, healed,
Thy earthly breast in streams of roseate dawn."
                                        (*He studies the sign.*)
Lo, single things inwoven, made to blend,
To work in oneness with the whole, and live
Members one of another, while ascend
Celestial powers, who ever take and give
Vessels of gold on heaven's living stair,
Their pinions fragrant with the bliss they bear,
Pervading all, that heaven and earth agree,
Transfixing all the world with harmony.

   O endless pageant,—but a pageant still,
A show, that mocks my touch or grasp or will!
Where are the nipples, Nature's springs, ah where
The living source that feeds the universe?
You flow, you give to drink, mysterious nurse,
And yet my soul is withered in despair. . . .

8. WORDSWORTH: The Poet Finds His Own Self

   The theme of returning to the source of life is repeated in William
Wordsworth (1770–1850), not because he had read *Faust* (it had been
written but not yet published) but because the theme was in the air.
We find it most concisely in *Ode on Intimations of Immortality from
Recollections of Early Childhood*, which holds in its epigraph a cardinal
line of Wordsworth's own, "The child is father to the man." From the
poem we read:

Our birth is but a sleep and a forgetting:
The Soul that rises with us, our life's Star,
    Hath had elsewhere its setting,
        And cometh from afar:
    Not in entire forgetfulness,
    And not in utter nakedness,
But trailing clouds of glory do we come
    From God, who is our home:
Heaven lies about us in our infancy!
Shades of the prison-house begin to close
    Upon the growing Boy,
But he beholds the light, and whence it flows,
    He sees it in his joy;
The Youth, who daily farther from the east
    Must travel, still is Nature's priest,
    And by the vision splendid
    Is on his way attended;
At length the Man perceives it die away,
And fade into the light of common day.

Later in the poem some hope of retrieve and salvation is presented through "primal sympathy" and "years that bring the philosophic mind." This "primal sympathy" is tied, I think, to what we might call emotive perception or feeling intellect. Recall that the child "sees" the light "in his joy." Of course, these phrases ring strangely in twentieth-century ears, since most of us have grown accustomed to the positivist doctrine that the emotive is precisely the noncognitive, the nonperceptive. In fact the poem runs counter to a bias of our time which has been building for centuries: Science gives us knowledge and science requires the non-intervention of emotion.

For Wordsworth there are important aspects of the *world*, not just our-selves, which we cannot know without the correct emotion. Indeed, the dualism of self and world is just as misleading in the interpretation of Wordsworth as is that of emotion and knowledge; the self was regarded by him as deriving its sense from the meaning that things in the world have for it, and this in turn derives in part from the emotional response that the self gives to them. That is, *things* can be joyous or, again, dangerous, and we fail in knowing them if we have never *felt* joy or danger.

If this sounds simpleminded, then greater complexity can be produced. Wordsworth declared that the passions of men are "incorporated with the beautiful and permanent forms of nature," i.e., they are not sealed up in a psychical container. With this reference to permanent forms of nature we can explicate both his incipient Platonism and the further reaches of his "feeling intellect." In *The Prelude*, the poet, hiking through a mountain pass, sees "The immeasurable height/Of woods decaying, never to be decayed,/The stationary blasts of waterfalls." How can a decaying wood go undecayed or a waterfall be still and stationary?

Let us try to unravel the paradox. A waterfall is still and stationary only in that its change is *constant* (the Idea of change does not itself change, we recall from Plato). And if this waterfall falls and changes constantly there is something changeless both about the Idea in which the waterfall participates and the self which grasps the Idea. Hence, the Idea binds up the self and the not-self. In other words, the self is transported by these perceptions, and it is automatically expanded by them; receptivity means expansion; to know is to grow. And, concurrent with the receptivity and expansion is an inexpugnable emotional component, for example, exaltation or elation. The self finds itself beyond itself, so emotion and intellect are not antagonistic, at least not as the common man experiences them in that daily and primal way which is actually the point of departure for all of us, even for reflecting and refining scientists.

Thus in the passage from Wordsworth's Preface to the Second Edition of *Lyrical Ballads* (1800) we find "the spontaneous overflow of powerful feeling" inextricably intermixed with thought. The poet's "habits of meditation" have wedded with his feelings, and the combination is so omnipresent in his work that one must inevitably think he uses it with a purpose. If by reading his poetry we are made to feel the importance and value of things, then Nature will be seen to be purposive for us (just because it is important for us), the disclosure of this purposiveness being the purpose of the poet.* But Wordsworth is not a philosopher as such and so the purposiveness just happens; it comes about in the natural course of events; it is not contrived or premeditated; it is spontaneous. The poet is one who "hath put his heart to school" in the very act of learning about the world.

In the selections from *The Prelude* (1795–1805), Wordsworth clearly expressed major themes of romanticism.

FROM BOOK III

I looked for universal things; perused
The common countenance of earth and sky:
Earth, nowhere unembellished by some trace
Of that first Paradise whence man was driven;

---

* Compare this to Kant's idea that the beautiful seems to have a purpose but we do not know exactly what the purpose is.

And sky, whose beauty and bounty are expressed
By and proud name she bears—the name of Heaven.
I called on both to teach me what they might;
Or turning the mind in upon herself,
Pored, watched, expected, listened, spread my thoughts
And spread them with a wider creeping; felt
Incumbencies more awful, visitings
Of the Upholder of the tranquil soul,
That tolerates the indignities of Time,
And, from the centre of Eternity
All finite motions overruling, lives
In glory immutable. But peace! enough
Here to record that I was mounting now
To such community with highest truth—
A track pursuing, not untrod before,
From strict analogies by thought supplied
Or consciousnesses not to be subdued.
To every natural form, rock, fruit, or flower,
Even the loose stones that cover the highway,
I gave a moral life: I saw them feel,
Or linked them to some feeling: the great mass
Lay bedded in a quickening soul, and all
That I beheld respired with inward meaning.
And that whate'er of Terror or of Love
Or Beauty, Nature's daily face put on
From transitory passion, unto this
I was as sensitive as waters are
To the sky's influence in a kindred mood
Of passion; was obedient as a lute
That waits upon the touches of the wind.
Unknown, unthought of, yet I was most rich—
I had a world about me—'twas my own;
I made it, for it only lived to me,
And to the God who sees into the heart. . . .

FROM BOOK IV

　　　　　　　　'Mid a throng
Of maids and youths, old men, and matrons staid,
A medley of all tempers, I had passed

The night in dancing, gaiety, and mirth,
With din of instruments and shuffling feet,
And glancing forms, and tapers glittering,
And unaimed prattle flying up and down;
Spirits upon the stretch, and here and there
Slight shocks of young love-liking interspersed,
Whose transient pleasure mounted to the head,
And tingled through the veins. Ere we retired,
The cock had crowed, and now the eastern sky
Was kindling, not unseen, from humble copse
And open field, through which the pathway wound,
And homeward led my steps. Magnificent
The morning rose, in memorable pomp,
Glorious as e'er I had beheld—in front,
The sea lay laughing at a distance; near,
The solid mountains shone, bright as the clouds,
Grain-tinctured, drenched in empyrean light;
And in the meadows and the lower grounds
Was all the sweetness of a common dawn—
Dews, vapors, and the melody of birds,
And laborers going forth to till the fields.
Ah! need I say, dear friend! that to the brim
My heart was full; I made no vows, but vows
Were then made for me; bond unknown to me
Was given, that I should be, else sinning greatly,
A dedicated Spirit. On I walked
In thankful blessedness, which yet survives. . . .

FROM BOOK V

These mighty workmen of our later age,
Who, with a broad highway, have overbridged
The froward chaos of futurity,
Tamed to their bidding; they who have the skill
To manage books, and things, and make them act
On infant minds as surely as the sun
Deals with a flower; the keepers of our time,
The guides and wardens of our faculties,
Sages who in their prescience would control
All accidents, and to the very road

Which they have fashioned would confine us down,
Like engines; when will their presumption learn,
That in the unreasoning progress of the world
A wiser spirit is at work for us,
A better eye than theirs, most prodigal
Of blessings, and most studious of our good,
Even in what seem our most unfruitful hours?. . .
A race of real children: not too wise,
Too learned or too good; but wanton, fresh,
And banded up and down by love and hate;
Not unresentful where self-justified;
Fierce, moody, patient, venturous, modest, shy;
Mad at their sports like withered leaves in winds;
Though doing wrong and suffering, and full oft
Bending beneath our life's mysterious weight
Of pain, and doubt, and fear, yet yielding not
In happiness to the happiest upon earth.
Simplicity in habit, truth in speech,
Be these the daily strengtheners of their minds;
May books and Nature be their early joy!
And knowledge, rightly honored with that name—
Knowledge not purchased by the loss of power! . . .

From Book VI

    Imagination—here the Power so called
Through sad incompetence of human speech,
That awful Power rose from the mind's abyss
Like an unfathered vapor that enwraps,
At once, some lonely traveller. I was lost;
Halted without an effort to break through;
But to my conscious soul I now can say—
"I recognize thy glory:" in such strength
Of usurpation, when the light of sense
Goes out, but with a flash that has revealed
The invisible world, doth greatness make abode,
There harbors; whether we be young or old,
Our destiny, our being's heart and home,
Is with infinitude, and only there;
With hope it is, hope that can never die,

Effort, and expectation, and desire,
And something evermore about to be.
Under such banners militant, the soul
Seeks for no trophies, struggles for no spoils
That may attest her prowess, blest in thoughts
That are their own perfection and reward,
Strong in herself and in beatitude
That hides her, like the mighty flood of Nile
Poured from his fount of Abyssinian clouds
To fertilize the whole Egyptian plain.

    The melancholy slackening that ensued
Upon those tidings by the peasant given
Was soon dislodged. Downwards we hurried fast,
And with the half-shaped road which we had missed,
Entered a narrow chasm. The brook and road
Were fellow-travellers in this gloomy strait,
And with them did we journey several hours
At a slow pace. The immeasurable height
Of woods decaying, never to be decayed,
The stationary blasts of waterfalls,
And in the narrow rent at every turn
Winds thwarting winds, bewildered and forlorn,
The torrent shooting from the clear blue sky,
The rocks that muttered close upon our ears,
Black drizzling crags that spake by the way-side
As if a voice were in them, the sick sight
And giddy prospect of the raving stream,
The unfettered clouds and region of the heavens,
Tumult and peace, the darkness and the light—
Were all like workings of one mind, the features
Of the same face, blossoms upon one tree;
Characters of the great Apocalypse,
The types and symbols of Eternity,
Of first, and last, and midst, and without end. . . .

FROM BOOK VIII

What sounds are those, Helvellyn, that are heard
Up to thy summit, through the depth of air
Ascending, as if distance had the power

To make the sounds more audible? What crowd
Covers, or sprinkles o'er, yon village green?
Crowd seems it, solitary hill! to thee,
Though but a little family of men,
Shepherds and tillers of the ground—betimes
Assembled with their children and their wives,
And here and there a stranger interspersed.
They hold a rustic fair—a festival,
Such as, on this side now, and now on that,
Repeated through his tributary vales,
Helvellyn, in the silence of his rest,
Sees annually, if clouds towards either ocean
Blown from their favorite resting-place, or mists
Dissolved, have left him in unshrouded head.
Delightful day it is for all who dwell
In this secluded glen, and eagerly
They give it welcome. Long ere heat of noon,
From byre or field the kine were brought; the sheep
Are penned in cotes; the chaffering is begun.
The heifer lows, uneasy at the voice
Of a new master; bleat the flocks aloud.
Booths are there none; a stall or two is here;
A lame man or a blind, the one to beg,
The other to make music; hither, too,
From far, with basket, slung upon her arm,
Of hawker's wares—books, pictures, combs, and pins—
Some aged woman finds her way again,
Year after year, a punctual visitant!
There also stands a speech-maker by rote,
Pulling the strings of his boxed raree-show;
And in the lapse of many years may come
Prouder itinerant, mountebank, or he
Whose wonders in a covered wain lie hid.
But one there is, the loveliest of them all,
Some sweet lass of the valley, looking out
For gains, and who that sees her would not buy?
Fruits of her father's orchard are her wares,
And with the ruddy produce she walks round
Among the crowd, half pleased with, half ashamed
Of her new office, blushing restlessly.

The children now are rich, for the old today
Are generous as the young; and, if content
With looking on, some ancient wedded pair
Sit in the shade together, while they gazed
"A cheerful smile unbends the wrinkled brow,
The days departed start again to life,
And all the scenes of childhood reappear,
Faint, but more tranquil, like the changing sun
To him who slept at noon and wakes at eve."
Thus gaiety and cheerfulness prevail,
Spreading from young to old, from old to young,
And no one seems to want his share.—Immense
Is the recess, the circumambient world
Magnificent, by which they are embraced:
They move about upon the soft green turf:
How little they, they and their doings, seem,
And all that they can further or obstruct!
Through utter weakness pitiably dear,
As tender infants are: and yet how great!
For all things serve them; them the morning light
Loves, as it glistens on the silent rocks;
And them the silent rocks; which now from high
Looks down upon them; the reposing clouds;
The wild brooks prattling from invisible haunts;
And old Helvellyn, conscious of the stir
Which animates this day their calm abode. . . .

The selection which follows is taken from the Preface to *Lyrical Ballads* (Second Edition, 1800), and in it Wordsworth presents his romantic theory of poetry.

. . . The principal object, then, proposed in these poems was to choose incidents and situations from common life, and to relate or describe them throughout, as far as was possible, in a selection of language really used by men, and, at the same time, to throw over them a certain coloring of imagination, whereby ordinary things should be presented to the mind in an unusual aspect; and, further, and above all, to make these incidents and situations interesting by tracing in them, truly though not ostentatiously, the primary laws of nature: chiefly, as far as regards the manner in which we associate ideas in a state of excitement. Humble and rustic life was generally chosen, because, in that condition, the essential passions of the heart find a better soil in which they can attain their maturity, are less under restraint, and speak a plainer and more emphatic language; because in that condition of life our elementary feelings coexist in a state of greater simplicity, and, consequently, may be more accurately contemplated, and more forcibly communicated; because the manners of rural life germinate from those elementary feelings, and, from the necessary character of rural occupations, are more easily comprehended, and are more durable; and, lastly, because in that condition the passions of men are incorporated with the beautiful and permanent forms of nature. The language, too, of these men has been adopted (purified indeed from what appear to be its real defects, from all lasting and rational causes of dislike or disgust) because such men hourly communicate with the best objects from which the best part of language is originally derived; and because, from their rank in society and the sameness and narrow circle of their intercourse, being less under the influence of social vanity, they convey their feelings and notions in simple and unelaborated expressions. Accordingly, such a language, arising out of repeated experience and regular feelings, is a more permanent, and a far more philosophical language, than that which is frequently substituted for it by poets, who think that they are conferring honor upon themselves and their art, in proportion as they separate themselves from the sympathies of men, and indulge in arbitrary and capricious habits of expression, in order to furnish food for fickle tastes and fickle appetites of their own creation.

I cannot, however, be insensible to the present outcry against the triviality and meanness, both of thought and language, which some of my contemporaries have occasionally introduced into their metrical compositions; and I acknowledge that this defect, where it exists, is more dishonorable to the writer's own character than false refinement or arbitrary innovation, though I should contend at the same time, that it is far less pernicious in the sum of its consequences. From such verses the poems in these volumes will be found distinguished at least by one mark of difference, that each of them has a worthy *purpose*. Not that I always began to write with a distinct purpose formally conceived; but habits of meditation have, I trust, so prompted and regulated my feelings, that my descriptions of such objects as strongly excite those feelings, will be found to carry along with them a *pur-*

pose. If this opinion be erroneous, I can have little right to the name of a poet. For all good poetry is the spontaneous overflow of powerful feelings: and though this be true, poems to which any value can be attached were never produced on any variety of subjects but by a man who, being possessed of more than usual organic sensibility, had also thought long and deeply. For our continued influxes of feeling are modified and directed by our thoughts, which are indeed the representatives of all our past feelings; and as by contemplating the relation of these general representatives to each other, we discover what is really important to men, so, by the repetition and continuance of this act, our feelings will be connected with important subjects, till at length, if we be originally possessed of much sensibility, such habits of mind will be produced that, by obeying blindly and mechanically the impulses of those habits, we shall describe objects, and utter sentiments, of such a nature, and in such connection with each other, that the understanding of the reader must necessarily be in some degree enlightened, and his affections strengthened and purified.

It has been said that each of these poems has a purpose. Another circumstance must be mentioned which distinguishes these poems from the popular poetry of the day; it is this, that the feeling therein developed gives importance to the action and situation, and not the action and situation to the feeling.

A sense of false modesty shall not prevent me from asserting that the reader's attention is pointed to this mark of distinction far less for the sake of these particular poems than from the general importance of the subject. The subject is indeed important! For the human mind is capable of being excited without the application of gross and violent stimulants; and he must have a very faint perception of its beauty and dignity who does not know this, and who does not further know that one being is elevated above another, in proportion as he possesses this capability. It has therefore appeared to me that to endeavor to produce or enlarge this capability is one of the best services in which, at any period, a writer can be engaged; but this service, excellent at all times, is especially so at the present day. For a multitude of causes, unknown to former times, are now acting with a combined force to blunt the discriminating powers of the mind, and, unfitting it for all voluntary exertion, to reduce it to a state of almost savage torpor. The most effective of these causes are the great national events which are daily taking place, and the increasing accumulation of men in cities, where the uniformity of their occupations produces a craving for extraordinary incident, which the rapid communication of intelligence hourly gratifies. To this tendency of life and manners the literature and theatrical exhibitions of the country have conformed themselves. The invaluable works of our elder writers, I had almost said the works of Shakespeare and Milton, are driven into neglect by frantic novels, sickly and stupid German tragedies, and deluges of idle and extravagant stories in verse. When I think upon this degrading thirst after outrageous stimulation, I am almost ashamed to have spoken of the feeble endeavor made in these volumes to counteract it; and, reflecting upon the magnitude of the general evil, I should be oppressed with no dishonorable melancholy, had I not a deep impression of certain inherent and indestructible qualities of the human mind, and likewise of certain powers in the great and permanent objects that act upon it, which are equally inherent and indestructible; and were there not added to this impression a belief that the time is approaching when the evil will be systematically opposed by men of greater powers, and with far more distinguished success. . . .

9. SCHLEIERMACHER: The New Significance of Religion

Romanticism is a rekindling of religion, however implicit or unorthodox the form. An explicitly religious thinker of the time is Friedrich Schleiermacher (1768–1834), who might be called the father of religious modernism. He, like other romantics, conceived of religion as the deepest love of the greatest beauty; and again, and with a vengeance, the theme is "back to the source." Rationalism, he said, with its deistic arguments and counterarguments, its pros and cons concerning a remote mechanical-engineer or watchmaker God, reduced religion to a "plaything of the mind" and deprived us of the total involvement in the universe with which original religion can sustain us. Intellectualistic dogmatizing and catechizing have also contributed to the deprivation.

For Schleiermacher as for Wordsworth, feelings are cognitive. When we *feel* dependent upon the universe, then we can be sure that is the way things are; that is, we really *are* dependent, contingent beings, incapable of creating ourselves or even maintaining ourselves in existence without the support of the not-self; indeed for each breath we take we are dependent upon something to be breathed, and for each mark we make we require something that can be marked. He describes the ultimate feeling-knowing of dependency as a religious experience: "the whole soul is dissolved in the immediate feeling of the Infinite and Eternal." This immediate feeling is knowledge of the divine.

Furthermore, we again find the theme that freedom is perfect necessity: the necessity of a course of action that locates and completes the self in that which transcends it. Here is a doctrine of positive freedom and a reformulation of the traditional Christian conception that man is most free when he is most "enslaved" to the will of God: it is only when a man is embraced by the righteous power of God that he is able to do the right.

The selection which I have despaired of translating literally is from the aptly titled *Talks on Religion to Its Cultured Despisers,* 1799.

Undoubtedly you are familiar with the history of human folly, and I am sure you have surveyed the various forms of religious doctrine —from the absurd fables of lawless peoples to the most refined deism, from the rude superstitions of human sacrifice to the poorly constructed scraps of metaphysics and ethics that we now call purified Christianity, and doubtless you have found them all without point or meaning. The last thing I want to do is contradict you. Instead, if you merely mean by your conclusion that the most cultured and refined religious system is no better than the rudest, if you have merely perceived that the divine cannot lie in a continuum both ends of which are mundane and despicable, then I will gladly relieve you of the trouble of bothering to evaluate what lies in between. Perhaps all religions appear to you to be transitions and stages toward the final form. Perhaps, due to the handiwork of its own age, each stage becomes better articulated and polished, until at last it has grown equal to that perfect plaything with which our century has presented history. However, this artful consummation of doctrines and systems is usually anything but a consummation of religion. . . .

If you have concerned yourselves exclusively with these dogmas and opinions, therefore, you do not yet know religion itself, and what you despise is not it. Why have you not cut deeper and located the kernel in this shell? Lazy seekers, your voluntary ignorance and your all-too-smug satisfaction over the first thing you turn up astonish me. Why don't you look at the religious life itself, and first at those blessed exaltations of the mind in which all other activities are set aside or almost suppressed, and in which the whole self is dissolved in the immediate feeling of the infinite and eternal? The inclination which you pretend to dislike reveals itself in basic and palpable form in such moments. Only someone who has studied and has really known man while he is subject to these emotions can recognize in the external manifestations of religion what is truly religious. He will surely perceive something more in the externals than you will. An integral part of these manifestations is something of that spiritual substance without which they could not have arisen. But when clumsy, ignorant hands try to unwrap a spiritual substance, and dissect it and examine it disdainfully, nothing but a cold dead mass will appear for their scrutiny.

If you consider academic philosophical systems, for instance, how often you find that they are merely homes for the perpetuation of the dead letter. The protean spirit of enraptured recognition is too ephemeral and too free for the rigid forms employed by those who wish to grasp and hold things that are strange to human beings. That anyone should in any unqualified sense regard the architects of such mammoth and unnatural thought systems as true philosophers is incredible. That one would seek to learn from them the spirit of their research is lamentable. Wouldn't you advise such a person, "Be careful, friend, that you have not hit upon those who merely follow and collect, those who are satisfied to quit while they have only second-hand information. With them you will never find the spirit of the art; you must go to the discoverers in whom the spirit rests"? The same advice must be given to those who seek true religion. It is even more necessary in the case of religion, since religion in its very essence is as far removed from what is systematic as philosophy is naturally disposed to it.

Let us for the moment consider only those who originated the ingenious, unnatural religious systems, the mutability of which you deprecate, and the incongruity of which (given your contemptuous tendency) strikes you as almost absurd. Have these systems come from the heroes of religion? Name one systematizer who has brought any kind of new revelation down to us . . . there are none. So you must not blame me that I do not count among the heroes of religion theologians of the letter who believe that salvation of the world and the light of wisdom are to be found in a new dressing of formulas, or a new arrangement of ingenious proofs. Only in isolation, when celestial feelings are unburdened, when sacred fires burst out from a supercharged spirit, only then can there be a mighty thunder of speech announcing that God is revealing Himself. There, in that state, ideas and words are simply the necessary and inextricable product of the heart, only to be understood by it and along with it.

10. FICHTE: Moral Obligation as Revelation of Reality

In Johann Fichte (1762–1814) and Friedrich von Schelling, both Germans, we encounter romantics who are philosophers in the more precise sense of the term. Their thought can only be understood as specific developments of particular doctrines in Kant.

According to Kant's *Critique of Pure Reason*, the world known by the senses and studied by natural science is a collection of appearances or phenomena presented to the mind. Since the mind has a definite structure, the phenomena must conform to this structure in certain general ways if they are to be known at all; that is, be presentations to the mind (something like light's being bent in a definite way when projected upon a mirror with a definite surface, or matter's being shaped in a definite way when pressed into a mold). By understanding the ways in which the mind is able to know things as they appear to it, we can have some infallible knowledge of phenomena, *i.e.*, things as they appear to us. But Kant maintained that there is always more to an object in the world than can be revealed by any sequence of its phenomenal presentations, however long the sequence; we must ever suppose that something is left over, unpresented. This he regarded as "the thing in itself," the "noumenon," as he called it, and this he thought to be unknowable.

One's self, according to Kant's *Critique of Pure Reason*, is a prime example of something noumenal or "in itself," and one can have no scientific knowledge of the self aside from knowing that some sort of subject for knowledge and some knower must be there. It is only in terms of his ethical philosophy, as elaborated in the *Critique of Practical Reason*, that he discussed the characteristics of the self. He inferred that because we know the moral law, we know what we ought to do; and since it is absurd to say that we ought to do what we cannot do, we know that the moral law must be something we are *able* to do; the noumenal or real self, then, must be free.

Both Fichte and Schelling rejected the limitations Kant placed on reason. In so doing, they did not just expand Kant's philosophy; they radically altered it. It was precisely by means of limiting infallible knowledge about the world to the range of sense experience or phenomena that Kant had tried to extricate himself from Hume's skepticism and build a foundation for his new, modest metaphysics in which reason is tamed but made usable.*

Schelling refers to Kant's dualism of knowable phenomena and unknowable noumena when he writes, "He estranges us—we are left with specters." Fichte's method of breaching the Kantian limitations on reason was radically to expand the jurisdiction of the practical reason so as to bring all of reality, as well as the whole throbbing, noumenal self, into its scope. Schelling's method, equally audacious and equally repugnant to Kant, was to apply to absolute reality itself what Kant applied to phenomena only: No object in the universe can be discussed outside of its relationship to the mind; each object is just an object for a knower.

Fichte's analysis of the self-conscious self fastens initially upon an awareness of a primal impulse to purposive, moral activity. Fichte notes, however, that this awareness can be doubted. Perhaps some unknown foreign power intervenes and the impulse to act is not ours at all. We can doubt whether our awareness of the impulse is truthful, and then we can doubt the truthfulness of the awareness of the awareness, *ad infinitum, ad nauseam*. Perhaps our entire experience is composed of distorted images, deceptive pictures and nothing is substantive. But if we proceed along this speculative tangent, our duty to act morally is never done; instead of acting on our impulse to moral activity, we doubt the impulse. And if this happens we fail to be moral, for we do what we ought not to do.

Fichte draws his grand conclusion: We do our duty then, and do not doubt it. And in so doing we must believe that other autonomous beings exist that have duties and rights like our own; it is part of our duty to believe this about them. Supposedly unknowable noumenal realities—in this case other selves—fall to the blade of reason and into its garner. Moreover, belief in duty involves the belief that there must be a whole world of want, need and physical and moral obstacles. For without something real to be overcome, the duty to overcome it cannot be real; but, Fichte says, the duty is real. So the noumenal *is* known.

"Practical reason is the root of all reason," he writes, and he writes provocative lines such as, "I do not hunger because food is present; but a thing becomes food for me because I hunger." His tendency to combine moral will, inclination and self-realization is understandable in the face of the Kantian critique, which struck him as alienating man from the world and from his own desiring, enthusiastic self. Fichte is in this way

* Kant could be certain that sense experience *alone must* conform to the structure of the mind on grounds remotely similar to one's being certain that soft but solid material *alone must* conform to a mold into which it is pressed.

a source for American pragmatism. As William James later maintained, what a thing is (its essence) is just its most important characteristics; and what is important about the thing cannot be discussed out of relationship to the human needs, purposes and interests which make certain characteristics important.

This selection is from Chapter 10 of *The Destiny of Man* (1800), sometimes translated, *The Vocation of Man.**

. . . Not merely to know, but according to thy knowledge to *do,* is the destiny of man. "Not for leisurely contemplation of thyself, not to brood over devout sensations, art thou here. Thine action, thine action alone, determines thy worth."

This voice, which sounds from the innermost recesses of my soul, leads me out of mere knowledge, to something lying beyond and entirely opposed to it; something which is higher than all knowledge, and contains within itself the end and object of all knowledge.

If I shall act, I shall doubtless know that I act, and how I act; but this knowledge will not be itself the act, but will merely behold it. This voice then announces to me what I sought, a something lying beyond knowledge, and in its nature entirely independent of it. Thus it is, I know this immediately, intuitively, but I have entered on the territories of speculation, and doubt once awakened will continue secretly to disturb me, unless I can justify my belief even before this tribunal. I must ask myself therefore, how is it thus? Whence arises that voice in my soul which leads me beyond the boundaries of knowledge?

There is in me an impulse to absolute independent self-activity. Nothing is more insupportable to me, than to be merely by another, for another, and through another.

I will be something by my own unaided effort. This impulse is inseparably united with my self-consciousness.

I endeavour to explain this feeling, to give sight to this blind impulse by thought. It urges me to independent action. Who am I? Subject and object in one—contemplating and contemplated, thinking and thought of. As both must I have become what I am; as both must I originate ideas, and produce a state or mode of being beyond them. I ascribe to myself as an intelligence the power of originating the idea of a purpose, and further of manifesting this idea in action; a real effective productive power, which is something quite different from

* Translated by Mrs. Percy Sinnet, 1846.

the capacity of ideal conception. Those ideas of purpose or design are not, like the ideas of knowledge, imitations or representations of something already given, but much rather types of something yet to be produced. The power or force which produces them lies beyond them, and only becomes manifest in them. Such an independent energy it is that in consequence of this impulse I ascribe to myself.

Here then, it appears, does the consciousness of all reality begin; the real efficacy of my idea, and the real power of action which in consequence of it I am compelled to ascribe to myself, commences at this point. Let it be as it may with the reality of the sensual world, I have reality in myself.

I can make this active power the subject of thought, but I do not produce it from my thought. The immediate feeling of this impulse to activity lies at the foundation of my thought, and thought does no more than conceive this feeling according to its own laws. . . .

I understand thee now, sublime Spirit! I have found the organ by which to apprehend this reality, and probably all other. It is not knowledge, for knowledge can only demonstrate and establish itself; every knowledge supposes some higher knowledge on which it is founded, and of this ascent there is no end. It is Faith, that voluntary reposing on the views naturally presenting themselves to us, because through these views only we can fulfil our destiny; which approves of knowledge, and raises to certainty and conviction that which without it might be mere delusion. It is no knowledge, but a resolution of the will to admit this knowledge. This is no mere verbal distinction, but a true and deep one, pregnant with the most important consequences for my whole character. Let me for ever hold fast by it. . . .

Thus also has it been with every human creature who has been born into the world. Unconsciously they have all seized on the reality which exists for them only through faith, and this intuitive faith forces itself on them simultaneously with their existence. If in mere knowledge, in mere perception and thought, we can discover no ground for regarding our mental presentations as more than mere pictures, why do we all nevertheless regard them as more, and imagine for them a basis, a *substratum* independent of all their modifications? If we all possess the capacity and the instinct to go beyond this natural view of things, why do so few follow this instinct, exercise this capacity, nay, even resist, with a sort of bitterness, when one seeks to urge them towards this path? What holds them imprisoned in these natural boundaries? Not inferences of reason, for there are none which could do this. It is our deep interest in reality that does this; in the good that is to be produced, in the common and sensuous that is to be enjoyed. From this interest, this concern in reality, can no one who lives detach himself, and just as little from the faith which that brings with it. We are all born in faith, and he who is blind, follows blindly the secret and irresistible attraction; he who sees, follows by sight, and believes because he will believe.

What unity and completeness, what dignity, does our human nature receive from this view. Our thought is not based on itself, independently of our instincts and inclinations; man does not consist of two existences running parallel to each other; he is absolutely one. Our entire system of thought is founded on intuition, and as is the heart of the individual, so is his knowledge. Our instinct forces on us a certain mode of thought, only so long as we do not perceive the constraint; the moment the constraint appears, it vanishes, and it is no longer the instinct by itself, but we ourselves through our instinct, who form our system of thought.

But it is appointed that I shall open my eyes; shall learn to know myself; shall perceive the constraint, and that I shall thus of necessity form my own mode of thought. I am absolutely free—the source of my own spiritual life as of my thought. I would not that my character should be the production of Nature, but of myself, and I have become that which I would be.

By the unlimited pursuit of sophistical subtilties I might have darkened and made doubtful the natural view of my own spiritual nature, but I have chosen the system I have now adopted with foresight and deliberation from other possible modes of thought, because I regarded it as the most worthy the dignity of my nature and destiny. Freely and consciously I have returned to the point at which Nature had abandoned me. I admit her declaration, not because I must, but because I will.

The noble destiny to which my understanding is appointed, fills me with reverence. It no longer serves merely to call forth an endless succession of representations proceeding from nothing and tending to nothing; it is entrusted to me for a great purpose. Its cultivation to this end is confided to my hands, and will be at my hands again required. I know immediately, and my faith requires no further confirmation of this than my immediate consciousness that I am not necessitated to a blind and aimless succession of thoughts, but that I can voluntarily direct my attention to one object, and turn it from another; that it is I who think, and that I can choose the subject of my thought. By reflection I have found that my whole manner of thinking, and the views which I take of truth, depend only on myself, since I can choose whether I will go on subtilising till I lose all power of recognising truth, or whether I will yield myself to it with faithful obedience. My mode of thinking, the cultivation of my understanding, and the objects to which I direct it, depend entirely on my will. True insight is merit; the perversion of my capacity for knowledge, thoughtlessness, error, and unbelief, are culpable.

There is but one point towards which I should unceasingly direct my thoughts,—namely, what is appointed for me to do, and what is the most suitable mode of doing it.

My thoughts must bear relation to my actions, and must be regarded as means to this end, otherwise they are idle and aimless, a mere waste of time and strength, and the perversion of a noble power.

I may hope, I may surely promise myself success in this purpose. The Nature on which I have to act is not a system foreign to myself, into which I cannot penetrate. It is regulated by my own laws of thought, and cannot but agree with them; its interior must be transparent, penetrable, and knowable to me. It expresses everywhere nothing more than the relations of my own being, and I may hope as certainly to know it as to know myself. Let me seek only what I should seek, and I shall find; let me ask only what I should ask, and I shall receive an answer.

The voice in my soul in which I will have faith, and for the sake of which I have faith in all else, does not merely command me generally to act, but in every particular situation it declares what I shall do and what leave undone; it accompanies me through every event of my life, and it is impossible for me to contend against it. To listen to it and obey it honestly and impartially, without fear or equivocation, is the business of my existence. My life is no longer an empty play without truth or significance. It is appointed that what conscience ordains me shall be done, and for this purpose am I here. I have understanding to know, and power to execute it.

By conscience alone comes truth and reality into my representations. I cannot refuse to it my attention and my obedience, if I would not renounce the end of my existence. It is true, and the foundation of all other truth and reality, that its voice is to be obeyed, and consequently all is true which is assumed in the possibility of such an obedience.

There appear before me in space, certain phenomena, to which I transfer the idea of myself. I conceive them as being like myself. A certain speculative system has indeed taught me, or would teach me, that these rational beings outside myself are but the productions of my own power of representative perception; that according to the laws of my thought I am compelled to carry my ideas thus out of myself, and that by the same laws I can only apply them to certain conceptions of space, time and the like. But the law of my conscience requires me to regard them as free substantive existences, entirely independent of myself, and declares that the purposes of their being lie in themselves, and that I dare by no means interfere with their fulfilment, nay, that I am bound to forward it to the utmost of my power. It commands me to reverence their freedom, and to sympathise in their destiny as similar to my own. In this manner will and must I act towards them, if I have resolved to obey the voice of my conscience; and regarding them from this point, the speculations which perplexed me vanish like an empty dream. I think of them as beings like myself, I have said; but strictly speaking, it is not by mere thought that they are presented to me as such. It is by the voice of my conscience saying, "This is the limit of thy freedom; here know and reverence the aims of others." This is but translated into the thought, here is another being free and independent like thyself, thy fellow creature!

There appear before me other phænomena, which I do not regard as beings like myself, but as things irrational. Speculation finds no difficulty in showing how these are developed from, and are the necessary productions of, my own representative perceptions. But I apprehend these things, also, by want, and desire, and enjoyment. Not by the mental conception alone, but by hunger, and thirst, and satiety, does anything become for me food and drink. I am necessitated to believe in the reality of that which threatens my sensuous existence, or in that which alone is able to maintain it. Conscience comes to the assistance of this natural instinct, and consecrates and limits it. Thou shalt preserve, exercise, strengthen thy sensuous power, for it has been counted upon in the plans of reason; but thou canst only preserve it by employing it in a manner conformable to the inward laws of these things. There are, also, other beings in thy likeness, upon whose force, also, calculation has been made, as upon thine. Permit to them the same use of all that has been allowed to thee. Respect, as their right, what is destined for them; what is destined for thee, as thine. Thus shall I act—according to this action must I think. I am compelled to regard these things as standing under their own laws, independent of, though perceivable by, me—the laws of nature, and therefore to ascribe to them an independent existence. I am compelled to believe in such laws, the task of investigating them is set before me, and that empty speculation vanishes like a mist before the sun. In short, there is for me no such thing as a pure existence, in which I have no concern, and which I contemplate merely for the sake of the contemplation. It exists for me merely by its relation to me, and there is one relation to which all others are subordinate—that of moral action. My world is the object and sphere of my duties, and absolutely nothing more; my capacity, and the capacity of all finite beings, is sufficient to comprehend any other. . . .

To the question, whether, in deed and in fact, such a world is present as I represent to myself, can I give no more fundamental answer—none more raised above doubt, than this. I have, most certainly, such and such determinate duties, and they cannot be otherwise fulfilled than in such a world as I represent to myself. Even to any who had never meditated on his moral destiny, if there could be such a one, or who had never formed any resolution concerning it, even with a view to an indefinite future, even for him, his sensuous world, and his belief in its reality, arises in no other manner than from his ideas of a moral world. If he should not apprehend this by the thought of his duties, he certainly will by the demand for his rights. What he does not require of himself he will certainly require of others; that they should treat him with consideration, not as an irrational thing, but as a free and intelligent being; and thus, that they may be enabled to meet his own claims, he will be necessitated to regard them, also, as free and independent of mere natural agency. If he proposes to himself no other object in his relations to things surrounding him than that of enjoyment, he at least requires this enjoyment as a right, and demands from others that they should leave him undisturbed in this enjoyment; and thus embraces even the world of sense in his moral idea. These claims of regard for the preservation of his own existence, for his freedom and rationality, no one will willingly renounce; and in his ideas of these claims, at least, is found earnestness and belief in reality, and denial of doubt, if even they are not associated with the acknowledgment of a moral law in his heart.

It is not therefore the operation of what we regard as things external, which do indeed exist for us only inasmuch as we know of them, and just as little the play of imagination and thought, whose products as such are no more than empty pictures, but the necessary faith in our own freedom and energy, and in the reality of our actions, and of certain laws of human action, which lie at the root of all our consciousness of external reality, a consciousness which is itself only belief, founded on another unavoidable belief. We are compelled to admit that we act, and that we ought to act, in a certain manner; we are compelled to assume a certain sphere for this action—this sphere is the actual world as we find it. From the necessity of action proceeds the consciousness of the external world, and not the reverse way, from the consciousness of the external world the necessity of action. From the latter is the former deduced. We do not act because we know, but we know because we are destined to act; practical reason is the root of all reason. The laws of action for rational creatures are of *immediate certainty*; and their world is only certain so far as these are so. We cannot deny them without annihilating the world, and ourselves with it. We raise ourselves from nothing, and maintain ourselves above it solely by our moral agency.

I am required to act, but can I act without having in view something beyond the action itself, without directing my intentions to something which could only be attained by my action? Can I will, without willing some particular thing? To every action is united in thought, immediately and by the laws of thought itself, some future existence—a state of being related to my action as effect to cause. This object of my action is not, however, to determine my mode of action—I am not to place the object before me, and then determine how I am to act that I may attain it—my action is not to be dependent on the object, but I am to act in a certain manner, merely because it is my duty so to act; this is the first point. That some consequence will follow this action I know, and this consequence necessarily becomes an object to me, since I am bound to perform the action which must bring it to pass. I will that something shall happen, because I am to act so that it may happen. As I do not hunger because food is present, but a thing becomes food for me because I hunger, so I do not act thus, or thus, because a certain end is to be attained, but the end is to be attained since I must act in the manner to attain it. I do not observe a certain point, and allow its position to determine the direction of my line, and the angle that it shall make; but I draw simply a right angle, and by that determine the points through which my line must pass. The end does not determine the commandment, but the commandment the end. . . .

11. SCHELLING: Artistic Talent as Revelation of Reality

"Prince of romanticists"—that is Josiah Royce's happy characterization of Friedrich von Schelling (1775–1854), a badly neglected thinker. Nearly all the romantic themes are fully present in Schelling's work: union of mind and world; art as the key to this union, and to the union of freedom and necessity as well; interdependence of opposites; spontaneous, evolutionary development of the religiously conceived whole.

Schelling's contention that mind and world have a common center, and in the last analysis are identical, cannot be dismissed as mere childish anthropomorphism which animates the inanimate, personifies the impersonal, sets animals to talking, etc. It is a development, rather, of a core theme in western thought: What we think of (in its essence or whatness, at least) must characterize the thought thinking it as well, for thought can be characterized only as thought of this determinate thing. This is similar to Aristotle and St. Thomas. However, Schelling came after Kant and took his point of departure from him; he gave Kantian philosophy an interpretation that Kant himself would have vehemently repudiated: The mind-world relationship is construed as symmetrical; the world is relative to mind in the sense that there are no determinate things at all unless they are objects for actual, active mind. There is no thing in itself or noumenon. Matter, as studied by physics, is merely extinguished mind; only this accounts for the intelligibility which physics can find there. Thus world and mind are two poles of one reality, with mind being the positive one which supplies final intelligibility.*

Ultimate reality for Schelling is immanent in our experience and it evolves: One creative energy flows through both mind and world. Things cannot be understood in isolation of the evolving context in which they participate. The logic of identity, in the Aristotelian sense that "A is A," is adequate for abstract entities like numbers, but it is inadequate for things of nature which are what they are, not only relative to mind but, within this encompassing relativity, relative as well both to what they are not and to what they are not yet.† Although Schelling would main-

---

* Schelling's equation of intelligibility and intelligence suggests that the psychical and objective aspects of thought have been lumped together; it suggests that the doctrine of "intentionality," as found, for example, in St. Thomas has been imperfectly understood. It is not until Husserl appears in the early twentieth century that the doctrine of intentionality is fully restored.

† I do not know whether Schelling denies the law of contradiction. I do know that he writes in *Of Human Freedom* (trans. by Guttman, p. 33), "Nothing is the 'other' and yet no being has being without the other."

tain that all is included in one Absolute mind, we nevertheless do find a triple relativity.

What is prior in time is not a most perfect actual Being (like a transcendent God), but a gnawing potency which strains toward realization. Things have not been settled; ultimate reality is in the making and we are in on the creative process with all its struggles. Ordinary theism Schelling stigmatizes as "a God that is alien to nature and a nature that is devoid of God." Moreover, evil for Schelling is no stumbling block, but a challenge which prompts the creation of moral value—a good in the making. God himself evolves through strife and travail.

Live dangerously—that is romantic, I suppose (though the world-process is necessary, it is no less dangerous). And it is romantic too to think that the way of salvation lies through esthetic experience, as Schelling does: In good sculpture, say, we emulate nature, but we do not so by passively mirroring a form which has been preunderstood in the quantitative terms of physics; we do so by a logically prior grasping and expressing of its essence, which, as a process, is analogous to the process by which the thing itself is expressed in nature. Like is known by like and art explicates the universe.

Schelling teaches that the world comes to self-consciousness in artistically creative men, but nature is not yet wholly self-conscious. Some essences are embodied as actually existing things because of a primordial, unreflecting, spontaneous divine mind and will. Great works of art, Schelling says, are those which emulate nature in this respect also: more gets expressed than was consciously intended. Like nature, this art is a "life self-supported and independent of the producer." An "unconscious action" has combined with the conscious one.

Disregarding his metaphysics, Schelling certainly gives us a more realistic account of the unconscious than the current and popular "cellar view," which conceives as something cut off from consciousness or "beneath" or "behind" it. It is more realistic because there is more to *any* act than what is revealed in focally conscious intention. There are shadowy and fleeting fringes and margins in the stream of consciousness, as William James was later to point out, which are difficult to grasp reflectively in a succeeding instant, and which probably account for the fact that spontaneous action begets more consequences than were consciously intended. That, and not caprice, would seem to be the true spice, flare and dividend of freedom; it requires the connection of the unconscious and the conscious, not their separation.

But, as later nineteenth-century thinkers were better to discern, there is more in subconsciousness than artistic impulse; there is much that is opaque, inartistic and terrifying. So even in Schelling, who is the apparent apogee of romanticism, we can gain the summit only to see beyond it.

The first selection is from the opening pages of Schelling's *The Relation of Plastic Art to Nature* (1807), translated by Bruce Wilshire.

According to the oldest account, plastic art is silent poetry. The originator of this definition doubtless meant that the former is to express spiritual thoughts just like the latter; except not by speech, but by shape, by form, by corporeal, independent works—like silent nature.

Therefore it is evident that plastic art stands as a uniting link between the soul and nature, and can only be grasped in the living center of both. Indeed, since plastic art relates to the soul in the same way that every other art does, and especially poetry, its only peculiarity is its mode of connection with nature. . . .

We hope, therefore, in considering plastic art in relation to its true prototype and original source, nature, to be able to contribute something new to its theory—to give greater exactness and clearness to the conceptions of it; but, most importantly, to elucidate the coherence of the whole structure of art in the light of a higher necessity.

But has not science always recognized this relation? Has not the point of departure of every modern theory been that art should imitate nature? Certainly this is true. But what good is this sweeping generality to the artist when the concept of nature is so diversely interpreted? . . . To one person nature is nothing but the lifeless aggregate of an indeterminable crowd of objects, or the space in which he imagines things placed, as in a container; to another nothing but the soil from which he derives his nourishment and support; to the inspired seeker alone, the holy and continuously creative original energy of the world which generates and busily evolves all things out of itself.

The proposition would have a towering significance indeed if it taught art to emulate this creative force; but the sense in which it was meant can scarcely be doubted by anybody apprised of the universal condition of science at the time that it was first advanced. How singular that the very persons who denied all life to nature should set it up for imitation in art! At them might be directed the words of a profound writer: "Your deceitful philosophy has deposed nature; so why do you call upon us to imitate her? Is it so you can wreak the same violence on the disciples of nature and renew the pleasure?"

To them nature was not only a dumb but a totally lifeless image in whose inmost being no living word dwelt—a hollow scaffolding of forms from which a similarly hollow image was to be transferred to the canvas or cut out of stone. . . .

How can we spiritually melt, so to speak, this apparently rigid form, so that the pure energy of things may flow together with the power of our spirit and both become one single casting. We must surpass form in order to gain it again as intelligible, living and truly felt. Take the most beautiful forms. After you have abstracted from the inward creative principle, what remains? Nothing but mere unessential qualities such as extension and spatial relations. Does the fact that one portion of matter exists near another, but distinct from it, contribute anything to its inner essence—or does it not rather contribute nothing? Evidently the last. Not mere contiguous existence but the manner of it makes form. And this can be determined only by a positive force, which subordinates the manifold of parts to the unity of one idea. . . . From the force that works in the crystal to the force comparable to a gentle magnetic current which gives to the particles of matter in the human form that position and arrangement among themselves—through this the idea, the essential unity and beauty, can become visible. . . .

All unity must be spiritual in origin and nature. And what is the aim of all investigation of nature but to find science within it? . . . The science by which nature operates is not, however, like human science, which is connected with reflection on itself; in the science of nature the conception is not separate from the act, nor the design from its execution. Raw matter strives blindly, so to speak, for regular shape and unwittingly achieves pure stereometric forms, which belong nevertheless to the realm of ideas and are something spiritual in the material. . . .

The link that binds idea and form, body and soul, is this formative science in nature and art. First of all there stands an eternal idea framed in the infinite understanding—but how does this idea flow into actuality and incarnation? Only by virtue of the creative science, which is as necessarily connected with the infinite understanding as the principle in the artist that grasps the idea that unsensuous beauty is linked with that which presents it to the senses. . . .

Long ago it was recognized that in art not everything is performed with consciousness; that with the conscious activity an unconscious activity must combine; and that the loftiest in art is born of the perfect unity and interpenetration of the two. Works that lack the seal of unconscious knowing are detectable by the clear absence of a life that is self-sufficient and independent of the producer; whereas on the contrary, when the unconscious acts, art imparts to its work, along with the greatest clarity to the understanding, that unfathomable reality in which it resembles a work of nature.

This second selection is taken from the beginning of Schelling's chief work, *System of Transcendental Idealism* (1800). It affords an introduction to his technical philosophy.*

Section I. Idea of Transcendental Philosophy

1. All knowledge is based upon the agreement of an objective with a subjective. For we *know* only the true, and the truth is universally held to be the agreement of representations with their objects.

2. The sum of all that is purely objective in our knowledge we may call Nature; whereas the sum of everything subjective may be termed the *Ego*, or Intelligence. These two concepts are mutually opposed. Intelligence is originally conceived as that which solely represents, and nature as that which is merely capable of representation; the former as the conscious—the latter as the unconscious. But in all knowledge there is necessary a mutual agreement of the two—the conscious and the unconscious *per se*. The problem is to explain this agreement.

3. In knowledge itself, in that I know, the objective and subjective are so united that one cannot say which of the two has priority. There is here no first and no second—the two are contemporaneous and one. In any attempt to explain this identity, I must already have resolved it. In order to explain it, inasmuch as there is nothing else given me as a principle of explanation except these two factors of knowledge, I must of necessity place the one before the other, that is to say, must set out from the one in order to arrive at the other. From which of the two I shall set out is not determined by the problem.

4. There are, consequently, only two cases possible:

A. *Either the objective is made first, and the question arises how a subjective agreeing with it is superinduced.*

The idea of the subjective is not contained in the idea of the objective; on the contrary they mutually exclude each other. The

* Translated by Benjamin Rand in his *Modern Classical Philosophers* (Boston: Houghton Mifflin Company, 1908).

subjective must therefore be *superinduced* upon the objective. It forms no part of the conception of Nature that there must be likewise an intelligence to represent it. Nature, to all appearance, would exist even if there were nothing to represent it. The problem may therefore likewise be expressed thus: How is the Intelligent superinduced upon Nature? or, How does Nature come to be represented?

The problem assumes Nature, or the objective, as the first. It is, therefore, undoubtedly the task of natural science, which does the same. That natural science actually, and without knowing it, approximates, at least, to the solution of this problem, can here be only briefly shown.

If all knowledge has, as it were, two poles, which mutually presuppose and demand each other, then they must seek each other in all sciences. There must, therefore, of necessity, exist two fundamental sciences; and it must be impossible to set out from one pole without being driven to the other. The necessary tendency of all natural science, therefore, is to proceed from Nature to the intelligent. This, and this alone, lies at the foundation of the effort to bring theory into natural phenomena. The final perfection of natural science would be the complete intellectualization of all the laws of Nature into laws of intuition and of thought. The phenomena, that is, the material, must completely vanish, and leave only the laws,—that is, the formal. Hence it happens that the more the conformity to law is manifested in Nature, so much the more the wrapping disappears—the phenomena themselves become more intellectualized, and at length entirely cease. Optical phenomena are nothing more than a geometry whose lines are drawn by aid of the light; and even this light itself is already of doubtful materiality. In the phenomena of magnetism every trace of matter has already vanished; and of the phenomena of gravitation, which even the natural philosopher believed could be attributed only to direct spiritual influence, there remains nothing but their law, whose performance on a large scale is the mechanism of the heavenly motions. The complete theory of Nature would be that by virtue of which the whole of Nature should be resolved into an intelligence. The dead and unconscious products of Nature are only unsuccessful attempts of Nature to reflect itself, but the so-called dead Nature is merely an unripe Intelligence; hence in its phenomena the intelligent character appears, though still unconscious. Its highest aim, that is of becoming wholly self-objective, Nature does not attain, except in its highest and last reflection, which is none other than man, or more generally what we call reason. By its means Nature first turns completely back upon itself, and thereby it is manifest that Nature is originally identical with what in us is known as intelligent and conscious.

This may suffice to prove that natural science has a necessary tendency to render Nature intelligent. By this very tendency it becomes natural philosophy, which is one of the two necessary fundamental sciences of philosophy.

B. *Or the subjective is made first, and the problem is, how an objective is superinduced agreeing with it.*

If all knowledge is based upon the agreement of these two, then the problem to explain this agreement is undoubtedly the highest for all knowledge; and if, as is generally admitted, philosophy is the highest and loftiest of all sciences, it becomes certainly the chief task of philosophy.

But the problem demands only the explanation of that agreement generally, and leaves it entirely undetermined where the explanation shall begin, what it shall make its first, and what its second. Since also the two opposites are mutually necessary, the result of the operation is the same, from whichever point one sets out. To make the objective first, and to derive the subjective from it, is, as has just been shown, the task of natural philosophy.

If, therefore, there is a transcendental philosophy, the only direction remaining for it is the opposite, that is: to proceed from the subjective as the first and the absolute, and to deduce the origin of the objective from it. Natural and transcendental philosophy have divided between themselves these two possible directions of philosophy. And if all philosophy must have for an aim to make either an Intelligence out of Nature or a Nature out of Intelligence, then transcendental philosophy, to which this latter problem belongs, is the other necessary fundamental science of philosophy.

SECTION II. COROLLARIES

In the foregoing we have not only deduced the concept of transcendental philosophy, but have at the same time afforded the reader a glance into the whole system of philosophy. It is composed, as has been shown, of two fundamental sciences, which though opposed to one another in principle and direction, reciprocally demand and supplement each other. Not the entire system of philosophy, but only the one fundamental science of it, is here to be set up, and, in the first place, to be more strictly characterized in accordance with the idea of it already deduced.

1. If, for transcendental philosophy, the subjective is the first and only ground of all reality, and the sole principle of explanation of everything else, then it necessarily begins with universal doubt regarding the reality of the objective.

As the natural philosopher, wholly intent upon the objective, seeks nothing so much as to exclude every admixture of the subjective in his knowledge, so, on the other hand, the transcendental philosopher seeks nothing so much as the entire exclusion of the objective from the purely subjective principle of knowledge. The means of separation is absolute scepticism—not that partial scepticism which is directed merely against the common prejudices of men and never sees the foundation—but the radical scepticism which aims not at the individual prejudices, but against the fundamental prejudice, with which all others must stand or fall. For beyond the artificial and inculcated prejudices of man, there exist others of deeper origin which have been placed in him not by art or education, but by nature itself. These are regarded by all except the philosopher, as the principles of knowledge, and by the mere thinker of self, as the test of all truth.

The one fundamental prejudice, to which all others may be reduced, is this: that there exist things outside of us. This is an opinion, which, although it rests neither on proofs nor on conclusions (for there is not a single valid proof of it), yet as it cannot be uprooted by any opposite proof (*naturam furcâ expellas, tamen usque redibit*), lays claim to immediate certainty. But since it refers to something wholly distinct from us, and, in fact, opposed to us, of which there is no evidence how it came into immediate consciousness, it must be regarded as nothing more than a prejudice—a natural and original one, to be sure, but nevertheless a prejudice.

The contradiction that a conclusion which in its nature cannot be immediately certain, is, nevertheless, blindly and without grounds, accepted as such, cannot be solved by transcendental philosophy, except on the assumption that this conclusion is implicitly, and without our being aware of it, not founded upon, but identical, and one and the same with an affirmation which is immediately certain. To demonstrate this identity will in reality be the task of transcendental philosophy.

2. Now, even for the ordinary use of reason, there exists nothing

immediately certain except the affirmation *I am*, which, since it loses all significance outside of immediate consciousness, is the most individual of all truths, and the absolute prejudice, which must be assumed, if anything else is to be made certain. The affirmation *There are things outside of us*, will therefore be certain for the transcendental philosopher, solely because of its identity with the affirmation *I am*; and its certainty will also only be equal to the certainty of the affirmation from which it derives its own.

According to this view transcendental knowledge would be distinguished from common knowledge in two particulars.

First.—That for it the certainty of the existence of external things is a mere prejudice, which it transcends, in order to investigate the grounds of it. (It can never be the task for transcendental philosophy to prove the existence of things in themselves, but only to show that it is a natural and necessary prejudice to assume external objects as real.)

Second.—That it separates the two affirmations, *I am* and *There are things outside of me*, which run together in the ordinary consciousness, and places the one before the other, in order to prove their identity and that immediate connection which in the other is only felt. By this act of separation, when it is completed, one transports one's self in the transcendental act of contemplation, which is by no means a natural, but an artificial one.

3. If the subjective alone has reality for the transcendental philosopher he will also make only the subjective directly his object. The objective will be for him only indirectly an object, and, whereas, in ordinary knowledge, knowledge itself—the act of knowing—disappears in the object, in transcendental knowledge, on the contrary, the object as such disappears in the act of knowing. Transcendental knowledge is therefore a knowledge of knowing, in so far as it is purely subjective.

Thus, for example, in intuition it is the objective only that reaches the ordinary consciousness; the act of intuition is itself lost in the object; whereas on the contrary the transcendental mode of observation gets only a glimpse of the object of intuition by the act of intuition. Thus the ordinary thinking is a mechanism, in which ideas prevail, without, however, being distinguished as ideas; whereas the transcendental act of thought interrupts this mechanism, and in becoming conscious of the idea as an act, rises to the idea of the idea. In ordinary action, the acting is itself forgotten in the object of the action; philosophizing is also an action, but not an action only. It is likewise a continued self-intuition in this action.

The nature of the transcendental mode of thought must consist, therefore, in general in this: that, in it, that which in all other thinking, knowing, or acting escapes the consciousness, and is absolutely non-objective, is brought into consciousness, and becomes objective. In brief, it consists in a continuous act of becoming an object to itself on the part of the subjective.

The transcendental art will therefore consist in the ability to maintain one's self constantly in this duplicity of acting and thinking.

Section III. Preliminary Division of Transcendental Philosophy

This division is preliminary, because the principles of the division can be derived only from the science itself.

We return to the idea of science.

Transcendental philosophy has to explain how knowledge is possible at all, assuming that the subjective in it is accepted as the ruling or first element.

It is therefore, not a single part, nor a special object of knowledge, but knowledge itself, and knowledge in general, that it takes for its object.

Now all knowledge can be reduced to certain original convictions or original prejudices. These different convictions transcendental philosophy must trace to one original conviction. This ultimate conviction from which all others are derived, is expressed in the first principle of this philosophy, and the task of finding such is none other than to find the absolutely certain by which all other certainty is attained.

The division of transcendental philosophy is determined through those original convictions, whose validity it affirms. These convictions must, in the first place, be sought in the common understanding. If, therefore, we go back to the standpoint of the ordinary view, we find the following convictions deeply engraven in the human understanding:—

A. That not only does there exist a world of things independent of us, but also that our representations agree with them in such a manner that there is nothing else in the things beyond what we represent by them. The necessity in our objective representations is explained by the belief that the things are unalterably determined, and that by this determination of things our representations appear to be mediately determined. By this first and most original conviction, the first problem of philosophy is determined, *viz:* to explain how representations can absolutely agree with objects which exist entirely independent of them. Since it is upon the assumption that things are exactly as we represent them, and that we therefore certainly know things as they are in themselves, that the possibility of all experience rests (for what would experience be, and where would physics, for example, stray to, without that presupposition of the absolute identity of being and seeming?), the solution of this problem is identical with theoretical philosophy, which has to investigate the possibility of experience.

B. The second equally original conviction is, that representations which originate in us freely and without necessity can pass over from the world of thought into the real world, and attain objective reality.

This conviction is opposed to the first. According to the first, it is assumed that objects are unalterably determined, and our representations by them; according to the other, that objects are changeable, and that, too, by the causality of representations in us. According to the first conviction, a transition takes place within us from the real world into the world of representations, or a determining of the representations by the objective; according to the second, a transition takes place from the world of representations into the world of reality, or a determining of the objective by a (freely conceived) representation in us.

By this second conviction, a second problem is determined, *viz.* how, by something merely thought, an objective is changeable, so as entirely to correspond with that something thought.

Since the possibility of all free action rests upon that assumption, the solution of this problem is practical philosophy.

C. But with these two problems we find ourselves involved in a contradiction. According to B, the supremacy of thought (the ideal) over the world of sense is demanded. But how is such supremacy conceivable, if (according to A) the idea in its origin is already only the slave of the objective? On the other hand, if the real world is something wholly independent of us, and is something with which our ideas must conform as their pattern (by A), then it becomes inconceivable how, on the other hand, the real world can conform to the ideas in us (by B). In brief, in the theoretical certainty we lose the practical; in the practical we lose the theoretical. It is impossible that at the same time there should be truth in our knowledge and reality in our volition.

This contradiction must be solved; if there is to be a philosophy at all. The solution of this problem, or the answering of the question: How can ideas be conceived as conforming to objects, and at the same time objects as conforming to ideas?—is not the first, but is the chief task of transcendental philosophy.

It is easy to see that this problem cannot be solved either in theoretical or practical philosophy, but in a higher one, which is the connecting link of both, and is neither theoretical nor practical, but both at the same time.

How at the same time the objective world conforms to representations in us, and representations in us conform to the objective world, cannot be conceived, unless there exists a preestablished harmony between the two worlds of the ideal and the real. But this preestablished harmony is itself not conceivable unless the activity by which the objective world is produced, is originally identical with that which displays itself in volition, and *vice versa*.

Now it is certainly a *productive* activity which manifests itself in volition. All free action is productive, but productive only with consciousness. If, then, since the two activities are only one in principle, we suppose that the same activity which is productive *with* consciousness in free action, is productive *without* consciousness in the production of the world, this preestablished harmony is a reality, and the contradiction is solved. If we suppose that all this is actually the case, then that original identity of the activity which is engaged in the production of the world, with that which exhibits itself in volition, must manifest itself in the productions of the former, and these must necessarily appear as the productions of an activity at once conscious and unconscious.

Nature, as a whole, no less than in its different productions, will of necessity appear as a work produced with consciousness and yet at the same time as the production of the blindest mechanism. It is the result of purpose without being explainable as such. The philosophy of the aims of Nature, or teleology, is therefore the required point of union of theoretical and practical philosophy.

D. Heretofore, we have posited only in general terms the identity of the unconscious activity which has produced Nature, and the conscious activity which manifests itself in volition, without having decided where the principle of this activity lies, whether in Nature or in us.

But now the system of knowledge can be regarded as complete only when it reverts to its principle. Transcendental philosophy would therefore be completed only when it also could demonstrate that identity—the highest solution of its entire problem—in its principle (the *Ego*).

It is therefore postulated, that activity, at once conscious and unconscious, can be shown in the subjective, that is in consciousness itself.

Such an activity can be no other than the *æsthetic,* and every work of art can only be conceived as the product of such. The ideal work of art and the real world of objects are therefore products of one and the same activity. The meeting of the two (of the conscious and the unconscious) gives *without* consciousness the real, *with* consciousness the æsthetic world.

The objective world is only the original still unconscious poetry of the soul. The universal organum of philosophy—the keystone of its entire arch—is the philosophy of art.

12. COLERIDGE: Transcendence by Imagination and Language

A central theme of romanticism is our intimacy with nature. A central problem for romanticism is to explain just what this means. Samuel Taylor Coleridge's (1772–1834) critique of Wordsworth's theory of poetry suggests that it is a problem which Wordsworth has not solved—at least not on the level of theory.

According to Wordsworth's theory, good poetry is comprised of selections from the actual language of rustic men "as far as possible" (we are reminded of Rousseau's "natural man"). Coleridge, the English philosopher, critic and poet, maintained that the language of good poetry—even if the poetry be about rustic life—is quite different from the language an unlettered rustic would actually speak. Rich, poetical language, descriptive of nature, is not a function of merely prolonged sensory exposure to a rich and luxurious nature (the mind is not like a camera which passively registers stimuli), else the savage in the jungle would have the richest poetry; he apparently does not. Rather, such poetry is a function of the symbolical, linguistic and cultural tradition; for example, the rustic who knows the Bible experiences nature differently from the one who does not, because he participates in the cultural tradition in a way which the other does not.

Implicit in Coleridge's critique is a view of mind and language which casts doubt on the very ideal of the natural man. As with Kant—and Coleridge knew Kantian philosophy—Coleridge's doctrine of the creative imagination suggests that the mind "legislates" forms to nature, not the reverse, that the imagination ranges beyond the present and actual universe into the region of the possible before the mind can know the universe at all.

Almost before the reader knows it, Coleridge has suggested several disturbing questions: Isn't there something *unnatural* about a being so endowed with imagination that he stands to present and actual nature in such a remote and indirect relationship? Should we not formulate an *un*natural ideal for man? But Coleridge does not press these questions, and he nearly always avoids the issue of the open-ended and man-centered universe by falling back on the cultural tradition, particularly Christianity.

With the questions, however, Coleridge, like Blake, has planted seeds of thought which are given room to grow later in the age. One thinks of Nietzsche and his fears about the wide-open future, and of Baudelaire (*see* Chapter 20) and his ideal of the unnatural man in an unnatural world: "It is by the sea; they say it is built of marble, and that the people have such a horror of vegetation that they tear up all the trees. There is a country after your own soul." One thinks of the glass and metal of New York City. Well, what *is* natural for man? An infant does not become a man as an acorn becomes an oak. Consciousness, education and the process of becoming civilized are required. If man does not have a fixed essence or nature but only a history and cultural tradition, if his history changes radically or his cultural attachments are disrupted—what then? Coleridge opens the door a crack and we glimpse the anxieties of our own age, as we see in the selection from *Biographia Literaria*, Chapters XVII and XVIII.

CHAPTER XVII

. . . My own differences from certain supposed parts of Mr. Wordsworth's theory ground themselves on the assumption that his words had been rightly interpreted, as purporting that the proper diction for poetry in general consists altogether in a language taken, with due exceptions, from the mouths of men in real life, a language which actually constitutes the natural conversation of men under the influence of natural feelings. My objection is, first, that in any sense this rule is applicable only to certain classes of poetry; secondly, that even to these classes it is not applicable, except in such a sense, as hath never by any one (as far as I know or have read) been denied or doubted; and lastly, that as far as, and in that degree in which it is practicable, it is yet as a rule useless, if not injurious, and therefore either need not or ought not to be practised. The poet informs his reader that he had generally chosen low and rustic life; but not as low and rustic, or in order to repeat that pleasure of doubtful moral effect, which persons of elevated rank and of superior refinement oftentimes derive from a happy imitation of the rude unpolished manners and discourse of their inferiors. For the pleasure so derived may be traced to three exciting causes. The first is the naturalness, in fact, of the things represented. The second is the apparent naturalness of the representation, as raised and qualified by an imperceptible infusion of the author's own knowledge and talent, which infusion does, indeed, constitute it an imitation as distinguished from a mere copy. The third cause may be found in the reader's conscious feeling of his superiority awakened by the contrast presented to him; even as for the same purpose the kings and great barons of yore retained, sometimes actual clowns and fools, but more frequently shrewd and witty fellows in that character. These, however, were not Mr. Wordsworth's objects. *He* chose low and rustic life, "because in that condition the essential passions of the heart find a better soil, in which they can attain their maturity, are less under restraint, and speak a plainer and more emphatic language; because in that condition of life our elementary feelings coexist in a state of greater simplicity, and consequently may be more accurately contemplated, and more forcibly communicated; because the manners of rural life germinate from those elementary feelings; and from the necessary character of rural occupations are more easily comprehended, and are more durable; and lastly, because in that condition the passions of men are incorporated with the beautiful and permanent forms of nature."

Now it is clear to me that in the most interesting of the poems, in which the author is more or less dramatic, as *The Brother*, *Michael*, *Ruth*, *The Mad Mother*, and others, the persons introduced are by no means taken from low or rustic life in the common acceptation of those words; and it is not less clear that the sentiments and language, as far as they can be conceived to have been really transferred from the minds and conversation of such persons, are attributable to causes and circumstances not necessarily connected with "their occupations and abode." The thoughts, feelings, language, and manners of the shepherd-farmers in the vales of Cumberland and Westmoreland, as far as they are actually adopted in those poems, may be accounted for from causes, which will and do produce the same results in every state of life, whether in town or country. As the two principal I rank that independence which raises a man above servitude, or daily toil for the profit of others, yet not above the necessity of industry and a frugal simplicity of domestic life; and the accompanying unambitious, but solid and religious, education, which has rendered few books familiar, but the Bible, the Liturgy or Hymn book. To this latter cause, indeed, which is so far accidental that it is the blessing of particular countries and a particular age, not the product of particular places or employments, the poet owes the show of probability that his personages might really feel, think, and talk with any tolerable resemblance to his representation. It is an excellent remark of Dr. Henry More's that "a man of confined education, but of good parts, by constant reading of the Bible will naturally form a more winning and commanding rhetoric than those that are learned: the intermixture of tongues, and of artificial phrases debasing *their* style."

It is, moreover, to be considered that to the formation of healthy feelings, and a reflecting mind, negations involve impediments not less formidable than sophistication and vicious intermixture. I am convinced that for the human soul to prosper in rustic life a certain vantage-ground is prerequisite. It is not every man that is likely to be improved by a country life or by country labors. Education, or original sensibility, or both, must pre-exist, if the changes, forms, and incidents of nature are to prove a sufficient stimulant. And where these are not sufficient, the mind contracts and hardens by want of stimulants: and the man becomes selfish, sensual, gross, and hardhearted. Let the management of the Poor Laws in Liverpool, Manchester, or Bristol be compared with the ordinary dispensation of the poor rates in agricultural villages, where the farmers are the overseers and guardians of the poor. If my own experience have not been particularly unfortunate, as well as that of the many respectable country clergymen with whom I have conversed on the subject, the result would engender more than scepticism concerning the desirable influences of low and rustic life in and for itself. Whatever may be concluded on the other side, from the stronger local attachments and enterprising spirit of the Swiss, and other mountaineers, applies to a particular mode of pastoral life, under forms of property that permit and beget manners truly republican, not to rustic life in general, or to the absence of artificial cultivation. On the contrary the mountaineers, whose manners have been so often eulogized, are in general better educated and greater readers than men of equal rank elsewhere. But where this is not the case, as among the peasantry of North Wales, the ancient mountains, with all their terrors and all their glories, are pictures to the blind, and music to the deaf.

I should not have entered so much into detail upon this passage, but here seems to be the point to which all the lines of difference converge as to their source and center;—I mean, as far as, and in whatever respect, my poetic creed *does* differ from the doctrines promulgated in this preface. I adopt with full faith the principle of Aristotle, that poetry, as poetry, is essentially ideal, that it avoids and excludes all accident; that its apparent individualities of rank, character, or occupation must be representative of a class; and that the persons of poetry must be clothed with generic attributes, with the common attributes of the class: not with such as one gifted individual might possibly possess, but such as from his situation it is most probable before-hand that he would possess. If my premises are right and my deductions legitimate, it follows that there can be no poetic medium between the swains of Theocritus and those of an imaginary golden age. . . .

As little can I agree with the assertion that from the objects with which the rustic hourly communicates the best part of language is formed. For first, if to communicate with an object implies such an acquaintance with it, as renders it capable of being discriminately reflected on, the distinct knowledge of an uneducated rustic would furnish a very scanty vocabulary. The few things and modes of action requisite for his bodily conveniences would alone be individualized, while all the rest of nature would be expressed by a small number of confused general terms. Secondly, I deny that the words and combinations of words derived from the objects with which the rustic is familiar, whether with distinct or confused knowledge, can be justly said to form the best part of language. It is more than probable that many classes of the brute creation possess discriminating sounds, by which they can convey to each other notices of such objects as concern their food, shelter, or safety. Yet we hesitate to call the aggregate of such sounds a language, otherwise than metaphorically. The best part of human language, properly so called, is derived from reflection on the acts of the mind itself. It is formed by a voluntary appropriation of fixed symbols to internal acts, to processes and results of imagination, the greater part of which have no place in the consciousness of uneducated man; though in civilized society, by imitation and passive remembrance of what they hear from their religious instructors and other superiors, the most uneducated share in the harvest which they neither sowed, nor reaped. If the history of the phrases in hourly currency among our peasants were traced, a person not previously aware of the fact would be surprised at finding so large a number, which three or four centuries ago were the exclusive property of the universities and the schools; and, at the commencement of the Reformation, had been transferred from the school to the pulpit, and thus gradually passed into common life. The extreme difficulty, and often the impossibility, of finding words for the simplest moral and intellectual processes of the languages of uncivilized tribes has proved perhaps the weightiest obstacle to the progress of our most zealous and adroit missionaries. Yet these tribes are surrounded by the same nature as our peasants are; but in still more impressive forms; and they are, moreover, obliged to particularize many more of them. When, therefore, Mr. Wordsworth adds, "accordingly, such a language"—(meaning, as before, the language of rustic life purified from provincialism)—"arising out of repeated experience and regular feelings, is a more permanent, and a far more philosophical language than that which is frequently substituted for it by Poets, who think that they are conferring honor upon themselves and their art in proportion as they indulge in arbitrary and capricious habits of expression," it may be answered that the language which he has in view can be attributed to rustics with no greater right than the style of Hooker or Bacon to Tom Brown or Sir Roger L'Estrange. Doubtless, if what is peculiar to each were omitted in each, the result must needs be the same. Further, that the poet, who uses an illogical diction, or a style fitted to excite only the low and changeable pleasure of wonder by means of groundless novelty, substitutes a language of folly and vanity, not for that of the rustic, but for that of good sense and natural feeling.

Here let me be permitted to remind the reader that the positions, which I controvert, are contained in the sentences—"a selection of the real language of men;"—"the language of these men" (that is, men in low and rustic life) "has been adopted; I have proposed to myself to imitate, and, as far as is possible, to adopt the very language of men."

"Between the language of prose and that of metrical composition, there neither is, nor can be, any *essential difference:*" it is against these exclusively that my opposition is directed.

I object, in the very first instance, to an equivocation in the use of the word "real." Every man's language varies, according to the extent of his knowledge, the activity of his faculties, and the depth or quickness of his feelings. Every man's language has, first, its individualities; secondly, the common properties of the class to which he belongs; and thirdly, words and phrases of universal use. The language of Hooker, Bacon, Bishop Taylor, and Burke differs from the common language of the learned class only by the superior number and novelty of the thoughts and relations which they had to convey. The language of Algernon Sidney differs not at all from that which every well-educated gentleman would wish to write, and (with due allowances for the undeliberateness, and less connected train, of thinking natural and proper to conversation) such as he would wish to talk. Neither one nor the other differ half as much from the general language of cultivated society as the language of Mr. Wordsworth's homeliest composition differs from that of a common peasant. For "real" therefore, we must substitute ordinary, or *lingua communis.* And this, we have proved, is no more to be found in the phraseology of low and rustic life than in that of any other class. Omit the peculiarities of each and the result of course must be common to all. And assuredly the omissions and changes to be made in the language of rustics, before it could be transferred to any species of poem, except the drama or other professed imitation, are at least as numerous and weighty as would be required in adapting to the same purpose the ordinary language of tradesmen and manufacturers. Not to mention that the language so highly extolled by Mr. Wordsworth varies in every county, nay in every village, according to the accidental character of the clergyman, the existence or non-existence of schools; or even, perhaps, as the exciseman, publican, and barber happen to be, or not to be, zealous politicians, and readers of the weekly newspaper *pro bono publico*. Anterior to cultivation the *lingua communis* of every country, as Dante has well observed, exists every where in parts, and no where as a whole.

Neither is the case rendered at all more tenable by the addition of the words, "in a state of excitement." For the nature of a man's words, where he is strongly affected by joy, grief, or anger, must necessarily depend on the number and quality of the general truths, conceptions and images, and of the words expressing them, with which his mind has been previously stored. For the property of passion is not to create; but to set in increased activity. At least, whatever new connections of thoughts or images, or—(which is equally, if not more than equally, the appropriate effect of strong excitement)—whatever generalizations of truth or experience the heat of passion may produce; yet the terms of their conveyance must have pre-existed in his former conversations, and are only collected and crowded together by the unusual stimulation. It is indeed very possible to adopt in a poem the unmeaning repetitions, habitual phrases, and other blank counters, which an unfurnished or confused understanding interposes at short intervals, in order to keep hold of his subject, which is still slipping from him, and to give him time for recollection; or, in mere aid of vacancy, as in the scanty companies of a country stage the same player pops backwards and forwards, in order to prevent the appearance of empty spaces, in the procession of Macbeth, or Henry VIII. But what assistance to the poet, or ornament to the poem, these can supply, I am at a loss to conjecture. Nothing assuredly can differ either in origin or in mode more widely from the apparent tautologies of intense and turbulent feeling, in which the passion is greater and of longer endurance than to be exhausted or satisfied by a single representation of the image or incident exciting it. Such repetitions I admit to be a beauty of the highest kind; as illustrated by Mr. Wordsworth himself from the song of Deborah. *At her feet he bowed, he fell, he lay down: at her feet he bowed, he fell: where he bowed, there he fell down dead.* (Judges V, 27.)

CHAPTER XVIII

I conclude, therefore, that the attempt is impracticable; and that, were it not impracticable, it would still be useless. For the very power of making the selection implies the previous possession of the language selected. Or where can the poet have lived? And by what rules could he direct his choice, which would not have enabled him to select and arrange his words by the light of his own judgment? We do not adopt the language of a class by the mere adoption of such words exclusively, as that class would use, or at least understand; but likewise by following the order, in which the words of such men are wont

to succeed each other. Now this order, in the intercourse of uneducated men, is distinguished from the diction of their superiors in
knowledge and power, by the greater disjunction and separation in
the component parts of that, whatever it be, which they wish to
communicate. There is a want of that prospectiveness of mind, that
surview, which enables a man to foresee the whole of what he is to
convey, appertaining to any one point; and by this means so to subordinate and arrange the different parts according to their relative
importance, as to convey it at once, and as an organized whole.

Now I will take the first stanza, on which I have chanced to open,
in the *Lyrical Ballads*. It is one of the most simple and the least
peculiar in its language.

> In distant countries have I been,
> And yet I have not often seen
> A healthy man, a man full grown,
> Weep in the public roads, alone.
> But such a one, on English ground,
> And in the broad highway, I met;
> Along the broad highway he came,
> His cheeks with tears were wet:
> Sturdy he seemed, though he was sad;
> And in his arms a lamb he had.

The words here are doubtless such as are current in all ranks of
life; and of course not less so in the hamlet and cottage than in the
shop, manufactory, college, or palace. But is this the *order* in which
the rustic would have placed the words? I am grievously deceived, if
the following less compact mode of commencing the same tale be not
a far more faithful copy. "I have been in a many parts, far and near,
and I don't know that I ever saw before a man crying by himself in
the public road; a grown man I mean, that was neither sick nor hurt,"
etc., etc. But when I turn to the following stanza in *The Thorn:*

> At all times of the day and night
> This wretched woman thither goes;
> And she is known to every star,
> And every wind that blows:
> And there, beside the Thorn, she sits,
> When the blue day-light's in the skies,
> And when the whirlwind's on the hill,

> Or frosty air is keen and still,
> And to herself she cries,
> Oh misery! Oh misery!
> Oh woe is me! Oh misery!

and compare this with the language of ordinary men; or with that which I can conceive at all likely to proceed, in real life, from such a narrator as is supposed in the note to the poem; compare it either in the succession of the images or of the sentences; I am reminded of the sublime prayer and hymn of praise, which Milton, in opposition to an established liturgy, presents as a fair specimen of common extemporary devotion, and such as we might expect to hear from every self-inspired minister of a conventicle! And I reflect with delight, how a little mere theory, though of his own workmanship, interferes with the processes of genuine imagination in a man of true poetic genius, who possesses, as Mr. Wordsworth, if ever man did, most assuredly does possess,

> The Vision and the Faculty divine.

13. EMERSON: The Proclamation of Intellectual Self-Reliance

"The American Scholar" is an address delivered at Harvard in 1837 by the American thinker Ralph Waldo Emerson (1803–1882). It has been called the "Declaration of Independence of American intellectual life." As Emerson himself put it, "The millions that around us are rushing into life, cannot always be fed on the sere remains of foreign harvests."

But as one will immediately see, Emerson's very declaration is structured by concepts derived from a foreign harvest built up for decades; it is early romanticism. The individual establishes his identity by finding himself reflected in nature, and nature is inseparable from mind (the Oversoul). By 1837 European thinkers were following quite a different course. The concept of nature had broken down into the concepts of the organic state, nation, folk and history. In Hegel and the Hegelians, bucolic individualism had long since been replaced by "higher criticism" of the intellectual and cultural tradition and "total politics."

Of course, though, originality is not the only value. For sheer moral fervor and the peculiar eloquence which arises from it, Emerson is, with the possible exception of Fichte, without peer. One can speak the Word without coining it, and the "transcendentalists" in America heard it. This is made clear in the following paragraph from his address to the Harvard Divinity School in 1838.

> These laws execute themselves. They are out of time, out of space, and not subject to circumstance: Thus, in the soul of man there is a justice whose retributions are instant and entire. He who does a good deed is instantly ennobled. He who does a mean deed is by the action itself contracted. He who puts off impurity thereby puts on purity. If a man is at heart just, then in so far is he God; the safety of God, the immortality of God, the majesty of God, do enter into that man with justice. If a man dissemble, deceive, he deceives himself, and goes out of acquaintance with his own being. Character is always known. Thefts never enrich; alms never impoverish; murder will speak out of stone walls. The least admixture of a lie— for example, the taint of vanity, any attempt to make a good impression, a favorable appearance—will instantly vitiate the effect. But speak the truth, and all things alive or brute are vouchers, and the very roots of the grass underground there do seem to stir and move to bear your witness. For all things proceed out of the same spirit, which is differently named love, justice, temperance, in its different applications, just as the ocean receives different names on the several shores which it washes. In so far as he roves from these ends, a man bereaves himself of power, of auxiliaries. His being shrinks . . . he becomes less and less, a mote, a point, until absolute badness is absolute death. . . .

. . . The millions that around us are rushing into life, cannot always be fed on the sere remains of foreign harvests. Events, actions arise, that must be sung, that will sing themselves. Who can doubt that poetry will revive and lead in a new age, as the star in the constellation Harp, which now flames in our zenith, astronomers announce, shall one day be the pole-star for a thousand years?

In this hope I accept the topic which not only usage but the nature of our association seem to prescribe to this day,—the AMERICAN SCHOLAR. Year by year we come up hither to read one more chapter of his biography. Let us inquire what light new days and events have thrown on his character and his hopes.

It is one of those fables which out of an unknown antiquity convey an unlooked-for wisdom, that the gods, in the beginning, divided Man into men, that he might be more helpful to himself; just as the hand was divided into fingers, the better to answer its end.

The old fable covers a doctrine ever new and sublime; that there is One Man,—present to all particular men only partially, or through one faculty; and that you must take the whole society to find the whole man. Man is not a farmer, or a professor, or an engineer, but he is all. Man is priest, and scholar, and statesman, and producer, and soldier. In the *divided* or social state these functions are parcelled out to individuals, each of whom aims to do his stint of the joint work, whilst each other performs his. The fable implies that the individual, to possess himself, must sometimes return from his own labor to embrace all the other laborers. But, unfortunately, this original unit, this fountain of power, has been so distributed to multitudes, has been so minutely subdivided and peddled out, that it is spilled into drops, and cannot be gathered. The state of society is one in which the members have suffered amputation from the trunk, and strut about so many walking monsters,—a good finger, a neck, a stomach, an elbow, but never a man.

Man is thus metamorphosed into a thing, into many things. The planter, who is Man sent out into the field to gather food, is seldom cheered by any idea of the true dignity of his ministry. He sees his bushel and his cart, and nothing beyond, and sinks into the farmer, instead of Man on the farm. The tradesman scarcely ever gives an ideal worth to his work, but is ridden by the routine of his craft, and the soul is subject to dollars. The priest becomes a form; the attorney a statute-book; the mechanic a machine; the sailor a rope of the ship.

In this distribution of functions the scholar is the delegated intellect. In the right state he is *Man Thinking*. In the degenerate state, when the victim of society, he tends to become a mere thinker, or still worse, the parrot of other men's thinking.

In this view of him, as Man Thinking, the theory of his office is contained. Him Nature solicits with all her placid, all her monitory pictures; him the past instructs; him the future invites. Is not indeed every man a student, and do not all things exist for the student's behoof? And, finally, is not the true scholar the only true master? But the old oracle said, "All things have two handles: beware of the wrong one." In life, too often, the scholar errs with mankind and forfeits his privilege. Let us see him in his school, and consider him in reference to the main influences he receives.

I. The first in time and the first in importance of the influences upon the mind is that of nature. Every day, the sun; and, after sunset, Night and her stars. Ever the winds blow; ever the grass grows. Every day, men and women, conversing—beholding and beholden. The scholar is he of all men whom this spectacle most engages. He must settle its value in his mind. What is nature to him? There is never a beginning, there is never an end, to the inexplicable continuity of this web of God, but always circular power returning into itself. Therein it resembles his own spirit, whose beginning, whose ending, he never can find,—so entire, so boundless. Far too as her splendors shine, system on system shooting like rays, upward, downward, without centre, without circumference,—in the mass and in the particle, Nature hastens to render account of herself to the mind. Classification begins. To the young mind every thing is individual, stands by itself. By and by, it finds how to join two things and see in them one nature; then three, then three thousand; and so, tyrannized over by its own unifying instinct, it goes on tying things together, diminishing anomalies, discovering roots running under ground whereby contrary and remote things cohere and flower out from one stem. It presently learns that since the dawn of history there has been a constant accumulation and classifying of facts. But what is classification but the perceiving that these objects are not chaotic, and are not foreign, but have a law which is also a law of the human mind? The astronomer discovers that geometry, a pure abstraction of the human mind, is the measure of planetary motion. The chemist finds proportions and intelligible method throughout matter; and science is nothing but the finding of analogy, identity, in the most remote parts. The ambitious soul sits down before each refractory fact; one after another reduces all strange constitutions, all new powers, to their class and their law, and goes on forever to animate the last fibre of organization, the outskirts of nature, by insight.

Thus to him, to this schoolboy under the bending dome of day, is suggested that he and it proceed from one root; one is leaf and one is flower; relation, sympathy, stirring in every vein. And what is that root? Is not that the soul of his soul? A thought too bold; a dream too wild. Yet when this spiritual light shall have revealed the law of more earthly natures,—when he has learned to worship the soul, and to see that the natural philosophy that now is, is only the first gropings of its gigantic hand, he shall look forward to an ever expanding knowledge as to a becoming creator. He shall see that nature is the opposite of the soul, answering to it part for part. One is seal and one is print. Its beauty is the beauty of his own mind. Its laws are the laws of his own mind. Nature then becomes to him the measure of his attainments. So much of nature as he is ignorant of, so much of his own mind does he not yet possess. And, in fine, the ancient precept, "Know thyself," and the modern precept, "Study nature," becomes at last one maxim.

II. The next great influence into the spirit of the scholar is the mind of the Past,—in whatever form, whether of literature, of art, of institutions, that mind is inscribed. Books are the best type of the influence of the past, and perhaps we shall get at the truth,—learn the amount of this influence more conveniently,—by considering their value alone.

The theory of books is noble. The scholar of the first age received into him the world around; brooded thereon; gave it the new arrangement of his own mind, and uttered it again. It came into him life; it went out from him truth. It came to him short-lived actions; it went out from him immortal thoughts. It came to him business; it went from him poetry. It was dead fact; now, it is quick thought. It can stand, and it can go. It now endures, it now flies, it now inspires. Precisely in proportion to the depth of mind from which it issued, so high does it soar, so long does it sing.

Or, I might say, it depends on how far the process had gone, of transmuting life into truth. In proportion to the completeness of the distillation, so will the purity and imperishableness of the product be. But none is quite perfect. As no air-pump can by any means make a perfect vacuum, so neither can any artist entirely exclude the conventional, the local, the perishable from his book, or write a book of pure thought, that shall be as efficient, in all respects, to a remote posterity, as to contemporaries, or rather to the second age. Each age, it is found, must write its own books; or rather, each generation for the next succeeding. The books of an older period will not fit this.

Yet hence arises a grave mischief. The sacredness which attaches to the act of creation, the act of thought, is transferred to the record. The poet chanting was felt to be a divine man: henceforth the chant is divine also. The writer was a just and wise spirit: henceforward it is settled the book is perfect; as love of the hero corrupts into worship of his statue. Instantly the book becomes noxious: the guide is a tyrant. The sluggish and perverted mind of the multitude, slow to open to the incursions of Reason, having once so opened, having once received this book, stands upon it, and makes an outcry if it is disparaged. Colleges are built on it. Books are written on it by thinkers, not by Man Thinking; by men of talent, that is, who start wrong, who set out from accepted dogmas, not from their own sight of principles. Meek young men grow up in libraries, believing it their duty to accept the views which Cicero, which Locke, which Bacon, have given; forgetful that Cicero, Locke, and Bacon were only young men in libraries when they wrote these books.

Hence, instead of Man Thinking, we have the bookworm. Hence the book-learned class, who value books, as such; not as related to nature and the human constitution, but as making a sort of Third Estate with the world and the soul. Hence the restorers of readings, the emendators, the bibliomaniacs of all degrees.

Books are the best of things, well used; abused, among the worst. What is the right use? What is the one end which all means go to effect? They are for nothing but to inspire. I had better never see a book than to be warped by its attraction clean out of my own orbit, and make a satellite instead of a system. The one thing in the world, of value, is the active soul. This every man is entitled to; this every man contains within him, although in almost all men obstructed and as yet unborn. The soul active sees absolute truth and utters truth, or creates. In this action it is genius; not the privilege of here and there a favorite, but the sound estate of every man. In its essence it is progressive. The book, the college, the school of art, the institution of any kind, stop with some past utterance of genius. This is good, say they,—let us hold by this. They pin me down. They look backward and not forward. But genius looks forward: the eyes of man are set in his forehead, not in his hindhead: man hopes: genius creates. Whatever talents may be, if the man create not, the pure afflux of the Deity is not his;—cinders and smoke there may be, but not yet flame. There are creative manners, there are creative actions, and creative words; manners, actions, words, that is, indicative of no custom or authority, but springing spontaneous from the mind's own sense of good and fair.

On the other part, instead of being its own seer, let it receive from another mind its truth, though it were in torrents of light, without periods of solitude, inquest, and self-recovery, and a fatal disservice is done. Genius is always sufficiently the enemy of genius by over-influence. The literature of every nation bears me witness. The English dramatic poets have Shakespearized now for two hundred years.

Undoubtedly there is a right way of reading, so it be sternly subordinated. Man Thinking must not be subdued by his instruments. Books are for the scholar's idle times. When he can read God directly, the hour is too precious to be wasted in other men's transcripts of their readings. But when the intervals of darkness come, as come they must,—when the sun is hid and the stars withdraw their shining, —we repair to the lamps which were kindled by their ray, to guide our steps to the East again, where the dawn is. We hear, that we may speak. The Arabian proverb says, "A fig tree, looking on a fig tree, becometh fruitful."

It is remarkable, the character of the pleasure we derive from the best books. They impress us with the conviction that one nature wrote and the same reads. We read the verses of one of the great English poets, of Chaucer, of Marvell, of Dryden, with the most modern joy,—with a pleasure, I mean, which is in great part caused by the abstraction of all *time* from their verses. There is some awe mixed with the joy of our surprise, when this poet, who lived in some past world, two or three hundred years ago, says that which lies close to my own soul, that which I also had well-nigh thought and said. But for the evidence thence afforded to the philosophical doctrine of the identity of all minds, we should suppose some pre-established harmony, some foresight of souls that were to be, and some preparation of stores for their future wants, like the fact observed in insects, who lay up food before death for the young grub they shall never see.

I would not be hurried by any love of system, by any exaggeration of instincts, to underrate the Book. We all know, that as the human body can be nourished on any food, though it were boiled grass and the broth of shoes, so the human mind can be fed by any knowledge. And great and heroic men have existed who had almost no other information than by the printed page. I only would say that it needs a strong head to bear that diet. One must be an inventor to read well. As the proverb says, "He that would bring home the wealth of the Indies, must carry out the wealth of the Indies." There is then creative reading as well as creative writing. When the mind is braced by labor and invention, the page of whatever book we read becomes luminous with manifold allusion. Every sentence is doubly significant, and the sense of our author is as broad as the world. We then see, what is always true, that as the seer's hour of vision is short and rare among heavy days and months, so is its record, perchance, the least part of his volume. The discerning will read, in his Plato or Shakespeare, only that least part,—only the authentic utterances of the oracle;—all the rest he rejects, were it never so many times Plato's and Shakespeare's.

Of course there is a portion of reading quite indispensable to a wise man. History and exact science he must learn by laborious reading. Colleges, in like manner, have their indispensable office,—to teach elements. But they can only highly serve us when they aim not to drill, but to create; when they gather from far every ray of various genius to their hospitable halls, and by the concentrated fires, set the hearts of their youth on flame. Thought and knowledge are natures in which apparatus and pretension avail nothing. Gowns and pecuniary foundations, though of towns of gold, can never countervail the least sentence or syllable of wit. Forget this, and our American colleges will recede in their public importance, whilst they grow richer every year.

III. There goes in the world a notion that the scholar should be a recluse, a valetudinarian,—as unfit for any handiwork or public labor as a penknife for an axe. The so-called "practical men" sneer at speculative men, as if, because they speculate or *see,* they could do nothing. I have heard it said that the clergy,—who are always, more universally than any other class, the scholars of their day,—are addressed as women; that the rough spontaneous conversation of men they do not hear, but only a mincing and diluted speech. They are often virtually disfranchised; and indeed there are advocates for their celibacy. As far as this is true of the studious classes, it is not just and wise. Action is with the scholar subordinate, but it is essential. Without it he is not yet man. Without it thought can never ripen into truth. Whilst the world hangs before the eye as a cloud of beauty, we cannot even see its beauty. Inaction is cowardice, but there can be no scholar without the heroic mind. The preamble of thought, the transition through which it passes from the unconscious to the conscious, is action. Only so much do I know, as I have lived. Instantly we know whose words are loaded with life, and whose not.

The world,—this shadow of the soul, or *other me,*—lies wide around. Its attractions are the keys which unlock my thoughts and make me acquainted with myself. I run eagerly into this resounding tumult. I grasp the hands of those next me, and take my place in the ring to suffer and to work, taught by an instinct that so shall the dumb abyss be vocal with speech. . . .

I have now spoken of the education of the scholar by nature, by books, and by action. It remains to say somewhat of his duties.

They are such as become Man Thinking. They may all be comprised in self-trust. The office of the scholar is to cheer, to raise, and to guide men by showing them facts amidst appearances. He plies the slow, unhonored, and unpaid task of observation. Flamsteed and Herschel, in their glazed observatories, may catalogue the stars with the praise of all men, and the results being splendid and useful, honor is sure. But he, in his private observatory, cataloguing obscure and nebulous stars of the human mind, which as yet no man has thought of as such,—watching days and months sometimes for a few facts; correcting still his old records;—must relinquish display and immediate fame. In the long period of his preparation he must betray often an ignorance and shiftlessness in popular arts, incurring the disdain of the able who shoulder him aside. Long he must stammer in his speech; often forgo the living for the dead. Worse yet, he must accept —how often!—poverty and solitude. For the ease and pleasure of treading the old road, accepting the fashions, the education, the religion of society, he takes the cross of making his own, and, of course, the self-accusation, the faint heart, the frequent uncertainty and loss of time, which are the nettles and tangling vines in the way of the self-relying and self-directed; and the state of virtual hostility in which he seems to stand to society, and especially to educated society. For all this loss and scorn, what offset? He is to find consolation in exercising the highest functions of human nature. He is one who raises himself from private considerations and breathes and lives on public and illustrious thoughts. He is the world's eye. He is the world's heart. He is to resist the vulgar prosperity that retrogrades ever to barbarism, by preserving and communicating heroic sentiments, noble biographies, melodious verse, and the conclusions of history. Whatsoever oracles the human heart, in all emergencies, in all solemn hours, has uttered as its commentary on the world of actions,—these he shall receive and impart. And whatsoever new verdict Reason from her inviolable seat pronounces on the passing men and events of to-day, —this he shall hear and promulgate.

These being his functions, it becomes him to feel all confidence in himself, and to defer never to the popular cry. He and he only knows the world. The world of any moment is the merest appearance. Some great decorum, some fetish of a government, some ephemeral trade, or war, or man, is cried up by half mankind and cried down by the other half, as if all depended on this particular up or down. The odds are that the whole question is not worth the poorest thought which the scholar has lost in listening to the controversy. Let him not quit his belief that a popgun is a popgun, though the ancient and honorable of the earth affirm it to be the crack of doom. In silence, in steadiness, in severe abstraction, let him hold by himself; add observation to observation, patient of neglect, patient of reproach, and bide his own time,—happy enough if he can satisfy himself alone that this day he has seen something truly. Success treads on every right step. For the instinct is sure, that prompts him to tell his brother what he thinks. He then learns that in going down into the secrets of his own mind he has descended into the secrets of all minds. He learns that he who has mastered any law in his private thoughts, is master to that extent of all men whose language he speaks, and of all into whose language his own can be translated. The poet, in utter solitude remembering his spontaneous thoughts and recording them, is found to have recorded that which men in crowded cities find true for them also. The orator distrusts at first the fitness of his frank confessions, his want of knowledge of the persons he addresses, until he finds that he is the complement of his hearers;—that they drink his words because he fulfils for them their own nature; the deeper he dives into his privatest, secretest presentiment, to his wonder he finds this is the most acceptable, most public, and universally true. The people delight in it; the better part of every man feels, This is my music; this is myself.

In self-trust all the virtues are comprehended. Free should the scholar be,—free and brave. Free even to the definition of freedom, "without any hindrance that does not arise out of his own constitution." Brave; for fear is a thing which a scholar by his very function puts behind him. Fear always springs from ignorance. It is a shame to him if his tranquillity, amid dangerous times, arises from the presumption that like children and women his is a protected class; or if he seek a temporary peace by the diversion of his thoughts from politics or vexed questions, hiding his head like an ostrich in the flowering bushes, peeping into microscopes, and turning rhymes, as a boy whistles to keep his courage up. So is the danger a danger still; so is the fear worse. Manlike let him turn and face it. Let him look into its eye and search its nature, inspect its origin,—see the whelping of this lion,—which lies no great way back; he will then find in himself a perfect comprehension of its nature and extent; he will have made his hands meet on the other side, and can henceforth defy it and pass on superior. The world is his who can see through its pretension. What deafness, what stone-blind custom, what overgrown error you behold is there only by sufferance,—by your sufferance. See it to be a lie, and you have already dealt it its mortal blow.

Yes, we are the cowed,—we the trustless. It is a mischievous notion that we are come late into nature; that the world was finished a long time ago. As the world was plastic and fluid in the hands of God, so it is ever to so much of his attributes as we bring to it. To ignorance and sin, it is flint. They adapt themselves to it as they may; but in proportion as a man has any thing in him divine, the firmament flows before him and takes his signet and form. Not he is great who can alter matter, but he who can alter my state of mind. They are the kings of the world who give the color of their present thought to all nature and all art, and persuade men by the cheerful serenity of their carrying the matter, that this thing which they do is the apple which the ages have desired to pluck, now at last ripe, and inviting nations to the harvest. The great man makes the great thing. . . .

III.

Evolution of the State:
Institutionalizing Freedom

14. HEGEL: The State as the Ground of Individual Freedom

Georg Wilhelm Friedrich Hegel (1770–1831) is the massive central figure who sits astride the age; he dominates it philosophically, dates it and divides it into an opening and a closing phase. His philosophy is designed to overcome antagonism between philosophies and to synthesize them—or what is left of them—into a larger whole. In his thought romanticism is tempered in the waters of systematic study and reflection, though doubtless some would say blunted and made brittle. Be that as it may, the result is an ingenious instrument of thought.

How do we gain an initial entrée to Hegel, one of the most difficult of all thinkers to understand? We simply apply one of his own lessons and attempt to grasp him in the proper context: His is a rationalism every bit as audacious as Leibniz's or Spinoza's, but it is fundamentally different from theirs because of his absorption of certain elements from Kant, from the romantics, and even from the early Greeks. The separate strands of romanticism—unity, history, interdependence of opposites, spontaneity, community—are developed, augmented and woven into a world-girdling metaphysical system, with his philosophy of mind and his logic supplying the keys to the pattern.

Although a brief account cannot possibly be complete, we can find the first and most important key to his system in his first major work, *Phenomenology of Mind*. Apparent at the outset, Hegel's theory of mind is inseparable from his theory of knowledge: consciousness is always *of* an object, and this is the relationship in which real objects become known. Hegel regards any theory as absurd which sets mind over and against reality, which divides the realm of being in two and which asks as its initial question how anything can ever become known. Such dualism contradicts itself: Mind must grasp reality in order to perpetuate the deception that it is cut off from it—for how else could it know that it is cut off from anything? For Hegel, any account which is honest to the bare appearance (phenomena) of the world must admit that something is immediately known.

In the *Phenomenology* he examines first the simplest fact disclosed in the simplest kind of immediate sensory awareness: We open our eyes and see that something appears to be there. The object seen, presented in its phenomenal immediacy, first "gives itself out to be" a particular something-or-other which is outside of and other than mind—that is, it appears to be *not* mind. We have knowledge of the appearance *as* appearance.

But when we examine the object more closely, we see that it is an instance of what we mean by "immediately perceived object," and we see that we can know that an instance is an instance only if we know the generality instanced. Furthermore, nothing we can say about the object, no attribute we can give it, is a particular. If we say, "It is here and now," then "now" is merely an instance of a changeless universal Now. A specific Now-point can be distinguished from other Nows only in terms of what happens in it; intrinsically, any Now is no more this Now than that one; aside from its events, an abstract Now is any Now. So Now cannot be a particular, it must be a generality, a universal, an essence.

Next comes the crucial turn in Hegel's analysis of mind. Since what first presents itself as immediate and other than mind is really indescribable without essences and universals, it is really indescribable without using terms relating to mind. The object must be described in terms of a general nature shared with other things, which can be expressed only by abstract mental concepts; thereby the object is always related to mind. The immediately presented is an object-for-mind; that is, it is *not* an immediate object which is other than mind; it is one mediated by mind. (Hegel declares that exposition of essence becomes exposition of a moment of mind.) Negation twice plays a key role: Phenomenal knowledge that the immediate object of consciousness is *not* consciousness generates in philosophical reflection the further knowledge that the opposition between consciousness and its object is *not* final, but is overcome in the larger object of a reflecting, mediating consciousness. To know what immediate consciousness is not, it must be bound to what it is not; but this is done only on the reflective, philosophical level of consciousness itself. Thus, in dramatic fashion, it is the very inadequacy of a dualism of consciousness and its object which prompts the entrance of its own reinforcements.

Here Hegel's philosophy of mind supplies a key both to his logic and his metaphysics. When mind reflects upon itself, it acts as a synthesis which gathers up negations and oppositions in a larger whole, and it is negation which drives this dialectical process. Reflection reveals a dynamism in the primitive mode of sense consciousness (or phenomenology) which generates other modes of consciousness like logic and history. Hegel's dialectical logic follows (thesis, antithesis, synthesis): The object is both immediate and independent of mind (thesis); the object is both an instance of a universal and is not independent of mind (antithesis); reflective mind recognizes that parts which are distinct on one level are not distinct on another level (synthesis). The method of thinking (logic) must ultimately determine what is thought about—since all objects are objects-for-mind. So we can see how Hegel's metaphysics follows: Absolute reality is the "Notion" of the whole which comprises the identity of the whole *in and through* the differences within it.

Here also Hegel's philosophy of mind supplies the key to understanding the title of this chapter: the institutionalizing of freedom. If positive freedom is found in self-determination and self-realization, if consciousness finds itself only in the universal (much as Rousseau and Kant had taught), then Hegel draws the conclusion that conscious man finds himself and determines himself only when he wills the achievement of the most universal and at the same time most concrete of all objects— for Hegel, the state. Thus man is free when he allies himself with the laws of the state, since only then is his mind brought home to itself. If a man sees the state as other than himself and independent of him (like a mere thing and not a universal), then he must also see himself as a thing and not a mind. Truly, Hegel's *Phenomenology of Mind* is his "voyage of discovery" and is perhaps the most breathtaking *tour de force* in the annals of philosophy.

In Hegel romanticism is intellectualized and brought to full, gigantic flower—although with colors drawn and faded in the process. Opposition is overcome or transcended without destroying the historical reality of the opposing elements and their interdependence; indeed, it is just *because* of the reality of these opposing elements and of the binding tension between them that transcendence or synthesis is possible. But—and the reservation falls with a thud—what is the role of the revolutionary individual? Marx said Hegel would suppress him. Of this later.

For Hegel, all distinctions between particulars obtain only within an organic whole, with reality as a kind of organism. There is no fundamentally private and unknowable "thing in itself" or individual (in contrast to Kant) closed off from mind. With one stroke, Hegel sweeps everything into the single public objective mind. He asks, Do we know that "the thing in itself" is unknowable? Then either we do know it and it is an object for mind and not really an unknowable thing outside it, or we do not know anything about it, not even that it is unknowable. Either way it is a contradiction to assert an unknowable thing in itself.

Furthermore, the Notion or idea of the whole works itself out and develops in history; indeed in one of its aspects it *is* history, since history is just the evolving synthesis of ever-ramifying antitheses and distinctions which arise among the various objects of consciousness. Better, we should say that history is the way that we beings caught in the temporal process become aware of the Notion; for there is an Absolute consciousness which knows its own process absolutely, and thereby knows the process' end from its beginning, and in which the completed Notion is already present as such. Like Hegel's theory of reality, his theory of history emerges at the junction of his logic and philosophy of mind. The most fundamental immediate or nonmediated (simplest) object of consciousness is pure undifferentiated Being (thesis); it is not nothing, and yet is so like nothing (it is nothing in particular) that it generates Nothing as its antithesis; the synthesis of these two theses, Hegel asserts, is Becoming—time, change, history.

Now, this Becoming which is history is not invented by consciousness, only discovered; but it is an object *for* consciousness, so not fundamentally alien to it. The past is often strange and hard to grasp, but it is a past *for* consciousness, and hence when mind overcomes the opposition and finds more of itself in its object mind is enriched; the past is nourishment for the growing organism. Furthermore, what the presently developed, reflective consciousness finds in the past are objects of consciousness within modes of consciousness operative then; for the history of the world is a history of the world *for* consciousness. There can be no world in itself, not at any time, but only a world-for-consciousness. So history is in part a history of man's evolving awareness of the world. But—it is not just that this awareness is an interesting part of history, nor that man-who-is-aware (the most important agent disclosed by history) cannot be accurately conceived as a mere object caught in a field of force since he must be conceived as a knowing subject whose knowing influences his behavior. The point is that the *world itself* is accessible only through multi-layers of consciousness-of-the-world and of consciousness of consciousness-of-the-world.

History itself, then, as a phenomenon of immediate consciousness which is an object for historically reflective consciousness, is a study of the development of consciousness for consciousness. We can never actually go back to an earlier people and earlier mode of consciousness, and knowing this defines both us and them: we *are not* them. Yet we must thoroughly know what we are not in order to know what we are. For example, to know the Greek language helps us to know ourselves, but only when we know that we are not Greeks. This is Hegel's safeguard against the danger of an escapist's copying of the past which lies like a trap in the neo-classicism of some of the earlier rationalists. The romantic sense of history is systematized by Hegel.

Finally, now, to recapitulate: Developing the romantics' idea of freedom as autonomy or self-determination, Hegel maintains that since man is the being who is capable of self-consciousness, he will be fully self-determined only when his self stands fully behind itself, as it were; only when he is self-conscious, will the person know what he is taking responsibility for when he takes responsibility for himself. Thus since history is a study of the development of consciousness toward self-consciousness, and since development of self-consciousness parallels development of freedom, history is the study of progress in the consciousness of freedom.

History, then, as a course of events-for-consciousness, is a development toward self-consciousness which is recapitulated by the dialectical movements within reflective consciousness itself, the latter being studied by philosophy of mind, logic and ontology. In a sense, ontogeny (the genesis of the individual) recapitulates phylogeny (the genesis of the species) as in evolutionary biology, except that in Hegel's evolutionary philosophy knowledge of reflective consciousness is logically prior to knowledge of history; history is just luxurious extra-corroboration for the former. Moreover, reflective consciousness is alleged to know already the end from the beginning, and thus the Notion, or absolute reality, is timeless. Hegel's philosophy of history is not logically prior, but it helps us to see what his more technical writing is driving at.

Hegel maintains that the ancient eastern civilizations are characterized by unreflective consciousness lost in its object; distinctions are slurred over and lost in the whole. Its political correlate is a despot: the *one* who is free. With the Greeks, consciousness steps into the first dawn of reflectiveness: Forces of nature as things known are separated from the mind that knows them; but full identity in difference and final overcoming of opposition, that is, the full Notion, is lacking. Its political correlate is democracy or aristocracy: *some* are free. Only with the Germanic-Christian era is the full network of distinctions and individualities grasped within the larger whole of self-consciousness and the completed Notion. Only when Christ is understood to be the God-man is it seen that mind per se is divine, and that God and man partake of one substance—self-consciousness. The final opposition—between God and man —is overcome! The political form is a constitutional monarchy in which civil rights are guaranteed by the state to each individual: *all* are free.

For Hegel, philosophy is "empirical" in the sense that the subject matter it reflects upon and finally makes sense of through a study of the past is the present and actual historical situation. Thus he expresses contempt for "the romantics" who, he claims, lose themselves through artistic experiences in a never-never land of pure possibility; they forget that art is not the ultimate expression of mind, but that reflective thought is, and that the latter dictates that if man is to achieve full individuality, he can do so only as part of an actual state in which he is guaranteed positive freedom (a state similar in some salient respects to the actual Prussian state of the time). In Hegel's own eyes, he is the hardest of hard-headed realists: Freedom is to be institutionalized in the state and romantic individualism curbed, because that is the only way that real freedom can be attained in the real world. This move is given a further, wrenching impetus by Karl Marx; it is redirected in another direction—into a democratic welfare state—by T. H. Green.

The first selection is from the *Philosophy of History*,* a work compiled largely by Hegel's students from their notes.

The *Sun*—the Light—rises in the East. Light is a simply self-involved existence; but though possessing thus in itself universality, it exists at the same time as an individuality in the Sun. Imagination has often pictured to itself the emotions of a blind man suddenly becoming possessed of sight, beholding the bright glimmering of the dawn, the growing light, and the flaming glory of the ascending Sun. The boundless forgetfulness of his individuality in this pure splendor, is his first feeling—utter astonishment. But when the Sun is risen, this astonishment is diminished; objects around are perceived, and from them the individual proceeds to the contemplation of his own inner being, and thereby the advance is made to the perception of the relation between the two. Then inactive contemplation is quitted for activity; by the close of day man has erected a building constructed from his own inner Sun; and when in the evening he contemplates this, he esteems it more highly than the original external Sun. For now he stands in a *conscious relation* to his Spirit, and therefore a *free* relation. If we hold this image fast in mind, we shall find it symbolizing the course of History, the great Day's work of Spirit.

The History of the World travels from East to West, for Europe is absolutely the end of History, Asia the beginning. The History of the World has an East χατ᾽ ᾽εξοχήν (the term East in itself is entirely relative); for although the Earth forms a sphere, History performs no circle round it, but has on the contrary a determinate East, viz. Asia. Here rises the outward physical Sun, and in the West it sinks down: here consentaneously rises the Sun of self-consciousness, which diffuses a nobler brilliance. The History of the World is the discipline of the uncontrolled natural will, bringing it into obedience to a Universal principle and conferring subjective freedom. The East knew and to the present day knows only that *One* is Free; the Greek and Roman World, that *some* are free; the German World knows that *All* are free. The first political form therefore which we observe in History is *Despotism,* the second, *Democracy* and *Aristocracy,* the third *Monarchy.*

* Translated by J. Sibree, 1905.

To understand this division we must remark that as the State is the universal spiritual life, to which individuals by birth sustain a relation of confidence and habit, and in which they have their existence and reality—the first question is, whether their actual life is an unreflecting use and habit combining them in this unity, or whether its constituent individuals are reflective and personal beings having a properly subjective and independent existence. In view of this, *substantial* [objective] freedom must be distinguished from *subjective* freedom. Substantial freedom is the abstract undeveloped Reason implicit in volition, proceeding to develop itself in the State. But in this phase of Reason there is still wanting personal insight and will, that is, subjective freedom; which is realized only in the Individual, and which constitutes the reflection of the Individual in his own conscience.* Where there is merely substantial freedom, commands and laws are regarded as something fixed and abstract, to which the subject holds himself in absolute servitude. These laws need not concur with the desire of the individual, and the subjects are consequently like children, who obey their parents without will or insight of their own. But as subjective freedom arises, and man descends from the contemplation of external reality into his own soul, the contrast suggested by reflection arises, involving the Negation of Reality. The drawing back from the actual world forms *ipso facto* an antithesis, of which one side is the absolute Being—the Divine—the other the human subject as an individual. In that immediate, unreflected consciousness which characterizes the East, these two are not yet distinguished. The substantial world is distinct from the individual, but the antithesis has not yet created a schism between [absolute and subjective] Spirit.

The first phase—that with which we have to begin—is the *East*. Unreflected consciousness—substantial, objective, spiritual existence —forms the basis; to which the subjective will first sustains a relation in the form of faith, confidence, obedience. In the political life of the

---

* The essence of Spirit is self-determination or "Freedom." Where Spirit has attained mature growth, as in the man who acknowledges the absolute validity of the dictates of Conscience, the Individual is "a law to himself," and his Freedom is "realized." But in lower stages of morality and civilization, he *unconsciously projects* this legislative principle into some "governing power" (one or several), and obeys it as if it were an alien, extraneous force, not the voice of that Spirit of which he himself (though at this stage imperfectly) is an embodiment. The Philosophy of History exhibits the successive stages by which he reaches the consciousness, that it is *his own inmost being* that thus governs him—*i.e.* a consciousness of self-determination or "Freedom." —Tr.

East we find a realized rational freedom, developing itself without advancing to *subjective* freedom. It is the childhood of History. Substantial forms constitute the gorgeous edifices of Oriental *Empires,* in which we find all rational ordinances and arrangements, but in such a way that individuals remain as mere accidents. These revolve round a centre, round the sovereign, who, as patriarch—not as despot in the sense of the *Roman* Imperial Constitution—stands at the head. For he has to enforce the moral and substantial: he has to uphold those essential ordinances which are already established; so that what among us belongs entirely to subjective freedom here proceeds from the entire and general body of the State. The glory of Oriental conception is the One Individual as that substantial being to which all belongs, so that no other individual has a separate existence, or mirrors himself in his subjective freedom. All the riches of imagination and Nature are appropriated to that dominant existence in which subjective freedom is essentially merged; the latter looks for its dignity *not* in itself, but in that absolute object. All the elements of a complete State—even subjectivity—may be found there, but not yet harmonized with the grand substantial being. For outside the One Power—before which nothing can maintain an independent existence —there is only revolting caprice, which, beyond the limits of the central power, roves at will without purpose or result. Accordingly we find the wild hordes breaking out from the Upland—falling upon the countries in question, and laying them waste, or settling down in them, and giving up their wild life; but in all cases resultlessly lost in the central substance. This phase of Substantiality, since it has not taken up its antithesis into itself and overcome it, directly divides itself into two elements. On the one side we see duration, stability— Empires belonging to mere space, as it were [as distinguished from Time]—unhistorical History;—as, for example, in China, the State based on the Family relation;—a paternal Government, which holds together the constitution by its provident care, its admonitions, retributive or rather disciplinary inflictions;—a prosaic Empire, because the antithesis of Form, viz. Infinity, Ideality, has not yet asserted itself. On the other side, the Form of Time stands contrasted with this spatial stability. The States in question, without undergoing any change in themselves, or in the principle of their existence, are constantly changing their position toward each other. They are in ceaseless conflict, which brings on rapid destruction. The opposing principle of individuality enters into these conflicting relations; but it is itself as yet only unconscious, merely natural Universality—Light, which is not yet the light of the personal soul. This History, too (*i.e.* of the struggles before mentioned), is, for the most part, really *unhistorical,* for it is only the repetition of the same majestic ruin. The new element, which in the shape of bravery, prowess, magnanimity, occupies the place of the previous despotic pomp, goes through the same circle of decline and subsidence. This subsidence is therefore not really such, for through all this restless change no advance is made. History passes at this point—and only outwardly, *i.e.* without connection with the previous phase—to Central Asia. Continuing the comparison with the ages of the individual man, this would be the boyhood of History, no longer manifesting the repose and trustingness of the child, but boisterous and turbulent. The Greek World may then be compared with the period of adolescence, for here we have individualities forming themselves. This is the *second* main principle in human History. Morality is, as in Asia, a principle; but it is morality impressed on individuality, and consequently denoting the free volition of Individuals. Here, then, is the Union of the Moral with the subjective Will, or the Kingdom of *Beautiful Freedom,* for the Idea is united with a plastic form. It is not yet regarded abstractedly, but immediately bound up with the Real, as in a beautiful work of Art; the Sensuous bears the stamp and expression of the Spiritual. This Kingdom is consequently true Harmony; the world of the most charming, but perishable or quickly passing bloom: it is the natural, unreflecting observance of what is *becoming*—not yet true *Morality.* The individual will of the Subject adopts unreflectingly the conduct and habit prescribed by Justice and the Laws. The Individual is therefore in unconscious unity with the Idea—the social weal. That which in the East is divided into two extremes—the substantial as such, and the individuality absorbed in it—meets here. But these distinct principles are only *immediately* in unity, and consequently involve the highest degree of contradiction; for this æsthetic Morality has not yet passed through the struggle of subjective freedom, in its second birth, its *palingenesis;* it is not yet purified to the standard of the free subjectivity that is the essence of true morality.

The third phase is the realm of abstract Universality (in which the Social aim absorbs all individual aims): it is the *Roman State,* the severe labors of the *Manhood* of History. For true manhood acts neither in accordance with the caprice of a despot, nor in obedience to a graceful caprice of its own; but works for a general aim, one in which the individual perishes and realizes his own private object only in that general aim. The State begins to have an abstract existence, and to develop itself for a definite object, in accomplishing which its members have indeed a share, but not a complete and concrete one [calling their whole being into play]. Free *individuals* are sacrificed to the severe demands of the *National* objects, to which they must surrender themselves in this service of abstract generalization. The Roman State is not a repetition of such a State of Individuals as the Athenian Polis was. The geniality and joy of soul that existed there have given place to harsh and rigorous toil. The interest of History is detached from individuals, but these gain for themselves abstract, formal Universality. The Universal subjugates the individuals; they have to merge their own interests in it; but in return the abstraction which they themselves embody—that is to say, their personality—is recognized: in their individual capacity they become persons with definite rights as such. In the same sense as individuals may be said to be incorporated in the abstract idea of Person, *National Individualities* (those of the Roman Provinces) have also to experience this fate: in this form of Universality their concrete forms are crushed, and incorporated with it as a homogeneous and indifferent mass. Rome becomes a Pantheon of all deities, and of all Spiritual existence, but these divinities and this Spirit do not retain their proper vitality.—The development of the State in question proceeds in two directions. On the one hand, as based on reflection—abstract Universality—it has the express outspoken antithesis in itself: it therefore essentially involves in itself the struggle which that antithesis supposes; with the necessary issue, that individual caprice—the purely contingent and thoroughly worldly power of *one despot*—gets the better of that abstract universal principle. At the very outset we have the antithesis between the Aim of the State as the abstract universal principle on the one hand, and the abstract personality of the individual on the other hand. But when subsequently, in the historical development, individuality gains the ascendant, and the breaking up of the community into its component atoms can only be restrained by external compulsion, then the subjective might of *individual despotism* comes forward to play its part, as if summoned to fulfil this task. For the mere abstract compliance with Law implies on the part of the subject of law the supposition that he has not attained to self-organization and self-control; and this principle of obedience, instead of being hearty and voluntary, has for its motive and ruling power only the arbitrary and contingent disposition of the individual; so that the latter is led to seek consolation for the loss of his freedom in exercising and developing his private right. This is the purely *worldly* harmonization of the antithesis. But in the next place, the pain inflicted by Despotism begins to be felt, and Spirit, driven back into its utmost depths, leaves the godless world, seeks for a harmony in itself, and begins now an inner life—a complete concrete subjectivity, which possesses at the same time a substantiality that is not grounded in mere external existence. Within the soul therefore arises the *Spiritual* pacification of the struggle, in the fact that the individual personality, instead of following its own capricious choice, is purified and elevated into universality;—a subjectivity that of its own free will adopts principles tending to the good of all—reaches, in fact, a divine personality. To that worldly empire, this Spiritual one wears a predominant aspect of opposition, as the empire of a subjectivity that has attained to the knowledge of itself—itself in its essential nature—the Empire of Spirit in its full sense.

The *German* World appears at this point of development—the fourth phase of World-History. This would answer in the comparison with the periods of human life to its *Old Age*. The Old Age of *Nature* is weakness; but that of *Spirit* is its perfect maturity and *strength,* in which it returns to unity with itself, but in its fully developed character as *Spirit*.—This fourth phase begins with the Reconciliation presented in Christianity; but only in the germ, without national or political development. We must therefore regard it as commencing rather with the enormous contrast between the spiritual, religious principle, and the barbarian Real World. For Spirit as the consciousness of an inner World is, at the commencement, itself still in an abstract form. All that is *secular* is consequently given over to rudeness and capricious violence. The *Mohammedan* principle—the enlightenment of the Oriental World—is the first to contravene this barbarism and caprice. We find it developing itself later and more rapidly than Christianity; for the latter needed eight centuries to grow up into a political form. But that principle of the German World which we are now discussing, attained concrete reality only in the history of the German Nations. The contrast of the Spiritual principle animating the *Ecclesiastical* State, with the rough and wild barbarism of the *Secular* State, is here likewise present. The Secular *ought* to be in harmony with the Spiritual principle, but we find nothing more than the *recognition* of that obligation. The Secular power forsaken by the Spirit, must in the first instance vanish in presence of the Ecclesiastical [as representative of Spirit]; but while this latter degrades itself to mere secularity, it loses its influence with the loss of its proper character and vocation. From this corruption of the Ecclesiastical element— that is, of the Church—results the higher form of rational thought. Spirit, once more driven back upon itself, produces its work in an intellectual shape, and becomes capable of realizing the Ideal of Reason from the Secular principle alone. Thus it happens, that in virtue of elements of Universality, which have the principle of Spirit as their basis, the empire of Thought is established actually and concretely. The antithesis of Church and State vanishes. The Spiritual becomes reconnected with the Secular, and develops this latter as an independently organic existence. The State no longer occupies a position of real inferiority to the Church, and is no longer subordinate to it. The latter asserts no prerogative, and the Spiritual is no longer an element foreign to the State. Freedom has found the means of realizing its Ideal—its true existence. This is the ultimate result which the process of History is intended to accomplish, and we have to traverse in detail the long track which has been thus cursorily traced out. Yet length of Time is something entirely relative, and the element of Spirit is Eternity. Duration, properly speaking, cannot be said to belong to it.

This second selection is taken from the Introduction and the first chapter of Hegel's *Phenomenology of Mind* (1807).*

INTRODUCTION

It is natural to suppose that, before philosophy enters upon its subject proper—namely, the actual knowledge of what truly is—it is necessary to come first to an understanding concerning knowledge, which is looked upon as the instrument by which to take possession of the Absolute, or as the means through which to get a sight of it. The apprehension seems legitimate, on the one hand that there may be various kinds of knowledge, among which one might be better adapted than another for the attainment of our purpose—and thus a wrong choice is possible: on the other hand again that, since knowing is a faculty of a definite kind and with a determinate range, without

* Translated by J. B. Baillie; revised edition 1931. By permission of George Allen & Unwin, Ltd., London.

the more precise determination of its nature and limits we might take hold on clouds of error instead of the heaven of truth.

This apprehensiveness is sure to pass even into the conviction that the whole enterprise which sets out to secure for consciousness by means of knowledge what exists *per se,* is in its very nature absurd; and that between knowledge and the Absolute there lies a boundary which completely cuts off the one from the other. For if knowledge is the instrument by which to get possession of absolute Reality, the suggestion immediately occurs that the application of an instrument to anything does *not* leave it as it is for itself, but rather entails in the process, and has in view, a moulding and alteration of it. Or, again, if knowledge is not an instrument which we actively employ, but a kind of passive medium through which the light of the truth reaches us, then here, too, we do not receive it as it is in itself, but as it is through and in this medium. In either case we employ a means which immediately brings about the very opposite of its own end; or, rather, the absurdity lies in making use of any means at all. It seems indeed open to us to find in the knowledge of the way in which the *instrument* operates, a remedy for this parlous state; for thereby it becomes possible to remove from the result the part which, in our idea of the Absolute received through that instrument, belongs to the instrument, and thus to get the truth in its purity. But this improvement would, as a matter of fact, only bring us back to the point where we were before. If we take away again from a definitely formed thing that which the instrument has done in the shaping of it, then the thing (in this case the Absolute) stands before us once more just as it was previous to all this trouble, which, as we now see, was superfluous. If the Absolute were only to be brought on the whole nearer to us by this agency, without any change being wrought in it, like a bird caught by a limestick, it would certainly scorn a trick of that sort, if it were not in its very nature, and did it not wish to be, beside us from the start. For a trick is what knowledge in such a case would be, since by all its busy toil and trouble it gives itself the air of doing something quite different from bringing about a relation that is merely immediate, and so a waste of time to establish. Or, again, if the examination of knowledge, which we represent as a medium, makes us acquainted with the law of its refraction, it is likewise useless to eliminate this refraction from the result. For knowledge is not the divergence of the ray, but the ray itself by which the truth comes in contact with us; and if this be removed, the bare direction or the empty place would alone be indicated.

Meanwhile, if the fear of falling into error introduces an element of distrust into science, which without any scruples of that sort goes to work and actually does know, it is not easy to understand why, conversely, a distrust should not be placed in this very distrust, and why we should not take care lest the fear of error is not just the initial error. As a matter of fact, this fear presupposes something, indeed a great deal, as truth, and supports its scruples and consequences on what should itself be examined beforehand to see whether it is truth. It starts with ideas of knowledge as an instrument, and as a medium; and presupposes a distinction of ourselves from this knowledge. More especially it takes for granted that the Absolute stands on one side, and that knowledge on the other side, by itself and cut off from the Absolute, is still something real; in other words, that knowledge, which, by being outside the Absolute, is certainly also outside truth, is nevertheless true—a position which, while calling itself fear of error, makes itself known rather as fear of the truth. . . .

If now our inquiry deals with the truth of knowledge, it appears that we are inquiring what knowledge is in itself. But in this inquiry knowledge is *our* object, it is *for us*; and the essential nature (*Ansich*) of knowledge, were this to come to light, would be rather its being *for us*: what we should assert to be its essence would rather be, not the truth of knowledge, but only our knowledge of it. The essence or the criterion would lie in us; and that which was to be compared with this standard, and on which a decision was to be passed as a result of this comparison, would not necessarily have to recognize that criterion.

But the nature of the object which we are examining surmounts this separation, or semblance of separation, and presupposition. Consciousness furnishes its own criterion in itself, and the inquiry will thereby be a comparison of itself with its own self; for the distinction, just made, falls inside itself. In consciousness there is one element *for* another, or, in general, consciousness implicates the specific character of the moment of knowledge. At the same time this "other" is to consciousness not merely *for it,* but also outside this relation, or has a being in itself, i.e. there is the moment of truth. Thus in what consciousness inside itself declares to be the essence or truth we have the standard which itself sets up, and by which we are to measure its knowledge. Suppose we call knowledge the notion, and the essence or truth "being" or the object, then the examination consists in seeing whether the notion corresponds with the object. But if we call the inner nature of the object, or what it is in itself, the notion, and, on the other side, understand by object the notion *qua* object, i.e. the way the notion is *for* another, then the examination consists in our seeing whether the object corresponds to its own notion. It is clear, of course, that both of these processes are the same. The essential fact, however, to be borne in mind throughout the whole inquiry is that both these moments, notion and object, "being for another" and "being in itself," themselves fall within that knowledge which we are examining. Consequently we do not require to bring standards with us, nor to apply *our* fancies and thoughts in the inquiry; and just by our leaving these aside we are enabled to treat and discuss the subject as it actually is in itself and for itself, as it is in its complete reality.

But not only in this respect, that notion and object, the criterion and what is to be tested, are ready to hand in consciousness itself, is any addition of ours superfluous, but we are also spared the trouble of comparing these two and of making an examination in the strict sense of the term; so that in this respect, too, since consciousness tests and examines itself, all we are left to do is simply and solely to look on. For consciousness is, on the one hand, consciousness of the object, on the other, consciousness of itself; consciousness of what to it is true, and consciousness of its knowledge of that truth. Since both are for the same consciousness, it is itself their comparison; it is the same consciousness that decides and knows whether its knowledge of the object corresponds with this object or not. The object, it is true, appears only to be in such wise for consciousness as consciousness knows it. Consciousness does not seem able to get, so to say, behind it as it is, not for consciousness, but in itself, and consequently seems also unable to test knowledge by it. But just because consciousness has, in general, knowledge of an object, there is already present the distinction that the inherent nature, what the object is in itself, is one thing to consciousness, while knowledge, or the being of the object *for* consciousness, is another moment. Upon this distinction, which is present as a fact, the examination turns. Should both, when thus compared, not correspond, consciousness seems bound to alter its knowledge, in order to make it fit the object. But in the alteration of the knowledge, the object itself also, in point of fact, is altered; for the knowledge which existed was essentially a knowledge of the object; with change in the knowledge, the object also becomes different, since it belonged essentially to this knowledge. Hence consciousness comes to find that what formerly to it was the essence is not what is *per se,* or what was *per se* was only *per se for consciousness.* Since, then, in the case of its object consciousness finds its knowledge not corresponding with this object, the object likewise fails to hold out; or the standard for examining is altered when that, whose criterion this standard was to be, does not hold its ground in the course of the examination; and the examination is not only an examination of knowledge, but also of the criterion used in the process.

This dialectic process which consciousness executes on itself—on its knowledge as well as on its object—in the sense that out of it the new and true object arises, is precisely what is termed Experience. In this connection, there is a moment in the process just mentioned which should be brought into more decided prominence, and by which a new light is cast on the scientific aspect of the following exposition. Consciousness knows something; this something is the essence or what is *per se*. This object, however, is also the *per se,* the inherent reality, *for consciousness*. Hence comes ambiguity of this truth. Consciousness, as we see, has now two objects; one is the first *per se,* the second is the existence *for consciousness* of this *per se*. The last object appears at first sight to be merely the reflection of consciousness into itself, i.e. an idea not of an object, but solely of its knowledge of that first object. But, as was already indicated, by that very process the first object is altered; it ceases to be what is *per se,* and becomes consciously something which is *per se* only *for consciousness*. Consequently, then, what this real *per se* is for consciousness is truth: which, however, means that this is the essential reality, or the object which consciousness has. This new object contains the nothingness of the first; the new object is the *experience* concerning that first object.

In this treatment of the course of experience, there is an element in virtue of which it does not seem to be in agreement with what is ordinarily understood by experience. The transition from the first object and the knowledge of it to the other object, in regard to which we say we have had experience, was so stated that the knowledge of the first object, the existence *for consciousness* of the first *ens per se,* is itself to be the second object. But it usually seems that we learn by experience the untruth of our first notion by appealing to some other object which we may happen to find casually and externally; so that, in general, what we have is merely the bare and simple apprehension of what is in and for itself. On the view above given, however, the new object is seen to have come about by a transformation or conversion of consciousness itself. This way of looking at the matter is *our* doing, what *we* contribute; by its means the series of experiences

through which consciousness passes is lifted into a scientifically constituted sequence, but this does not exist for the consciousness we
contemplate and consider. We have here, however, the same sort of
circumstance, again, of which we spoke a short time ago when dealing with the relation of this exposition to scepticism, viz. that the
result which at any time comes about in the case of an untrue mode
of knowledge cannot possibly collapse into an empty nothing, but
must necessarily be taken as the negation of that of which it is a
result—a result which contains what truth the preceding mode of
knowledge has in it. In the present instance the position takes this
form: since what at first appeared as object is reduced, when it passes
into consciousness, to what knowledge takes it to be, and the implicit
nature, the real in itself, becomes what this entity *per se* is *for consciousness*; this latter is the new object, whereupon there appears also
a new mode or embodiment of consciousness, of which the essence is
something other than that of the preceding mode. It is this circumstance which carries forward the whole succession of the modes or
attitudes of consciousness in their own necessity. It is only this necessity, this origination of the new object—which offers itself to consciousness without consciousness knowing how it comes by it—that
to us, who watch the process, is to be seen going on, so to say, behind
its back. Thereby there enters into its process a moment of being *per
se* or of being for us, which is not expressly presented to that consciousness which is in the grip of experience itself. The *content,* however, of what we see arising, exists for it, and we lay hold of and
comprehend merely its formal character, i.e. its *bare* origination; *for
it*, what has thus arisen has merely the character of object, while, *for
us*, it appears at the same time as a process and coming into being.

In virtue of that necessity this pathway to science is itself *eo ipso*
science, and is, moreover, as regards its content, Science of the Experience of Consciousness.

The experience which consciousness has concerning itself can, by
its essential principle, embrace nothing less than the entire system of
consciousness, the whole realm of the truth of mind, and in such wise
that the moments of truth are set forth in the specific and peculiar
character they here possess—i.e. not as abstract pure moments, but
as they are for consciousness, or as consciousness itself appears in its
relation to them, and in virtue of which they are moments of the
whole, are embodiments or modes of consciousness. In pressing forward to its true form of existence, consciousness will come to a point
at which it lays aside its semblance of being hampered with what is

foreign to it, with what is only for it and exists as another; it will reach a position where appearance becomes identified with essence, where, in consequence, its exposition coincides with just this very point, this very stage of the science proper of mind. And, finally, when it grasps this its own essence, it will connote the nature of absolute knowledge itself.

CHAPTER I

CERTAINTY AT THE LEVEL OF SENSE-EXPERIENCE
—THE "THIS," AND "MEANING"

The knowledge, which is at the start or immediately our object, can be nothing else than just that which is immediate knowledge, knowledge of the immediate, of what *is*. We have, in dealing with it, to proceed, too, in an immediate way, to accept what is given, not altering anything in it as it is presented before us, and keeping mere apprehension (*Auffassen*) free from conceptual comprehension (*Begreifen*).

The concrete content, which sensuous certainty furnishes, makes this *prima facie* appear to be the richest kind of knowledge, to be even a knowledge of endless wealth—a wealth to which we can as little find any limit when we traverse its *extent* in space and time, where that content is presented before us, as when we take a fragment out of the abundance it offers us and by dividing and dividing seek to penetrate its *intent*. Besides that, it seems to be the truest, the most authentic knowledge: for it has not as yet dropped anything from the object; it has the object before itself in its entirety and completeness. This bare fact of *certainty*, however, is really and admittedly the abstractest and the poorest kind of *truth*. It merely says regarding what it knows: it *is*; and its truth contains solely the *being* of the fact it knows. Consciousness, on its part, in the case of this form of certainty, takes the shape merely of pure Ego. In other words, I in such a case am merely *qua* pure This, and the object likewise is merely *qua* pure This. I, *this* particular conscious I, am certain of *this* fact before me, not because I *qua* consciousness have developed myself in connection with it and in manifold ways set thought to work about it: and not, again, because the fact, the thing, of which I am certain, in virtue of its having a multitude of distinct qualities, was replete with possible modes of relation and a variety of connections with other things. Neither has anything to do with the truth sensuous certainty contains: neither the I nor the thing has here the meaning of a manifold relation with a variety of other things, of mediation in a variety of ways. The I does not contain or imply a manifold of ideas, the I here does not *think*: nor does the thing mean what has a multiplicity of qualities. Rather, the thing, the fact, *is*; and it *is* merely because it *is*. It *is*—that is the essential point for sense-knowledge, and that bare fact of *being*; that simple immediacy, constitutes its truth. In the same way the certainty *qua relation*, the certainty "of" something, is an immediate pure relation; consciousness is I—nothing more, a pure *this*; the *individual* consciousness knows a pure *this*, or knows what is *individual*.

But, when we look closely, there is a good deal more implied in that bare pure being, which constitutes the kernel of this form of certainty, and is given out by it as its truth. A concrete actual certainty of sense is not merely this pure immediacy, but an example, an instance, of that immediacy. Amongst the innumerable distinctions that here come to light, we find in all cases the fundamental difference —viz. that in sense-experience pure being at once breaks up into the two "thises," as we have called them, one this as I, and one as object. When *we* reflect* on this distinction, it is seen that neither the one nor the other is merely immediate, merely *is* in sense-certainty, but is at the same time *mediated*; I have the certainty through the other, viz. through the actual fact; and this, again, exists in that certainty through another, viz. through the I.

It is not only we who make this distinction of essential truth and particular example, of essence and instance, immediacy and mediation; we *find* it in sense-certainty itself, and it has to be taken up in the form in which it exists there, not as we have just determined it. One of them is put forward in it as existing in simple immediacy, as the essential reality, the *object*. The other, however, is put forward as the non-essential, as *mediated*, something which is not *per se* in the certainty, but there through something else, ego, a state of knowledge which only knows the object because the *object* is, and which can as well be as *not* be. The object, however, is the real truth, is the essential reality; it *is*, quite indifferent to whether it is known or not; it remains and stands even though it is not known, while the knowledge does not exist if the object is not there.

We have thus to consider as to the object, whether in point of fact it does exist in sense-certainty itself as such an essential reality as that certainty gives it out to be; whether its meaning and notion, which is

---

* I.e. for the purposes of philosophical analysis.

to be essential reality, corresponds to the way it is present in that certainty. We have for that purpose not to reflect about it and ponder what it might be in truth, but to deal with it merely as sense-certainty contains it.

Sense-certainty itself has thus to be asked: What is the This? If we take it in the two-fold form of its existence, as the *Now* and as the *Here*, the dialectic it has in it will take a form as intelligible as the This itself. To the question, What is the Now? we reply, for example, the Now is night-time. To test the truth of this certainty of sense, a simple experiment is all we need: write that truth down. A truth cannot lose anything by being written down, and just as little by our preserving and keeping it. If we look again at the truth we have written down, look at it *now, at this noon-time,* we shall have to say it has turned stale and become out of date.

The Now that is night is kept fixed, i.e. it is treated as what it is given out to be, as something which *is*; but it proves to be rather a something which is *not*. The Now itself no doubt maintains itself, but as what is *not* night; similarly in its relation to the day which the Now is at present, it maintains itself as something that is also not day, or as altogether something negative. This self-maintaining Now is there-fore not something immediate but something mediated; for, *qua* something that remains and preserves itself, it is determined through and *by means* of the fact that something else, namely day and night, is *not*. Thereby it is just as much as ever it was before, Now, and in being this simple fact, it is indifferent to what is still associated with it; just as little as night or day is its being, it is just as truly also day and night; it is not in the least affected by this otherness through which it is what it is. A simple entity of this sort, which is by and through negation, which is neither this nor that, which is a *not-this*, and with equal indifference this as well as that—a thing of this kind we call a Universal. The Universal is therefore in point of fact the truth of sense-certainty, the true content of sense-experience. . . .

15. MARX: Economic Revolution as the Ground of Freedom

Hegel's august and scholarly system tended to hide its ambiguities and revolutionary tendencies. Karl Marx (1818–1883), a German sociologist and philosopher working in England, the father of modern communism, brought some of these out. Each synthesis, for Hegel, becomes a thesis which engenders in turn its own antithesis. What about the synthesis, then, which is Hegel's own system? This had not been discussed within the system itself, leaving thereby the impression that his synthesis was the final one. But this is inconsistent, thought Marx: Hegel should be saved from himself. An extreme synthesis becomes in time an extreme thesis which must engender an antithesis of equal extremity; of such tensions is history made. And what of a synthesis which purported to speak for all that was worth saving in all previous philosophy? The antithesis must be precisely nonphilosophical, in any traditional sense of that term. We enter the age of total revolution.

The ambiguities and instabilities of philosophical relativism are more obvious in Schelling than in Hegel; but Hegel's system proved more explosive and revolutionary—at least in his followers' hands—because of the way in which Hegel bore down on the present and actual historical situation. Hegel believed that his philosophy had not only historical import, but was an explication of God's timeless essence before the foundation of the world. But the younger Hegelians, of whom Marx was one, found difficulty in making sense of this. For most of them there are no structures outside of the historical process, and for those who still think of Him, God *explicitas* is just a possibility—the flying goal of the process. Moreover, just what this fractured Hegelian goal is, said Marx, is not always clear, and where it is clear it is not always correct.

An alleged ambiguity seized upon by the young Hegelians of the left is Hegel's concept of Being. Hegel had declared in his *Philosophy of Right* that whatever is, is rational. But what *is*? Reality is a union of essence and existence for Hegel,* with the prime example being self-consciousness; but it turns out that some existing things are not fully joined to essence and therefore not fully real. But *which things*? (Particular gobs of mud, hair and filth?) Hegel's intellectual descendants were not sure, and from this crucial doubt sprouted the seeds of strife. For if what *is* is what now exists, then *what is* is rational and should be conserved. But if what *is* is what is not yet—if the union of essence and existence must be forcibly brought about—then what now exists must be overturned by revolution.

This central ambiguity is aggravated by another: In surveying any polar tension of thesis and antithesis and plotting the resulting synthesis, the relative weight given the poles determines the difference between a conservative and a revolutionary interpretation of history. In the chaos of Hegel-interpretation no objective criterion appeared for adjudicating the many disputes arising over this point. Once Hegel's own conservative bias and general balance of mind were gone, the specter of subjectivism,

---

* *Logik,* II, ed. by Lasson (Leipzig, 1923), 156 ff.

opportunism and nihilism was loose. For who could tell what is right and rational save on the basis of what actually does happen? And what was to stop one from making things happen on the basis of the most cynical kind of success ethics—whatever advances my own cause is good?

Just how Marx attempted to cope with this situation, and perhaps exploit it, exceeds the scope of this volume. But a rough outline can be drawn: In quasi-Hegelian fashion Marx seeks to transcend Hegel, salvage certain elements from him and put Hegel "in his place." There is a dialectical development in Marx, but "de-mystified," for he claims that Hegel was blind to his own bias, that of a bourgeois intellectual Christian (so blind, in fact, that he does not realize that his pantheism undermines Christian theism). Marx continues his charge: Hegel did not see that the "culminating" bourgeois state is a creation of the capitalist social class in order to perpetuate its own business interests and suppress the working class. He did not see that his worship of consciousness is a remnant of Christian gnosticism* and hatred of the body. He did not see that consciousness is just the most complex effect of the matter which is its cause. In sum, Hegel did not see that his philosophy is an expression of cultural, physical and socio-economic conditions which it itself does not comprehend.

For Marx the dialectic is not internal to an absolute consciousness** but is comprised by historical socio-economic conditions (thesis), human needs and desires (antithesis) which project possibilities on the basis of these conditions, and, at a certain point, as a result of interaction between these conditions and the will and thought of a definite socio-economic class, revolutionary action (synthesis) results. He is thus a dialectical materialist.

Marx believes his materialism to be of the kind which liberates the human spirit from that common, degrading bourgeois sort of materialism wearing the disguise of spiritualism. Marx uses Hegel against Hegel: Marx agrees with him that "man only 'is' insofar as he is productive; he must produce himself and his world because his entire existence is . . . mediating and mediated."† Hence, take away his ability to control his own work and he is deprived of his very self; and this Marx claims is just what the capitalist state, be it Prussian or otherwise, has done.

Likewise in Hegelian fashion, Marx agrees that an antithesis and synthesis are possible only on the basis of a prior thesis. It is only be-

---

* The opposite of agnosticism: extensive knowledge claims about the spiritual realm.

** See Sidney Hook, *From Hegel to Marx* (New York: Humanities Press, 1950).

† See Karl Löwith, *From Hegel to Nietzsche* (London: Constable & Co., 1963).

cause capitalism has "unlocked the treasure house of the world" and fashioned immensely powerful tools of production that man *as such* now has the ability to free himself from the bonds of physical nature. A new ethics (synthesis) of social justice is to be founded on the objective possibilities *created* by capitalism: Marx is an evolutionist and fits into the age. But, says Marx, a synthesis reorganizes everything, even the admittedly good elements of capitalism such as personal initiative and resourcefulness. What was an achievement for its time is now but bonds and fetters for the masses—and must be thrown off.

For Marx, man as such, universal man, is the proletarian man. This, of course, is debatable. Do not such laborers have some very special needs and abilities? What is general about them? But, then, much else is debatable also. How do we know that a proletarian state (thus "classless" in the sense that it is without class conflict) is good? It has not happened yet. Who is to verify that claim before it is too late perhaps to have anything else?

It is the whole philosophical problem of verification and truth that is most fundamental and most debatable in Marxism. Along with Marx's brilliant insights into specific socio-economic situations, he exhibits both a Hegelian afterglow of system-arrogance and a naïve confidence in the ability of science to solve problems traditionally considered philosophical. If traditional philosophy is just an effect of specific socio-economic conditions acting as cause, then how is Marx's philosophy which asserts this fact any more than a similar effect of different specific socio-economic conditions? What makes it *true* of these conditions and their alleged effects? The causal genesis of a thought is irrelevant to its truth. All that is relevant is the intrinsic structure of the thought and the structure of the reality intended to be thought about. Now, Marx would assert that though standards of truth change, they can be applied to socio-economic conditions and their alleged effects because the standards change concurrently with more slowly changing generic structures of physical nature. But even assuming that standards of truth are so derived, it still remains to be shown how such standards could determine that communist philosophy is true despite its genesis in particular socio-economic conditions, while other philosophies are false because of their genesis in other socio-economic conditions. If it is replied that communist philosophy is true because it is aware of its socio-economic conditions, then this begs the question of truth; for what is assumed is that communism is *truly* aware of its conditions and that these are determinate—precisely the point to be proved.

Marxism is the first of a type: a "scientific" philosophy which despairs of traditional philosophy. It is born of two antagonistic ancestors: an ambitious philosophical rationalism which treats natural science with indifference, and an implicit adoration of the systematic nature and the success of that despised natural science. The result is an inability to account for science and to integrate it into a comprehensive philosophy of culture.

Marxism is a full-fledged modern philosophy which runs all the dangers inherent in scientism: reductionism, first of all, then process-product and causal-cognitive confusions in the area of epistemology, and relativism and indeterminacy in the area of ethics.* It is a *bona fide* member of the modern world and an odd descendant of romanticism, at least on one side of the house. Ironically, it makes the world shake with the power intrinsic to thought itself; no purely economic interpretation—not even its own—can account for that intellectual and political power it does possess today.

Nowhere do the possibilities turned up by nineteenth-century thought appear more truly or more portentously than when seen from the viewpoint of the Hegel-Marx interaction. Hegel turns away from the future with gray resignation and contends that philosophy comes too late to predict the future and to rejuvenate civilization.† Marx cuts off the past like a burden and leaps into the future with a kind of religious abandon. Despite the real differences of view, there is a common feeling that the future holds dreadful chances and strange new choices.

The selections are all taken from the third edition of the first volume of *Capital*, first published in 1867.‡ The first one, entitled "Historical Tendency of Capitalist Accumulation," outlines Marx's argument that capitalist expropriation of labor power and property sets in motion the very forces that eventually lead to capitalists' themselves being expropriated by the masses.

What does the primitive accumulation of capital *i.e.,* its historical genesis, resolve itself into? In so far as it is not immediate transformation of slaves and serfs into wage-labourers, and therefore a mere change of form, it only means the expropriation of the immediate producers, *i.e.,* the dissolution of private property based on the labour of its owner. Private property, as the antithesis to social, collective property exists only where the means of labour and the external conditions of labour belong to private individuals. But according as these private individuals are labourers or not labourers, private prop-

* The claims of Darwinism, which was soon to hit, are in this sense quite similar.

† See *Philosophy of Right*, Preface.

‡ Translated from the third German edition by S. Moore and E. Aveling, 1886.

erty has a different character. The numberless shades, that it at first sight presents, correspond to the intermediate stage lying between these two extremes. The private property of the labourer in his means of production is the foundation of petty industry, whether agricultural, manufacturing, or both; petty industry, again, is an essential condition for the development of social production and of the free individuality of the labourer himself. Of course, this petty mode of production exists also under slavery, serfdom, and other states of dependence. But it flourishes, it lets loose its whole energy, it attains its adequate classical form, only where the labourer is the private owner of his own means of labour set in action by himself: the peasant of the land which he cultivates, the artisan of the tool which he handles as a virtuoso. This mode of production presupposes parcelling of the soil, and scattering of the other means of production. As it excludes the concentration of these means of production, so also it excludes co-operation, division of labour within each separate process of production, the control over, and the productive application of the forces of Nature by society, and the free development of the social productive powers. It is compatible only with a system of production, and a society, moving within narrow and more or less primitive bounds. To perpetuate it would be, as Pecqueur rightly says, "to decree universal mediocrity." At a certain stage of development it brings forth the material agencies for its own dissolution. From that moment new forces and new passions spring up in the bosom of society; but the old social organization fetters them and keeps them down. It must be annihilated; it is annihilated. Its annihilation, the transformation of the individualized and scattered means of production into socially concentrated ones, of the pigmy property of the many into the huge property of the few, the expropriation of the great mass of the people from the soil, from the means of subsistence, and from the means of labour, this fearful and painful expropriation of the mass of the people forms the prelude to the history of capital. It comprises a series of forcible methods, of which we have passed in review only those that have been epoch-making as methods of the primitive accumulation of capital. The expropriation of the immediate producers was accomplished with merciless Vandalism, and under the stimulus of passions the most infamous, the most sordid, the pettiest, the most meanly odious. Self-earned private property, that is based, so to say, on the fusing together of the isolated, independent labouring-individual with the conditions of his labour, is supplanted by capitalistic private property, which rests on exploitation of the nominally free labour of others, *i.e.*, on wages-labour.

As soon as this process of transformation has sufficiently decomposed the old society from top to bottom, as soon as the labourers are turned into proletarians, their means of labour into capital, as soon as the capitalist mode of production stands on its own feet, then the further socialization of labour and further transformation of the land and other means of production into socially exploited and, therefore, common means of production, as well as the further expropriation of private proprietors, takes a new form. That which is now to be expropriated is no longer the labourer working for himself, but the capitalist exploiting many labourers. This expropriation is accomplished by the action of the immanent laws of capitalistic production itself, by the centralization of capital. One capitalist always kills many. Hand in hand with this centralization, or this expropriation of many capitalists by few, develop, on an ever-extending scale, the co-operative form of the labour-process, the conscious technical application of science, the methodical cultivation of the soil, the transformation of the instruments of labour into instruments of labour only usable in common, the economizing of all means of production by their use as the means of production of combined, socialized labour, the entanglement of all peoples in the net of the world-market, and with this, the international character of the capitalistic régime. Along with the constantly diminishing number of the magnates of capital, who usurp and monopolize all advantages of this process of transformation, grows the mass of misery, oppression, slavery, degradation, exploitation; but with this too grows the revolt of the working-class, a class always increasing in numbers, and disciplined, united, organized by the very mechanism of the process of capitalist production itself. The monopoly of capital becomes a fetter upon the mode of production, which has sprung up and flourished along with, and under it. Centralization of the means of production and socialization of labour at last reach a point where they become incompatible with their capitalist integument. This integument is burst asunder. The knell of capitalist private property sounds. The expropriators are expropriated.

The capitalist mode of appropriation, the result of the capitalist mode of production, produces capitalist private property. This is the first negation of individual private property, as founded on the labour of the proprietor. But capitalist production begets, with the inexorability of a law of Nature, its own negation. It is the negation of negation. This does not reestablish private property for the producer, but gives him individual property based on the acquisitions of the capitalist era: *i.e.,* on co-operation and the possession in common of the land and of the means of production.

The transformation of scattered private property, arising from individual labour, into capitalist private property is, naturally, a process, incomparably more protracted, violent, and difficult, than the transformation of capitalistic private property, already practically resting on socialized production, into socialized property. In the former case, we had the expropriation of the mass of the people by a few usurpers; in the latter, we have the expropriation of a few usurpers by the mass of the people.*

The following charming and witty spoof on Hegel† (note Hegel's idea [p. 163] that man stands on his head and constructs the world accordingly; that is, the world for man is always the world-as-it-is-thought) expresses Marx's essentially grim contention that in capitalist society the social cooperation involved in producing commodities is suppressed, distorted and unconscious. What is really a relationship between *persons* who produce is given an unwitting, abridged, distorted and coded translation into the terms of the commodities produced. The producers in industrial society seldom meet, and thus fail to realize that they survive at all only by cooperating together; lack of conscious awareness goes hand in hand with lack of control over the social process. There emerge, Marx says, "material relations between persons and social relations between things": pernicious materialism sets in between persons, while tables cease being mere pieces of wood, but "stand on their heads" in

* The advance of industry, whose involuntary promoter is the bourgeoisie, replaces the isolation of the labourers, due to competition, by their revolutionary combination, due to association. The development of Modern Industry, therefore, cuts from under its feet the very foundation on which the bourgeoisie produces and appropriates products. What the bourgeoisie therefore produces, above all, are its own grave-diggers. Its fall and the victory of the proletariat are equally inevitable. . . . Of all the classes, that stand face to face with the bourgeoisie to-day, the proletariat alone is a really revolutionary class. The other classes perish and disappear in the face of Modern Industry, the proletariat is its special and essential product. . . . The lower middle-classes, the small manufacturers, the shopkeepers, the artisan, the peasant, all these fight against the bourgeoisie, to save from extinction their existence as fractions of the middle-class . . . they are reactionary, for they try to roll back the wheel of history. "Karl Marx and Frederick Engels, *Manifest der Kommunistischen Partei,*" London, 1847, pp. 9, 11.

† All selections are taken from *Capital,* Vol. I.

mystifying quasi-social and quasi-personal relationships to other com-modities. The tables dance; the producers of the tables stand like blocks of wood.

A commodity appears, at first sight, a very trivial thing, and easily understood. Its analysis shows that it is, in reality, a very queer thing, abounding in metaphysical subtleties and theological niceties. So far as it is a value in use, there is nothing mysterious about it, whether we consider it from the point of view that by its properties it is capable of satisfying human wants, or from the point that those prop-erties are the product of human labour. It is as clear as noon-day, that man, by his industry, changes the forms of the materials fur-nished by nature, in such a way as to make them useful to him. The form of wood, for instance, is altered, by making a table out of it. Yet, for all that, the table continues to be that common, every-day thing, wood. But, so soon as it steps forth as a commodity, it is changed into something transcendent. It not only stands with its feet on the ground, but, in relation to all other commodities, it stands on its head, and evolves out of its wooden brain grotesque ideas, far more wonderful than "table-turning" ever was.

The mystical character of commodities does not originate, there-fore, in their use-value. Just as little does it proceed from the nature of the determining factors of value. For, in the first place, however varied the useful kinds of labour, or productive activities, may be, it is a physiological fact that they are functions of the human organism, and that each such function, whatever may be its nature or form, is essentially the expenditure of human brain, nerves, muscles, &c. Sec-ondly, with regard to that which forms the groundwork for the quan-titative determination of value, namely, the duration of that expendi-ture, or the quantity of labour, it is quite clear that there is a palpable difference between its quantity and quality. In all states of society, the labour-time that it costs to produce the means of subsistence, must necessarily be an object of interest to mankind, though not of equal interest in different stages of development.* And lastly, from the moment that men in any way work for one another, their labour assumes a social form.

* Among the ancient Germans the unit for measuring land was what could be harvested in a day, and was called Tagwerk, Tagwanne (jurnale, or terra jurnalis, or diornalis), Mannsmaad, &c. (See G. L. von Maurer, *Einleitung zur Geschichte der Marke, &c.*, Verfassung, München, 1859, pp. 129–59.)

Whence, then, arises the enigmatical character of the product of labour, so soon as it assumes the form of commodities? Clearly from this form itself. The equality of all sorts of human labour is expressed objectively by their products all being equally values; the measure of the expenditure of labour-power by the duration of that expenditure takes the form of the quantity of value of the products of labour; and finally, the mutual relations of the producers, within which the social character of their labour affirms itself, take the form of a social relation between the products.

A commodity is therefore a mysterious thing, simply because in it the social character of men's labour appears to them as an objective character stamped upon the product of that labour; because the relation of the producers to the sum total of their own labour is presented to them as a social relation, existing not between themselves, but between the products of their labour. This is the reason why the products of labour become commodities, social things whose qualities are at the same time perceptible and imperceptible by the senses. In the same way the light from an object is perceived by us not as the subjective excitation of our optic nerve, but as the objective form of something outside the eye itself. But, in the act of seeing, there is at all events an actual passage of light from one thing to another, from the external object to the eye. There is a physical relation between physical things. But it is different with commodities. There, the existence of the thing *quâ* commodities, and the value relation between the products of labour which stamps them as commodities, have absolutely no connection with their physical properties and with the material relations arising therefrom. There it is a definite social relation between men that assumes, in their eyes, the fantastic form of a relation between things. In order, therefore, to find an analogy, we must have recourse to the mist-enveloped regions of the religious world. In that world the productions of the human brain appear as independent beings endowed with life, and entering into relation both with one another and the human race. So it is in the world of commodities with the products of men's hands. This I call the Fetishism which attaches itself to the products of labour, so soon as they are produced as commodities, and which is therefore inseparable from the production of commodities.

This Fetishism of commodities has its origin, as the foregoing analysis has already shown, in the peculiar social character of the labour that produces them.

As a general rule, articles of utility become commodities only because they are products of the labour of private individuals or groups of individuals who carry on their work independently of each other. The sum total of the labour of all these private individuals forms the aggregate labour of society. Since the producers do not come into social contact with each other until they exchange their products, the specific social character of each producer's labour does not show itself except in the act of exchange. In other words, the labour of the individual asserts itself as a part of the labour of society, only by means of the relations which the act of exchange establishes directly between the products, and indirectly, through them, between the producers. To the latter, therefore, the relations connecting the labour of one individual with that of the rest appear, not as direct social relations between individuals at work, but as what they really are, material relations between persons and social relations between things. It is only by being exchanged that the products of labour acquire, as values, one uniform social status, distinct from their varied forms of existence as objects of utility. This division of a product into a useful thing and a value becomes practically important only when exchange has acquired such an extension that useful articles are produced for the purpose of being exchanged, and their character as values has therefore to be taken into account, beforehand, during production. From this moment the labour of the individual producer acquires socially a two-fold character. On the one hand, it must, as a definite useful kind of labour, satisfy a definite social want, and thus hold its place as part and parcel of the collective labour of all, as a branch of a social division of labour that has sprung up spontaneously. On the other hand, it can satisfy the manifold wants of the individual producer himself only in so far as the mutual exchangeability of all kinds of useful private labour is an established social fact, and therefore the private useful labour of each producer ranks on an equality with that of all others. The equalization of the most different kinds of labour can be the result only of an abstraction from their inequalities, or of reducing them to their common denominator, viz., expenditure of human labour power or human labour in the abstract. The two-fold social character of the labour of the individual appears to him, when reflected in his brain, only under those forms which are impressed upon that labour in everyday practice by the exchange of products. In this way, the character that his own labour possesses of being socially useful takes the form of the condition that the product must be not only useful, but useful for others, and the social character that his particular labour has of being the equal of all other particular kinds of labour takes the form that all the physically different articles that are the products of labour have one common quality, viz, that of having value.

Hence, when we bring the products of our labour into relation with each other as values, it is not because we see in these articles the material receptacles of homogeneous human labour. Quite the contrary; whenever, by an exchange, we equate as values our different products, by that very act, we also equate, as human labour, the different kinds of labour expended upon them. We are not aware of this, nevertheless we do it.* Value, therefore, does not stalk about with a label describing what it is. It is value, rather, that converts every product into a social hieroglyphic. Later on, we try to decipher the hieroglyphic, to get behind the secret of our own social products; for to stamp an object of utility as a value is just as much a social product as language. The recent scientific discovery that the products of labour, so far as they are values, are but material expressions of the human labour spent in their production, marks, indeed, an epoch in the history of the development of the human race, but, by no means, dissipates the mist through which the social character of labour appears to us to be an objective character of the products themselves. The fact that in the particular form of production with which we are dealing, viz., the production of commodities, the specific social character of private labour carried on independently, consists in the equality of every kind of that labour, by virtue of its being human labour, which character, therefore, assumes in the product the form of value—this fact appears to the producers, notwithstanding the discovery above referred to, to be just as real and final, as the fact that after the discovery by science of the component gases of air, the atmosphere itself remained unaltered.

What, first of all, practically concerns producers when they make an exchange, is the question, how much of some other product they get for their own? When these proportions have, by custom, attained a certain stability, they appear to result from the nature of the prod-

* When, therefore, Galiani says: Value is a relation between persons—"La Ricchezza è una ragione tra due persone,"—he ought to have added: a relation between persons expressed as a relation between things. (Galiani: Della Moneta, p. 221, V. III. of Custodi's collection of "Scrittori Classici Italiani di Economia Politicia." Parte Moderna, Milano, 1803.)

ucts, so that, for instance, one ton of iron and two ounces of gold appear as naturally to be of equal value as a pound of gold and a pound of iron in spite of their different physical and chemical qualities appear to be of equal weight. The character of having value, when once impressed upon products, obtains fixity only by reason of their acting and re-acting upon each other as quantities of value. These quantities vary continually, independently of the will, foresight and action of the producers. To them, their own social action takes the form of the action of objects, which rule the producers instead of being ruled by them. It requires a fully developed production of commodities before, from accumulated experience alone, the scientific conviction springs up, that all the different kinds of private labour, which are carried on independently of each other, and yet as spontaneously developed branches of the social division of labour, are continually being reduced to the quantitive proportions in which society requires them. And why? Because, in the midst of all the accidental and ever fluctuating exchange-relations between the products, the labour-time socially necessary for their production forcibly asserts itself like an over-riding law of nature. The law of gravity thus asserts itself when a house falls about our ears.* The determination of the magnitude of value by labour-time is therefore a secret, hidden under the apparent fluctuations in the relative values of commodities. Its discovery, while removing all appearance of mere accidentality from the determination of the magnitude of the values of products, yet in no way alters the mode in which that determination takes place.

In the following selection from *Capital* (Vol. I) Marx sketches his theory of the driving motor of capitalist society: the production of surplus value, capital. It is only because of profit that the capitalist can build up money like water behind a dam, unleash it, and cut new channels of trade, profit and power.

The value of one pound of yarn being eighteenpence, if our capitalist buys 10 lbs. of yarn in the market, he must pay fifteen shillings for them. It is clear that, whether a man buys his house ready built, or

* "What are we to think of a law that asserts itself only by periodic revolutions? It is just nothing but a law of Nature, founded on the want of knowledge of those whose action is the subject of it." Friedrich Engels: "Umrisse zu einer Kritik der Nationa lökonomie," in the "Deutsch-französische Jahrbücher," edited by Arnold Ruge and Karl Marx. Paris, 1844.)

gets it built for him, in neither case will the mode of acquisition increase the amount of money laid out on the house.

Our capitalist, who is at home in his vulgar economy, exclaims: "Oh! but I advanced my money for the express purpose of making more money." The way to Hell is paved with good intentions, and he might just as easily have intended to make money, without producing at all.* He threatens all sorts of things. He won't be caught napping again. In future he will buy the commodities in the market, instead of manufacturing them himself. But if all his brother capitalists were to do the same, where would he find his commodities in the market? And his money he cannot eat. He tries persuasion. "Consider my abstinence; I might have played ducks and drakes with the 15 shillings; but instead of that I consumed it productively, and made yarn with it." Very well, and by way of reward he is now in possession of good yarn instead of a bad conscience; and as for playing the part of a miser, it would never do for him to relapse into such bad ways as that; we have seen before to what results such asceticism leads. Besides, where nothing is, the king has lost his rights; whatever may be the merit of his abstinence, there is nothing wherewith specially to remunerate it, because the value of the product is merely the sum of the values of the commodities that were thrown into the process of production. Let him therefore console himself with the reflection that virtue is its own reward. But no, he becomes importunate. He says: "The yarn is of no use to me: I produced it for sale." In that case let him sell it, or, still better, let him for the future produce only things for satisfying his personal wants, a remedy that his physician M'Culloch has already prescribed as infallible against an epidemic of over-production. He now gets obstinate. "Can the labourer," he asks, "merely with his arms and legs, produce commodities out of nothing? Did I not supply him with the materials, by means of which, and in which alone, his labour could be embodied? And as the greater part of society consists of such ne'er-do-weels, have I not rendered society incalculable service by my instruments of production, my cotton and my spindle, and not only society, but the labourer also, whom in addition I have provided with the necessaries of life? And am I to be allowed nothing in return for all this service?" Well, but has not the

---

* Thus from 1844–47 he withdrew part of his capital from productive employment, in order to throw it away in railway speculations; and so also, during the American Civil War, he closed his factory, and turned his workpeople into the streets, in order to gamble on the Liverpool cotton exchange.

labourer rendered him the equivalent service of changing his cotton and spindle into yarn? Moreover, there is here no question of service.* A service is nothing more than the useful effect of a use-value, be it of a commodity, or be it of labour. But here we are dealing with exchange-value. The capitalist paid to the labourer a value of 3 shillings, and the labourer gave him back an exact equivalent in the value of 3 shillings, added by him to the cotton: he gave him value for value. Our friend, up to this time so purse-proud, suddenly assumes the modest demeanour of his own workman, and exclaimed: "Have I myself not worked? Have I not performed the labour of superintendence and of overlooking the spinner? And does not this labour, too, create value?" His overlooker and his manager try to hide their smiles. Meanwhile, after a hearty laugh, he reassumes his usual mien. Though he chanted to us the whole creed of the economists, in reality, he says, he would not give a brass farthing for it. He leaves this and all such like subterfuges and juggling tricks to the professors of political economy, who are paid for it. He himself is a practical man; and though he does not always consider what he says outside his business, yet in his business he knows what he is about.

Let us examine the matter more closely. The value of a day's labour-power amounts to 3 shillings, because on our assumption half a day's labour is embodied in that quantity of labour-power, *i.e.,* because the means of subsistence that are daily required for the production of labour-power, cost half a day's labour. But the past labour that is embodied in the labour-power, and the living labour that it can call into action; the daily cost of maintaining it, and its daily expenditure in work, are two totally different things. The former determines the exchange-value of the labour-power, the latter is its use-value. The fact that half a day's labour is necessary to keep the labourer alive during 24 hours does not in any way prevent him from working

---

* "Extol thyself, put on finery and adorn thyself . . . but whoever takes more or better than he gives, that is usury, and is not service, but wrong done to his neighbour, as when one steals and robs. All is not service and benefit to a neighbour that is called service and benefit. For an adulteress and adulterer do one another great service and pleasure. A horseman does an incendiary a great service, by helping him to rob on the highway, and pillage land and houses. The papists do ours a great service, in that they don't drown, burn, murder all of them, or let them all rot in prison; but let some live, and only drive them out, or take from them what they have. The devil himself does his servants inestimable service. . . . To sum up, the world is full of great, excellent, and daily service and benefit."—(Martin Luther, *An die Pfarherrn, wider den Wucher zu predigen*, Wittenberg, 1540.)

a whole day. Therefore, the value of labour-power, and the value which that labour-power creates in the labour process, are two entirely different magnitudes; and this difference of the two values was what the capitalist had in view, when he was purchasing the labour-power. The useful qualities that labour-power possesses, and by virtue of which it makes yarn or boots, were to him nothing more than a conditio sine qua non; for in order to create value, labour must be expended in a useful manner. What really influenced him was the specific use-value which this commodity possesses of being *a source not only of value, but of more value than it has itself.* This is the special service that the capitalist expects from labour-power, and in this transaction he acts in accordance with the "eternal laws" of the exchange of commodities. The seller of labour-power, like the seller of any other commodity, realizes its exchange-value, and parts with its use-value. He cannot take the one without giving the other. The use-value of labour-power, or in other words, labour, belongs just as little to its seller as the use-value of oil after it has been sold belongs to the dealer who has sold it. The owner of the money has paid the value of a day's labour-power; his, therefore, is the use of it for a day; a day's labour belongs to him. The circumstance that on the one hand the daily sustenance of labour-power costs only half a day's labour, while on the other hand the very same labour-power can work during a whole day, that consequently the value which its use during one day creates is double what he pays for that use, this circumstance is, without doubt, apiece of good luck for the buyer, but by no means an injury to the seller.

Our capitalist foresaw this state of things, and that was the cause of his laughter. The labourer therefore finds, in the workshop, the means of production necessary for working, not only during six, but during twelve hours. Just as during the six hours' process our 10 lbs. of cotton absorbed six hours' labour, and became 10 lbs. of yarn, so now, 20 lbs. of cotton will absorb 12 hours' labour and be changed into 20 lbs. of yarn. Let us now examine the product of this prolonged process. There is now materialized in this 20 lbs. of yarn the labour of five days, of which four days are due to the cotton and the lost steel of the spindle, the remaining day having been absorbed by the cotton during the spinning process. Expressed in gold, the labour of five days is thirty shillings. This is therefore the price of the 20 lbs. of yarn, giving, as before, eighteenpence as the price of a pound. But the sum of the values of the commodities that entered into the process amounts to 27 shillings. The value of the yarn is 30 shillings. There-fore the value of the product is 1/9 greater than the value advanced for its production; 27 shillings have been transformed into 30 shill-ings; a surplus-value of 3 shillings has been created. The trick has at last succeeded; money has been converted into capital.

16. MILL: Political Limitation as the Ground of Freedom

John Stuart Mill (1806–1873) is an heir to the long English tradition of analytic and sensationalist psychology: John Locke, David Hume, Jeremy Bentham, his father, James Mill, and others. Thus some of his writings seem strangely wooden in the luxuriant setting of nineteenth-century thought. And yet there are aspects of his philosophy, including inconsistencies within it, which cannot be explained except through reference to its romantic elements. Most apparent is his sense of the variety and richness of experience and his zealous advocacy of social justice and liberty for all, *e.g.*, his championing of the rights of women and his work as a member of Parliament.

A significant inconsistency, or at least vagueness in his philosophy, is his utilitarian definition of good in terms of pleasure. He adds the qualifi-cation that mere intensity or quantity of pleasure is not enough, for some pleasures he concedes to be *better* (of a better quality) than others. But to define the good in terms of pleasure and then to say that one pleasure has more goodness than another is to get caught in a circle. Mill's only reply is that those with the broadest experience in the spectrum of pleasure just know that those pleasures which accord with, or stem from, "a sense of dignity" or the "higher faculties" are better than those which do not.

But is the experience of dignity (a romantic theme) a brute datum like a sensation of color? A Continental thinker would sense something incomplete and far too general here (it is a shibboleth to think that it is typical of the Continentals to get lost in abstractions and generalities while Englishmen are down-to-earth). *Why* are the pleasures of dignity better? Needn't we postulate a rational object which conforms to and advances a rational will? Are not the pleasures of dignity better (if "pleasure" can be properly used in this way) because they arise from a rational creature's ability to act contrary to much stronger inclinations toward other pleasures, and to do so just because it is right to do so?

Such queries tell us *why* it is that, as Mill himself says, Socrates dissatisfied is better than a fool satisfied. The English philosopher, Green, under the influence of Hegel, championed this point just a few years later.

Whatever may be said about the theory of Utilitarian Ethics, its innovation must be noted: for Mill recognizes the essential social context of the individual and therefore seeks the same principle as the ground of both individual ethics and social theory. In the essays "Liberty" and "Representative Government" he makes his conviction clear that the prime function of the state is to protect individual liberty. In sharpest contrast to Marx, he maintains that socio-economic problems are to be solved within the political arena. Government is not a mere function of economics. Economic questions constitute merely *some* of the questions which concern the entire society which finds its comprehensive organization in politial terms.

The first selection—on the Utilitarian Principle, in terms of which Mill sought to relate questions of individual and social ethics—is taken from Chapter II of his famous essay "Utilitarianism" (1863).

The creed which accepts as the foundation of morals *utility,* or the *greatest happiness principle,* holds that actions are right in proportion as they tend to promote happiness, wrong as they tend to produce the reverse of happiness. By "happiness" is intended pleasure, and the absence of pain; by "unhappiness," pain, and the privation of pleasure. To give a clear view of the moral standard set up by the theory, much more requires to be said; in particular, what things it includes in the ideas of pain and pleasure; and to what extent this is left an open question. But these supplementary explanations do not affect the theory of life on which this theory of morality is grounded— namely, that pleasure, and freedom from pain, are the only things desirable as ends; and that all desirable things (which are as numerous in the utilitarian as in any other scheme) are desirable either for the pleasure inherent in themselves, or as means to the promotion of pleasure and the prevention of pain.

Now such a theory of life excites in many minds, and among them in some of the most estimable in feeling and purpose, inveterate dislike. To suppose that life has (as they express it) no higher end than pleasure—no better and nobler object of desire and pursuit— they designate as utterly mean and groveling; as a doctrine worthy only of swine, to whom the followers of Epicurus were, at a very early period, contemptuously likened; and modern holders of the doctrine are occasionally made the subject of equally polite comparisons by its German, French, and English assailants.

When thus attacked, the Epicureans have always answered that it is not they but their accusers who represent human nature in a degrading light; since the accusation supposes human beings to be capable of no pleasures except those of which swine are capable. If this supposition were true, the charge could not be gainsaid, but would then be no longer an imputation; for if the sources of pleasure were precisely the same to human beings and to swine, the rule of life which is good enough for the one would be good enough for the other. The comparison of the Epicurean life to that of beasts is felt as degrading, precisely because a beast's pleasures do not satisfy a human being's conceptions of happiness. Human beings have faculties more elevated than the animal appetites, and when once made conscious of them, do not regard anything as happiness which does not include their gratification. I do not, indeed, consider the Epicureans to have been by any means faultless in drawing out their scheme of consequences from the utilitarian principle. To do this in any sufficient manner, many Stoic as well as Christian elements require to be included. But there is no known Epicurean theory of life which does not assign to the pleasures of the intellect, of the feelings and imagination, and of the moral sentiments, a much higher value as pleasures than to those of mere sensation. It must be admitted, however, that utilitarian writers in general have placed the superiority of mental over bodily pleasures chiefly in the greater permanency, safety, uncostliness, etc., of the former—that is, in their circumstantial advantages rather than in their intrinsic nature. And on all these points utilitarians have fully proved their case; but they might have taken the other, and, as it may be called, higher ground, with entire consistency. It is quite compatible with the principle of utility to recognize the fact that some *kinds* of pleasure are more desirable and more valuable than others. It would be absurd that while, in estimating all other things, quality is considered as well as quantity, the estimation of pleasures should be supposed to depend on quantity alone.

If I am asked what I mean by difference of quality in pleasures, or what makes one pleasure more valuable than another merely as a pleasure, except its being greater in amount, there is but one possible answer. Of two pleasures, if there be one to which all or almost all who have experience of both give a decided preference, irrespective of any feeling of moral obligation to prefer it, that is the more desirable pleasure. If one of the two is, by those who are competently acquainted with both, placed so far above the other that they prefer it, even though knowing it to be attended with a greater amount of discontent, and would not resign it for any quantity of the other pleasure which their nature is capable of, we are justified in ascribing to the preferred enjoyment a superiority in quality, so far outweighing quantity as to render it, in comparison, of small account.

Now it is an unquestionable fact that those who are equally acquainted with, and equally capable of appreciating and enjoying, both, do give a most marked preference to the manner of existence which employs their high faculties. Few human creatures would consent to be changed into any of the lower animals, for a promise of the fullest allowance of a beast's pleasures; no intelligent human being would consent to be a fool, no instructed person would be an ignoramus, no person of feeling and conscience would be selfish and base, even though they should be persuaded that the fool, the dunce, or the rascal is better satisfied with his lot than they are with theirs. They would not resign what they possess more than he for the most complete satisfaction of all the desires which they have in common with him. If they ever fancy they would, it is only in cases of unhappiness so extreme that to escape from it they would exchange their lot for almost any other, however undesirable in their own eyes. A being of higher faculties requires more to make him happy, is capable probably of more acute suffering, and certainly accessible to it at more points, than one of an inferior type; but in spite of these liabilities, he can never really wish to sink into what he feels to be a lower grade of existence. We may give what explanation we please of this unwillingness: we may attribute it to pride, a name which is given indiscriminately to some of the most and to some of the least estimable feelings of which mankind are capable; we may refer it to the love of liberty and personal independence, an appeal to which was with the Stoics one of the most effective means for the inculcation of it; to the love of power, or to the love of excitement, both of which do really enter into and contribute to it: but its most appropriate appellation is a sense of dignity, which all human beings possess in one form or other, and in some, though by no means in exact proportion to their higher faculties, and which is so essential a part of the happiness of those in whom it is strong that nothing which conflicts with it could be, otherwise than momentarily, an object of desire to them.

Whoever supposes that this preference takes place at a sacrifice of happiness—that the superior being, in anything like equal circumstances, is not happier than the inferior—confounds the two very different ideas, of *happiness* and *content*. It is indisputable that the being whose capacities of enjoyment are low has the greatest chance of having them fully satisfied; and a highly endowed being will always feel that any happiness which he can look for, as the world is constituted, is imperfect. But he can learn to bear its imperfections, if they are at all bearable; and they will not make him envy the being who is indeed unconscious of the imperfections, but only because he feels not at all the good which those imperfections qualify. It is better to be a human being dissatisfied than a pig satisfied; better to be Socrates dissatisfied than a fool satisfied. And if the fool, or the pig, are of a different opinion, it is because they only know their own side of the question. The other party to the comparison knows both sides.

It may be objected that many who are capable of the higher pleasures, occasionally, under the influence of temptation, postpone them to the lower. But this is quite compatible with a full appreciation of the intrinsic superiority of the higher. Men often, from infirmity of character, make their election for the nearer good, though they know it to be the less valuable; and this no less when the choice is between two bodily pleasures, than when it is between bodily and mental. They pursue sensual indulgences to the injury of health, though perfectly aware that health is the greater good. It may be further objected that many who begin with youthful enthusiasm for everything noble, as they advance in years sink into indolence and selfishness. But I do not believe that those who undergo this very common change, voluntarily choose the lower description of pleasures in preference to the higher. I believe that before they devote themselves exclusively to the one, they have already become incapable of the other. Capacity for the nobler feelings is in most natures a very tender plant, easily killed, not only by hostile influences, but by mere want of sustenance; and in the majority of young persons it speedily dies away if the occupations to which their position in life has devoted them, and the society into which it has thrown them, are not favorable to keeping that higher capacity in exercise. Men lose their high aspirations as they lose their intellectual tastes, because they have not time or opportunity for indulging them; and they addict themselves to inferior pleasures not because they deliberately prefer them, but because they are either the only ones to which they have access or the only ones which they are any longer capable of enjoying. It may be questioned whether anyone who has remained equally susceptible to both classes of pleasures, ever knowingly and calmly preferred the lower; though many, in all ages, have broken down in an ineffectual attempt to combine both.

From this verdict of the only competent judges I apprehend there can be no appeal. On a question which is the best worth having of two pleasures, or which of two modes of existence is the most grateful to the feelings, apart from its moral attributes and from its consequences, the judgment of those who are qualified by knowledge of both, or, if they differ, that of the majority among them, must be admitted as final. And there need be the less hesitation to accept this judgment respecting the quality of pleasures, since there is no other tribunal to be referred to even on the question of quantity. What means are there of determining which is the acutest of two pains, or the intensest of two pleasurable sensations, except the general suffrage of those who are familiar with both? Neither pains nor pleasures are homogeneous, and pain is always heterogeneous with pleasure. What is there to decide whether a particular pleasure is worth purchasing at the cost of a particular pain, except the feelings and judgment of the experienced? When, therefore, those feelings and judgment declare the pleasures derived from the higher faculties to be preferable *in kind,* apart from the question of intensity, to those of which the animal nature, disjoined from the higher faculties, is susceptible, they are entitled on this subject to the same regard.

I have dwelt on this point, as being a necessary part of a perfectly just conception of utility, or happiness, considered as the directive rule of human conduct. But it is by no means an indispensable condition to the acceptance of the utilitarian standard; for that standard is not the agent's own greatest happiness, but the greatest amount of happiness altogether; and if it may possibly be doubted whether a noble character is always the happier for its nobleness, there can be no doubt that it makes other people happier, and that the world in general is immensely a gainer by it. Utilitarianism, therefore, could only attain its end by the general cultivation of nobleness of character, even if each individual were only benefited by the nobleness of others, and his own, so far as happiness is concerned, were a sheer deduction from the benefit. But the bare enunciation of such an absurdity as this last renders refutation superfluous.

The next selection is from the first chapter of Mill's famous "On Liberty" (1859). Obviously, his view differs from that of the Hegelians and Marxists who maintain that the state should intervene in the affairs of the individual if the state judges it to be for his own good, *i.e.*, if it helps establish his "positive freedom" or his ability to do the good.

"On Liberty" is *the* classic statement of the liberal tradition in the defense of the priority of individual intellectual freedom. In contrast to Hegel, Marx and Green, Mill looks with a jaundiced eye on any particular intervention by the state in individual affairs. His emphasis on the importance of individual liberty of thought and expression is argued in terms of social utility. Increasingly sympathetic to a Fabian kind of socialism, and a foremost defender of political democracy, he regards the maximum amount of individual liberty and the protection of minority viewpoints as necessary for the social good and social progress.

The object of this essay is to assert one very simple principle, as entitled to govern absolutely the dealings of society with the individual in the way of compulsion and control, whether the means used be physical force in the form of legal penalties, or the moral coercion of public opinion. That principle is that the sole end for which mankind are warranted, individually or collectively, in interfering with the liberty of action of any of their number is self-protection. That the only purpose for which power can be rightfully exercised over any member of a civilized community, against his will, is to prevent harm to others. His own good, either physical or moral, is not a sufficient warrant. He cannot rightfully be compelled to do or forbear because it will be better for him to do so, because it will make him happier, because, in the opinions of others, to do so would be wise, or even right. These are good reasons for remonstrating with him, or reasoning with him, or persuading him, or entreating him, but not for compelling him, or visiting him with any evil in case he do otherwise. To justify that, the conduct from which it is desired to deter him must be calculated to produce evil to someone else. The only part of the conduct of anyone, for which he is amenable to society, is that which concerns others. In the part which merely concerns himself, his independence is, of right, absolute. Over himself, over his own body and mind, the individual is sovereign.

It is perhaps hardly necessary to say that this doctrine is meant to apply only to human beings in the maturity of their faculties. We are not speaking of children, or of young persons below the age which the law may fix as that of manhood or womanhood. Those who are still in a state to require being taken care of by others, must be protected against their own actions as well as against external injury. For the same reason, we may leave out of consideration those backward states of society in which the race itself may be considered as in its nonage. The early difficulties in the way of spontaneous progress are so great, and there is seldom any choice of means for overcoming them; and a ruler full of the spirit of improvement is warranted in the use of any expedients that will attain an end perhaps otherwise unattainable. Despotism is a legitimate mode of government in dealing with barbarians, provided the end be their improvement, and the means justified by actually effecting that end. Liberty, as a principle, has no application to any state of things anterior to the time when mankind have become capable of being improved by free and equal discussion. Until then, there is nothing for them but implicit obedience to an Akbar or a Charlemagne, if they are so fortunate as to find one. But as soon as mankind have attained the capacity of being guided to their own improvement by conviction or persuasion (a period long since reached in all nations with whom we need here concern ourselves), compulsion, either in the direct form or in that of pains and penalties for non-compliance, is no longer admissible as a means to their own good, and justifiable only for the security of others.

It is proper to state that I forego any advantage which could be derived to my argument from the idea of abstract right, as a thing independent of utility. I regard utility as the ultimate appeal on all ethical questions; but it must be utility in the largest sense, grounded on the permanent interests of a man as a progressive being. Those interests, I contend, authorized the subjection of individual spontaneity to external control, only in respect to those actions of each which concern the interest of other people. If anyone does an act hurtful to others, there is a *prima facie* case for punishing him, by law, or, where legal penalties are not safely applicable, by general disapprobation. There are also many positive acts for the benefit of others, which he may rightfully be compelled to perform: such as to give evidence in a court of justice; to bear his fair share in the common defense, or in any other joint work necessary to the interest of the society of which he enjoys the protection; and to perform certain acts of individual beneficence, such as saving a fellow-creature's life, or interposing to protect the defenseless against ill-usage, things which whenever it is obviously a man's duty to do, he may rightfully be made responsible to society for not doing. A person may cause evil to others not only by his actions but by his inaction, and in either case he is justly accountable to them for the injury. The latter case, it is true, requires a much more cautious exercise of compulsion than the former. To make anyone answerable for doing evil to others is the rule; to make him answerable for not preventing evil is, comparatively speaking, the exception. Yet there are many cases clear enough and grave enough to justify that exception. In all things which regard the external relations of the individual, he is *de jure* amenable to those whose interests are concerned, and, if need be, to society as their protector. There are often good reasons for not holding him to the responsibility; but these reasons must arise from the special expediencies of the case: either because it is a kind of case in which he is on the whole likely to act better, when left to his own discretion, than when controlled in any way in which society have it in their power to control him; or because the attempt to exercise control would produce other evils, greater than those which it would prevent. When such reasons as these preclude the enforcement of responsibility, the conscience of the agent himself should step into the vacant judgment seat, and protect those interests of others which have no external protection; judging himself all the more rigidly, because the case does not admit of his being made accountable to the judgment of his fellow-creatures.

But there is a sphere of action in which society, as distinguished from the individual, has, if any, only an indirect interest; comprehending all that portion of a person's life and conduct which affects only himself, or if it also affects others, only with their free, voluntary, and undeceived consent and participation. When I say only himself, I mean directly, and in the first instance; for whatever affects himself, may affect others through himself; and the objection which may be grounded on this contingency, will receive consideration in the sequel. This, then, is the appropriate region of human liberty. It comprises, *first,* the inward domain of consciousness; demanding liberty of conscience in the most comprehensive sense; liberty of thought and feeling; absolute freedom of opinion and sentiment on all subjects, practical or speculative, scientific, moral, or theological. The liberty of expressing and publishing opinions may seem to fall under a different principle, since it belongs to that part of the conduct of an individual which concerns other people; but, being almost of as much importance as the liberty of thought itself, and resting in great part on the same reasons, is practically inseparable from it. *Secondly,* the principle requires liberty of tastes and pursuits; of framing the plan of our life to suit our own character; of doing as we like, subject to such consequences as may follow: without impediment from our fellow-creatures, so long as what we do does not harm them, even though they should think our conduct foolish, perverse, or wrong. *Thirdly,* from this liberty of each individual, follows the liberty, within the same limits, of combination among individuals; freedom to unite, for any purpose not involving harm to others: the persons combining being supposed to be of full age, and not forced or deceived.

No society in which these liberties are not, on the whole, respected, is free, whatever may be its form of government; and none is completely free in which they do not exist absolute and unqualified. The only freedom which deserves the name is that of pursuing our own good in our own way, so long as we do not attempt to deprive others of theirs, or impede their efforts to obtain it. Each is the proper guardian of his own health, whether bodily, or mental and spiritual. Mankind are greater gainers by suffering each other to live as seems good to themselves, than by compelling each to live as seems good to the rest.

Though this doctrine is anything but new, and, to some persons, may have the air of a truism, there is no doctrine which stands more directly opposed to the general tendency of existing opinion and practice. Society has expended fully as much effort in the attempt (according to its lights) to compel people to conform to its notions of personal as of social excellence. The ancient commonwealths thought themselves entitled to practice, and the ancient philosophers countenanced, the regulation of every part of private conduct by public authority, on the ground that the State had a deep interest in the whole bodily and mental discipline of every one of its citizens: a mode of thinking which may have been admissible in small republics surrounded by powerful enemies, in constant peril of being subverted by foreign attack or internal commotion, and to which even a short interval of relaxed energy and self-command might so easily be fatal that they could not afford to wait for the salutary permanent effects of freedom. In the modern world, the greater size of political communities, and, above all, the separation between spiritual and temporal authority (which placed the direction of men's consciences in other hands than those which controlled their worldly affairs), prevented so great an interference by law in the details of private life; but the engines of moral repression have been wielded more strenuously against divergence from the reigning opinion in self-regarding, than even in social matters; religion, the most powerful of the elements which have entered into the formation of moral feeling, having almost always been governed either by the ambition of a hierarchy, seeking control over every department of human conduct, or by the spirit of Puritanism. And some of those modern reformers who have placed themselves in strongest opposition to the religions of the past, have been no way behind either churches or sects in their assertion of the right of spiritual domination: M. Comte, in particular, whose social system, as unfolded in his *Système de Politique Positive,* aims at establishing (though by moral more than by legal appliances) a despotism of society over the individual, surpassing anything contemplated in the political ideal of the most rigid disciplinarian among the ancient philosophers.

Apart from the peculiar tenets of individual thinkers, there is also in the world at large an increasing inclination to stretch unduly the powers of society over the individual, both by the force of opinion and even by that of legislation; and as the tendency of all the changes taking place in the world is to strengthen society, and diminish the power of the individual, this encroachment is not one of the evils which tend spontaneously to disappear, but, on the contrary, to grow more and more formidable. The disposition of mankind, whether as rulers or as fellow-citizens, to impose their own opinions and inclinations as a rule of conduct on others, is so energetically supported by some of the best and by some of the worst feelings incident to human nature, that it is hardly ever kept under restraint by anything but want of power; and as the power is not declining, but growing, unless a strong barrier of moral conviction can be raised against the mischief, we must expect, in the present circumstances of the world, to see it increase. . . .

17. GREEN: The Welfare State as Positive Freedom

One measure of the vitality of Continental thought in the nineteenth century was its ability to leap the Channel and to capture, for a while, the allegiance of the British. This is not wholly without precedent —Wordsworth and Coleridge had felt the influence earlier—and yet it is remarkable nevertheless.

Thomas Hill Green (1836–1882) was a distinguished English philosopher who taught at Oxford. In terms of technical philosophy, he brought Kant and Hegel to England. He stands at the fount of that British philosophic movement known as neo-Hegelianism or British Idealism, which carried into the twentieth century. In many ways comparable to the American Josiah Royce, he sought to mold the insights of the Kant-Hegel tradition to the thought and the social problems of his own country. In his *Lectures on the Principles of Political Obligation* he may be said to have provided the philosophic foundation of the democratic welfare state, on a ground largely derived from Rousseau, Kant and Hegel.

He also emerges as the first apostle in the English-speaking world of the doctrine of "positive freedom." Freedom, he has maintained, is not merely the absence of certain restraints but the affirmative opportunity to develop the individual self. Like Marx he regarded as farcical the classical English economists' contention that a lone laboring man is really free to bargain with his employer. Unlike Marx he saw the solution to problems of exploitation, class antagonism and social injustice in a new conception of the democratic state. Like Aristotle and Rousseau before him, he urged that we can find our individuality only within the context of our society, and that it is the function of government, the supreme organization of a society, to enhance the opportunities for its citizens to develop their potentials as mature, intelligent, social, moral beings.

He regarded the key question of social organization to be, "Why should I obey the law?" The answer he suggested, echoing Rousseau and Hegel, is that law is the expression of the society of which I am a member and through which I become the self I am. By my active participation in the society, through the various organizations to which I belong (church, union, club) and in its governmental structure as a voter, I am exercising my societal membership and participating in the formation of both myself and my society.

But in order to contribute my best to the society to which I belong, I need material sustenance; a sense of security; liberty of thought; the education to use that liberty; and the opportunity to make a contribution to the social good. Therefore, the function of government is active intervention in the name of the whole, not to dictate my moral conscience to me, but to open and keep open the channels for its development and free expression.

In a classic essay, "Liberal Legislation and Freedom of Contract" (1881), Green, who was active in civic affairs, enunciated this democratic Hegelianism in terms of specific social problems of the time.

We shall probably all agree that freedom, rightly understood, is the greatest of blessings; that its attainment is the true end of all our effort as citizens. But when we thus speak of freedom, we should consider carefully what we mean by it. We do not mean merely freedom from restraint or compulsion. We do not mean merely freedom to do as we like irrespectively of what it is that we like. We do not mean a freedom that can be enjoyed by one man or one set of men at the cost of a loss of freedom to others. When we speak of freedom as something to be so highly prized, we mean a positive power or capacity of doing or enjoying something worth doing or enjoying, and that, too, something that we do or enjoy in common with others. We mean by it a power which each man exercises through the help or security given him by his fellow-men, and which he in turn helps to secure for them. When we measure the progress of a society by its growth in freedom, we measure it by the increasing development and exercise on the whole of those powers of contributing to social good with which we believe the members of the society to be endowed; in short, by the greater power on the part of the citizens as a body to make the most and best of themselves. Thus, though of course there can be no freedom among men who act not willingly but under compulsion, yet on the other hand the mere removal of compulsion, the mere enabling a man to do as he likes, is in itself no contribution to true freedom. In one sense no man is so well able to do as he likes as the wandering savage. He has no master. There is no one to say him nay. Yet we do not count him really free, because the freedom of savagery is not strength, but weakness. The actual powers of the noblest savage do not admit of comparison with those of the humblest citizen of a law-abiding state. He is not the slave of man, but he is the slave of nature. Of compulsion by natural necessity he has plenty of experience, though of restraint by society none at all. Nor can he deliver himself from that compulsion except by submitting to this restraint. So to submit is the first step in true freedom, because the first step towards the full exercise of the faculties with which man is endowed. But we rightly refuse to recognise the highest development on the part of an exceptional individual or exceptional class, as an advance towards the true freedom of man, if it is founded on a refusal of the same opportunity to other men. The powers of the human mind have probably never attained such force and keenness, the proof of what society can do for the individual has never been so strikingly exhibited, as among the small groups of men who possessed civil privileges in the small republics of antiquity. The whole framework of our political ideas, to say nothing of our philos-

ophy, is derived from them. But in them this extraordinary efflores-
cence of the privileged class was accompanied by the slavery of the
multitude. That slavery was the condition on which it depended, and
for that reason it was doomed to decay. There is no clearer ordinance
of that supreme reason, often dark to us, which governs the course of
man's affairs, than that no body of men should in the long run be able
to strengthen itself at the cost of others' weakness. The civilisation
and freedom of the ancient world were shortlived because they were
partial and exceptional. If the ideal of true freedom is the maximum
of power for all members of human society alike to make the best of
themselves, we are right in refusing to ascribe the glory of freedom to
a state in which the apparent elevation of the few is founded on the
degradation of the many, and in ranking modern society, founded as
it is on free industry, with all its confusion and ignorant licence and
waste of effort, above the most splendid of ancient republics.

If I have given a true account of that freedom which forms the goal
of social effort, we shall see that freedom of contract, freedom in all
the forms of doing what one will with one's own, is valuable only as a
means to an end. That end is what I call freedom in the positive
sense: in other words, the liberation of the powers of all men equally
for contributions to a common good. No one has a right to do what
he will with his own in such a way as to contravene this end. It is only
through the guarantee which society gives him that he has property at
all, or, strictly speaking, any right to his possessions. This guarantee
is founded on a sense of common interest. Everyone has an interest in
securing to everyone else the free use and enjoyment and disposal of
his possessions, so long as that freedom on the part of one does not
interfere with a like freedom on the part of others, because such
freedom contributes to that equal development of the faculties of all
which is the highest good for all. This is the true and the only justification of rights of property. Rights of property, however, have been and
are claimed which cannot be thus justified. We are all now agreed that
men cannot rightly be the property of men. The institution of property being only justifiable as a means to the free exercise of the social
capabilities of all, there can be no true right to property of a kind
which debars one class of men from such free exercise altogether. We
condemn slavery no less when it arises out of a voluntary agreement
on the part of the enslaved person. A contract by which any one
agreed for a certain consideration to become the slave of another we
should reckon a void contract. Here, then, is a limitation upon freedom of contract which we all recognise as rightful. No contract is

vaild in which human persons, willingly or unwillingly, are dealt with as commodities, because such contracts of necessity defeat the end for which alone society enforces contracts at all.

Are there no other contracts which, less obviously perhaps but really, are open to the same objection? In the first place, let us consider contracts affecting labour. Labour, the economist tells us, is a commodity exchangeable like other commodities. This is in a certain sense true, but it is a commodity which attaches in a peculiar manner to the person of man. Hence restrictions may need to be placed on the sale of this commodity which would be unnecessary in other cases, in order to prevent labour from being sold under conditions which make it impossible for the person selling it ever to become a free contributor to social good in any form. This is most plainly the case when a man bargains to work under conditions fatal to health, *e.g.* in an unventilated factory. Every injury to the health of the individual is, so far as it goes, a public injury. It is an impediment to the general freedom; so much deduction from our power, as members of society, to make the best of ourselves. Society is, therefore, plainly within its right when it limits freedom of contract for the sale of labour, so far as is done by our laws for the sanitary regulations of factories, workshops, and mines. It is equally within its right in prohibiting the labour of women and young persons beyond certain hours. If they work beyond those hours, the result is demonstrably physical deterioration; which, as demonstrably, carries with it a lowering of the moral forces of society. For the sake of that general freedom of its members to make the best of themselves, which it is the object of civil society to secure, a prohibition should be put by law, which is the deliberate voice of society, on all such contracts of service as in a general way yield such a result. The purchase or hire of unwholesome dwellings is properly forbidden on the same principle. Its application to compulsory education may not be quite so obvious, but it will appear on a little reflection. Without a command of certain elementary arts and knowledge, the individual in modern society is as effectually crippled as by the loss of a limb or a broken constitution. He is not free to develop his faculties. With a view to securing such freedom among its members it is as certainly within the province of the state to prevent children from growing up in that kind of ignorance which practically excludes them from a free career in life, as it is within its province to require the sort of building and drainage necessary for public health.

Our modern legislation then with reference to labour, and education, and health, involving as it does manifold interference with freedom of contract, is justified on the ground that it is the business of the state, not indeed directly to promote moral goodness, for that, from the very nature of moral goodness, it cannot do, but to maintain the conditions without which a free exercise of the human faculties is impossible. It does not indeed follow that it is advisable for the state to do all which it is justified in going. We are often warned nowadays against the danger of over-legislation; or, as I heard it put in a speech of the present home secretary* in days when he was sowing his political wild oats, of "grandmotherly government." There may be good ground for the warning, but at any rate we should be quite clear what we mean by it. The outcry against state interference is often raised by men whose real objection is not to state interference but to centralisation, to the constant aggression of the central executive upon local authorities. As I have already pointed out, compulsion at the discretion of some elected municipal board proceeds just as much from the state as does compulsion exercised by a government office in London. No doubt, much needless friction is avoided, much is gained in the way of elasticity and adjustment to circumstances, by the independent local administration of general laws; and most of us would agree that of late there has been a dangerous tendency to override municipal discretion by the hard and fast rules of London "departments." But centralisation is one thing: over-legislation, or the improper exercise of the power of the state, quite another. It is one question whether of late the central government has been unduly trenching on local government, and another question whether the law of the state, either as administered by central or by provincial authorities, has been unduly interfering with the discretion of individuals. We may object most strongly to advancing centralisation, and yet wish that the law should put rather more than less restraint on those liberties of the individual which are a social nuisance. But there are some political speculators whose objection is not merely to centralisation, but to the extended action of law altogether. They think that the individual ought to be left much more to himself than has of late been the case. Might not our people, they ask, have been trusted to learn in time for themselves to eschew unhealthy dwellings, to refuse dangerous and degrading employment, to get their children the schooling

---

* *The present home secretary* was Sir William Harcourt (1827–1904), Liberal member of Parliament for Oxford; he became a leader of the Liberal Party after Gladstone's death.

necessary for making their way in the world? Would they not for their own comfort, if not from more chivalrous feeling, keep their wives and daughters from overwork? Or, failing this, ought not women, like men, to learn to protect themselves? Might not all the rules, in short, which legislation of the kind we have been discussing is intended to attain, have been attained without it; not so quickly, perhaps, but without tampering so dangerously with the independence and self-reliance of the people?

Now, we shall probably all agree that a society in which the public health was duly protected, and necessary education duly provided for, by the spontaneous action of individuals, was in a higher condition than one in which the compulsion of law was needed to secure these ends. But we must take men as we find them. Until such a condition of society is reached, it is the business of the state to take the best security it can for the young citizens' growing up in such health and with so much knowledge as is necessary for their real freedom. In so doing it need not at all interfere with the independence and self-reliance of those whom it requires to do what they would otherwise do for themselves. The man who, of his own right feeling, saves his wife from overwork and sends his children to school, suffers no moral degradation from a law which, if he did not do this for himself, would seek to make him do it. Such a man does not feel the law as constraint at all. To him it is simply a powerful friend. It gives him security for that being done efficiently which, with the best wishes, he might have much trouble in getting done efficiently if left to himself. No doubt it relieves him from some of the responsibility which would otherwise fall to him as head of a family, but, if he is what we are supposing him to be, in proportion as he is relieved of responsibilities in one direction he will assume them in another. The security which the state gives him for the safe housing and sufficient schooling of his family will only make him the more careful for their well-being in other respects, which he is left to look after for himself. We need have no fear, then, of such legislation having an ill effect on those who, without the law, would have seen to that being done, though probably less efficiently, which the law requires to be done. But it was not their case that the laws we are considering were especially meant to meet. It was the overworked women, the ill-housed and untaught families, for whose benefit they were intended. And the question is whether without these laws the suffering classes could have been delivered quickly or slowly from the condition they were in. Could the enlightened self-interest or benevolence of individuals, working under a system of unlimited freedom of contract, have ever brought them into a state compatible with the free development of the human faculties? No one considering the facts can have any doubt as to the answer to this question. Left to itself, or to the operation of casual benevolence, a degraded population perpetuates and increases itself. Read any of the authorised accounts, given before royal or parliamentary commissions, of the state of the labourers, especially of the women and children, as they were in our great industries before the law was first brought to bear on them, and before freedom of contract was first interfered with in them. Ask yourself what chance there was of a generation, born and bred under such conditions, ever contracting itself out of them. Given a certain standard of moral and material well-being, people may be trusted not to sell their labour, or the labour of their children, on terms which would not allow that standard to be maintained. But with large masses of our population, until the laws we have been considering took effect, there was no such standard. There was nothing on their part, in the way either of self-respect or established demand for comforts, to prevent them from working and living, or from putting their children to work and live, in a way in which no one who is to be a healthy and free citizen can work and live. No doubt there were many high-minded employers who did their best for their workpeople before the days of state-interference, but they could not prevent less scrupulous hirers of labour from hiring it on the cheapest terms. It is true that cheap labour is in the long run dear labour, but it is so only in the long run, and eager traders do not think of the long run. If labour is to be had under conditions incompatible with the health or decent housing or education of the labourer, there will always be plenty of people to buy it under those conditions, careless of the burden in the shape of rates and taxes which they may be laying up for posterity. Either the standard of well-being on the part of the sellers of labour must prevent them from selling their labour under those conditions, or the law must prevent it. With a population such as ours was forty years ago, and still largely is, the law must prevent it and continue the prevention for some generations, before the sellers will be in a state to prevent it themselves. . . .

IV.

Evolution of the Species:
The Impact of Science on Culture

18. LAMARCK and DARWIN:
Biological Mechanism

The romantic movement can be understood in part as a negative reaction to the advancing tide of mathematically oriented, mechanistic science. The romantics suspected that such science would eventually disrupt the springs of human action and produce an eccentric civilization. The age ends with a resurgent tide of this science, unexpectedly augmented by biology, advancing and producing an undercurrent of confusion and alarm.

Kant felt obliged to limit the area of competence of Newtonian science in order to protect the other spheres of man's rational life—for example, his moral and artistic pursuits. Schelling and Hegel were markedly less liberal and less arbitrational in tone. Schelling spoke demeaningly of "mere contiguity in space and time" and of the overriding priority of continuities of essences. Hegel called Newtonian science "the edifice of an understanding deserted by reason" whose unhampered expansion is unacceptable. For Hegel, the natural world is knowable only as an object for mind; man "stands upon his head," that is, upon his thoughts, and constructs the world accordingly. To turn him right side up and to put his feet on the ground—as natural scientists so proudly think they do—is to get things philosophically backward. Hegel's work feeds the suspicion that science for the most part has forgotten the very structure of mind, language, civilization which makes scientific investigation of the world possible, and that its discoveries and products will back up and obliterate its own ground.

But Hegel did not really offer much constructive criticism to natural science, and it is highly unlikely that scientists would have listened if he had. The sad fact is that Kant's initial attempt to arbitrate between the sciences and philosophy was not carried on by thinkers of the highest caliber. Even though the idea of evolution was itself of philosophical origin, most biologists were convinced that the progress of their science demanded divorce from philosophy, with its concern for consciousness, and required instead reliance exclusively on biological data.

Although the whole age had been in love with history and evolution and with biology, the impact of Charles Darwin's (1809–1882) discoveries caused a gaping rent in the intellectual fabric spun by the romantics. Living things had been seen as purposive and value-directed, as beyond mechanism. Darwin regarded the motor of evolution, natural selection, as nonpurposive, as mechanistic as physics in its own complex way. When he produced evidence to show that man had evolved through a natural biological process from an apelike ancestor, this was not just a new biological theory to be duly recorded in biology textbooks. It contained the vastly disruptive implication that man was no longer the master of creation set apart from the rest of the animals by his powers of conscious choice and reason, that he was just another primate caught in the slow-grinding evolutionary machine.

Of course, in denying that man was the result of a special divine creation, Darwin's theory endangered the religious person's sense of his own value as a God-made product. It also endangered his faith in the authority of revelation and the code of morals contained within that revelation. In seeming to deny man's special place and role in nature, the theory shook all values, religious and secular: the sense of the efficacy and dignity of purposive action and free will; the belief that evolving civilization cannot be understood in the terms of biology alone but requires the purposive and intentional terms of those paradigmatically purposive activities—art, religion, morals, philosophy and jurisprudence; and finally the general conviction that man can control his destiny. After all, Darwin maintained that human choice was feeble compared to the impersonal power of natural selection for the advancement of the species. He placed a comparatively low value on the role of creative thought and invention in altering the environment and in producing what might be called the unnatural selections characteristic of human life.

At bottom, the theory of evolution made it easy to forget that without the human mind there would be no such theory at all. The late romantic thinker C. G. Carus sang the swan song of romanticism when he contended that man *qua* thinking animal—he of the "winged psyche"—is separated from the rest of the animals by an impassable barrier. Friedrich Schlegel, who claimed that "man is the creative survey which nature makes of her own self," and Novalis, who wrote that "nature wanted to participate in the enjoyment of her own great beauty, and therefore she assumed the shape of man," had both long since passed from the scene.* The role of mind was increasingly less appreciated because natural scientists became increasingly absorbed in the special data of their special fields, and because, it must also be confessed, nineteenth-century philosophies of mind became too abstruse, or too one-sided, or too overweaning and even fantastic in some instances for most natural scientists and most ordinary men to either understand or accept.

The breakdown of communication between science and much of philosophy and the general culture was a prime element in the renewed sense of human malaise and impotence which breaks out again at the

* Alexander Gode von Aesche, *Natural Science and German Romanticism* (1941), pp. 201 and 211.

artificial antitheses prompted by scientific reflections stood unmolested by close of the romantic age. Inexhaustive framings of alternatives and reason. For example, take the common belief, still very much with us, that since man is an integral part of nature and his actions are determined, he cannot be free. Now, this would not have bothered Kant, for within the broad compass of his philosophy there is room for several spheres of human behavior concurrently.* In the natural-scientific analysis, man must appear determined by natural factors; but this is irrelevant to deciding whether he is free or not, since the criterion of difference relevant to the concept of freedom is not whether man is determined or not, but is rather a matter of *how* he is determined and *what* determines him. There is thus a third alternative. Everyone is determined and yet some are compulsive and unfree and some are not. To be determined by one's own self, by a self-imposed moral law, the very purpose of the imposition being conformity to moral law, is to be free. To be free is to be determined by practical reason; it is just to act intelligently. Another example of a pitfall commonly involved in scientific reflections is the simple matter of the genetic fallacy, which would be rectified as follows: The nature and value of a phenomenon (man, for example) is not necessarily determined by its genesis (in the primates), nor is the value of a rose determined by the manure out of which it grows.

The continuing challenge posed by science to philosophy, the challenge of repairing the conceptual framework within which and by which we understand the world and ourselves, is awesome. Since the romantics and the high tide of the new rationalism in Schelling and Hegel, the temptation has been for philosophy to become abstruse and aloof, or to submit and become a mere "underlaborer" in the scientific venture, or finally to give up entirely and let scientists do philosophy. Each way is untenable, for philosophic thought assesses the significance for civilization of all science and, in a way, encompasses it all, but it can do so only in its own unique way. No new disclosures of fact can solve problems which are really conceptual in nature—matters of essence and meaning. Science itself is quite unable to tell us what its brilliant discoveries *mean* for man. For example, suppose that someday a human organism is brought back to life by the insertion of an artificial brain. Now, is this the same man as before? The question of which facts count for which answer—yes or no— is not itself a matter of fact. It is a question of what is meant by "man" and "same," and this is a philosophical problem of the criteria and concepts involved, which can be handled only by appropriate philosophical methods, some of which may be historical. The ever more dazzling discoveries of the natural sciences cannot help us there; indeed, they simply provide us with more philosophical problems.

---

* A recent echo is heard in the "mutually compatible and complementary languages theory."

Julian Huxley, the biologist, has recently reflected that evolutionary studies now apprise us that man, as a result of his "new method" of evolving by "the cumulative transmission of experience," is the only type of animal capable of realizing important new possibilities in the evolutionary future.* These are interesting and encouraging words, but philosophically they leave much to be desired. The key phrase "cumulative transmission of experience" is really a metaphor which conceals more than it reveals and which awaits conceptual translation into literal terms before it can be adequately understood. Is an experience transmitted, say, from teacher to student like electricity is transmitted through a wire, or like foot pounds of force are transmitted from sprocket to sprocket via a chain? Obviously not. The conceptual translation of Huxley's phrase awaits a philosophical appraisal of persons, knowledge, language, mind, creative thought—in a word, civilization. And this is not whipped up at a moment's notice.

It is quite unlikely that the mild-mannered and highly civilized Charles Darwin intended any such disruption of western civilization. No such revolutionary intention is indicated by his words on religion from the "Conclusion" of *The Origin of Species*, first published in 1859 after more than twenty years of painstaking appraisal of the assembled evidence.

It must be emphasized, however, that the general theory of the evolution of species was not new. Some of the ancient Greek philosophers had suggested it. What was new in Darwin's theory was a plausible subsidiary theory of the empirical causes of the evolutionary process (natural selection by the environment) and a significant body of empirical evidence to support his contentions. One need only glance at the earlier French naturalist Jean Baptiste Lamarck (1744–1829) to see the theory itself clearly presented. This is readily seen in the selection which follows. But Lamarck lacked a sizable body of good evidence, and he advanced theories of the empirical causes of the evolutionary process upon which Darwin cast doubt. One of his theories involved the assumption that acquired characteristics could be inherited; for example, it was thought that a man who develops his muscles in the course of performing his occupation would tend to have children who are more heavily muscled than he himself was at birth. Another of his theories, rejected outright by Darwin, stipulated that want or need led directly to the formation of new organs which could satisfy that want.

The following passage is taken from the Introduction to *Animaux sans Vertèbres*.†

* See his Introduction, Charles Darwin, *The Origin of Species* (New York: Mentor, New American Library, 1958). p. xv.

† Alphens S. Packard, *Lamarck: The Founder of Evolution* (New York: Longmans Green, 1901), pp. 346–348.

"*First law:* Life, by its proper forces, continually tends to increase the volume of every body which possesses it, and to increase the size of its parts, up to a limit which brings it about.

"*Second law:* The production of a new organ in an animal body results from the supervision of a new want (*besoin*) which continues to make itself felt, and of a new movement which this want gives rise to and maintains.

"*Third law:* The development of organs and their power of action are constantly in ratio to the employment of these organs.

"*Fourth law:* Everything which has been acquired, impressed upon, or changed in the organization of individuals, during the course of their life is preserved by generation and transmitted to the new individuals which have descended from those which have undergone those changes."

In explaining the second law he says:

"The foundation of this law derives its proof from the third, in which the facts known allow of no doubt; for, if the forces of action of an organ, by their increase, further develop this organ—namely, increase its size and power, as is constantly proved by facts—we may be assured that the forces by which it acts, just originated by a new want felt, would necessarily give birth to the organ adapted to satisfy this new want, if this organ had not before existed.

"In truth, in animals so low as not to be able to *feel,* it cannot be that we should attribute to a felt want the formation of a new organ, this formation being in such a case the product of a mechanical cause, as that of a new movement produced in a part of the fluids of the animal.

"It is not the same in animals with a more complicated structure, and which are able to *feel.* They feel wants, and each want felt, exciting their inner feeling, forthwith sets the fluids in motion and forces them towards the point of the body where an action may satisfy the want experienced. Now, if there exists at this point an organ suitable for this action, it is immediately cited to act; and if the organ does not exist, and only the felt want be for instance pressing and continuous, gradually the organ originates, and is developed on account of the continuity and energy of its employment.

"If I had not been convinced: 1, that the thought alone of an action which strongly interests it suffices to arouse the *inner feeling* of an individual; 2, that a felt want can itself arouse the feeling in question; 3, that every emotion of *inner feeling,* resulting from a want which is aroused, directs at the same instant a mass of nervous fluid to the points to be set in activity, that it also creates a flow thither of the fluids of the body, and especially nutrient ones; that, finally, it then places in activity the organs already existing, or makes efforts for the formation of those which would not have existed there, and which a continual want would therefore render necessary—I should have had doubts as to the reality of the law which I have just indicated.

"But, although it may be very difficult to verify this law by observation, I have no doubt as to the grounds on which I base it, the necessity of its existence being involved in that of the third law, which is now well established.

"I conceive, for example, that a *gasteropod mollusc,* which, as it crawls along, finds the need of feeling the bodies in front of it, makes efforts to touch those bodies with some of the foremost parts of its head, and sends to these every time supplies of nervous fluids, as well as otherfluids—I conceive, I say, that it must result from this reiterated afflux towards the points in question that the nerves which abut at these points will, by slow degrees, be extended. Now, as in the same circumstances other fluids of the animal flow also to the same places, and especially nourishing fluids, it must follow that two or more tentacles will appear and develop insensibly under those circumstances on the points referred to.

"This is doubtless what has happened to all the races of *Gasteropods,* whose wants have compelled them to adopt the habit of feeling bodies with some part of their head.

"But if there occur, among the *Gasteropods,* any races which, by the circumstances which concern their mode of existence or life, do not experience such wants, then their head remains without tentacles; it has even no projection, no traces of tentacles, and this is what has happened in the case of *Bullæa, Bulla,* and *Chiton.*"

The first selection from Charles Darwin is from Chapter III, "Struggle for Existence," of *The Origin of Species,* sixth edition, 1872.

It may be asked, how is it that varieties, which I have called incipient species, become ultimately converted into good and distinct species which in most cases obviously differ from each other far more than do the varieties of the same species? How do those groups of species, which constitute what are called distant genera, and which differ from each other more than do the species of the same genus, arise? All these results . . . follow from the struggle for life. Owing to this struggle, variations, however slight and from whatever cause proceeding, if they be in any degree profitable to the individuals of a species, in their infinitely complex relations to other organic beings and to their physical conditions of life, will tend to the preservation of such individuals, and will generally be inherited by the offspring. The offspring, also, will thus have a better chance of surviving for, of the many individuals of any species which are periodically born, but a small number can survive. I have called this principle, by which each slight variation, if useful, is preserved by the term Natural Selection, in order to mark its relation to man's power of selection. But the expression often used by Mr. Herbert Spencer of the Survival of the Fittest is more accurate, and is sometimes equally convenient. We have seen that man by selection can certainly produce great results, and can adapt organic beings to his own uses, through the accumulation of slight but useful variations, given to him by the hand of Nature. But Natural Selection, as we shall hereafter see, is a power incessantly ready for action, and is as immeasurably superior to man's feeble efforts, as the works of Nature are to those of Art. . . .

A struggle for existence inevitably follows from the high rate at which all organic beings tend to increase. Every being, which during its natural lifetime produces several eggs or seeds, must suffer destruction during some period of its life, and during some season or occasional year, otherwise, on the principle of geometrical increase, its numbers would quickly become so inordinately great that no country could support the product. Hence, as more individuals are produced than can possibly survive, there must in every case be a struggle for existence, either one individual with another of the same species, or with the individuals of distinct species, or with the physical conditions of life. It is the doctrine of Malthus applied with manifold force to the whole animal and vegetable kingdoms; for in this case there can be no artificial increase of food, and no prudential restraint from marriage. Although some species may be now increasing, more or less rapidly, in numbers, all cannot do so, for the world would not hold them.

There is no exception to the rule that every organic being naturally increases at so high a rate, that, if not destroyed, the earth would soon be covered by the progeny of a single pair. Even slow-breeding man has doubled in twenty-five years, and at this rate, in less than a thousand years, there would literally not be standing-room for his progeny. Linnæus has calculated that if an annual plant produced only two seeds—and there is no plant so unproductive as this—and their seedlings next year produced two, and so on, then in twenty years there should be a million plants. The elephant is reckoned the slowest breeder of all known animals, and I have taken some pains to estimate its probable minimum rate of natural increase; it will be safest to assume that it begins breeding when thirty years old, and goes on breeding till ninety years old, bringing forth six young in the interval, and surviving till one hundred years old; if this be so, after a period of from 740 to 750 years there would be nearly nineteen million elephants alive, descended from the first pair. . . .

The dependency of one organic being on another, as of a parasite on its prey, lies generally between beings remote in the scale of nature. This is likewise sometimes the case with those which may be strictly said to struggle with each other for existence, as in the case of locusts and grass-feeding quadrupeds. But the struggle will almost invariably be most severe between the individuals of the same species, for they frequent the same districts, require the same food, and are exposed to the same dangers. . . .

The second selection, from the same book, is taken from the chapter entitled "Natural Selection; or The Survival of the Fittest."

How will the struggle for existence, briefly discussed in the last chapter,* act in regard to variation? Can the principle of selection, which we have seen is so potent in the hands of man, apply under nature? I think we shall see that it can act most efficiently. Let the endless number of slight variations and individual differences occurring in our domestic productions, and, in a lesser degree, in those under nature, be borne in mind; as well as the strength of the hereditary tendency. Under domestication, it may be truly said that the whole organisation becomes in some degree plastic. But the variability, which we almost universally meet with in our domestic productions, is not directly produced, as Hooker and Asa Gray have well remarked, by man; he can neither originate varieties, nor prevent their occurrence; he can reserve and accumulate such as do occur. Unintentionally he exposes organic beings to new and changing conditions of life, and variability ensues; but similar changes of condi-

* See pp. 222–231. Ed.

tions might and do occur under nature. Let it also be borne in mind how infinitely complex and close-fitting are the mutual relations of all organic beings to each other and to their physical conditions of life; and consequently what infinitely varied diversities of structure might be of use to each being under changing conditions of life. Can it, then, be thought improbable, seeing that variations useful to man have undoubtedly occurred, that other variations useful in some way to each being in the great and complex battle of life, should occur in the course of many successive generations. If such do occur, can we doubt (remembering that many more individuals are born than can possibly survive) that individuals having any advantage, however slight, over others, would have the best chance of surviving and of procreating their kind? On the other hand, we may feel sure that any variation in the least degree injurious would be rigidly destroyed. This preservation of favourable individual differences and variations, and the destruction of those which are injurious, I have called Natural Selection, or the Survival of the Fittest. Variations neither useful nor injurious would not be affected by natural selection, and would be left either a fluctuating element, as perhaps we see in certain polymorphic species, or would ultimately become fixed, owing to the nature of the organism and the nature of the conditions.

Several writers have misapprehended or objected to the term Natural Selection. Some have even imagined that natural selection induces variability, whereas it implies only the preservation of such variations as arise and are beneficial to the being under its conditions of life. No one objects to agriculturists speaking of the potent effects of man's selection; and in this case the individual differences given by nature, which man for some object selects, must of necessity first occur. Others have objected that the term selection implies conscious choice in the animals which become modified; and it had even been urged that, as plants have no volition, natural selection is not applicable to them! In the literal sense of the word, no doubt, natural selection is a false term; but who ever objected to chemists speaking of the elective affinities of the various elements?—and yet an acid cannot strictly be said to elect the base with which it in preference combines. It has been said that I speak of natural selection as an active power or Deity; but who objects to an author speaking of the attraction of gravity as ruling the movements of the planets? Every one knows what is meant and is implied by such metaphorical expressions; and they are almost necessary for brevity. So again it is difficult to avoid personifying the word Nature; but I mean by Nature, only the aggregate action and product of many natural laws, and by laws the sequence of events as ascertained by us. With a little familiarity such superficial objections will be forgotten.

We shall best understand the probable course of natural selection by taking the case of a country undergoing some slight physical change, for instance, of climate. The proportional numbers of its inhabitants will almost immediately undergo a change, and some species will probably become extinct. We may conclude, from what we have seen of the intimate and complex manner in which the inhabitants of each country are bound together, that any change in the numerical proportions of the inhabitants, independently of the change of climate itself, would seriously affect the others. If the country were open on its borders, new forms would certainly immigrate, and this would likewise seriously disturb the relations of some of the former inhabitants. Let it be remembered how powerful the influence of a single introduced tree or mammal has been shown to be. But in the case of an island, or of a country partly surrounded by barriers, into which new and better adapted forms could not freely enter, we should then have places in the economy of nature which would assuredly be better filled up, if some of the original inhabitants were in some manner modified; for, had the area been open to immigration, these same places would have been seized on by intruders. In such cases, slight modifications, which in any way favoured the individuals of any species, by better adapting them to their altered conditions, would tend to be preserved; and natural selection would have free scope for the work of improvement.

We have good reason to believe, as shown in the first chapter, that changes in the conditions of life give a tendency to increased variability; and in the foregoing cases the conditions have changed, and this would manifestly be favourable to natural selection, by affording a better chance of the occurrence of profitable variations. Unless such occur, natural selection can do nothing. Under the term of "variations," it must never be forgotten that mere individual differences are included. As man can produce a great result with his domestic animals and plants by adding up in any given direction individual differences, so could natural selection, but far more easily from having incomparably longer time for action. Nor do I believe that any great physical change, as of climate, or any unusual degree of isolation to check immigration, is necessary in order that new and unoccupied places should be left, for natural selection to fill up by improving some of the varying inhabitants. For as all the inhabitants of each country are struggling together with nicely balanced forces, extremely slight modifications in the structure or habits of one species would often give it an advantage over others; and still further modifications of the same kind would often still further increase the advantage, as long as the species continued under the same conditions of life and profited by similar means of subsistence and defence. No country can be named in which all the native inhabitants are now so perfectly adapted to each other and to the physical conditions under which they live, that none of them could be still better adapted or improved; for in all countries, the natives have been so far conquered by naturalised productions, that they have allowed some foreigners to take firm possession of the land. And as foreigners have thus in every country beaten some of the natives, we may safely conclude that the natives might have been modified with advantage, so as to have better resisted the intruders.

As man can produce, and certainly has produced, a great result by his methodical and unconscious means of selection, what may not natural selection effect? Man can act only on external and visible characters: Nature, if I may be allowed to personify the natural preservation or survival of the fittest, cares nothing for appearances, except in so far as they are useful to any being. She can act on every internal organ, on every shade of constitutional difference, on the whole machinery of life. Man selects only for his own good: Nature only for that of the being which she tends. Every selected character is fully exercised by her, as is implied by the fact of their selection. Man keeps the natives of many climates in the same country; he seldom exercises each selected character in some peculiar and fitting manner; he feeds a long and a short beaked pigeon on the same food; he does not exercise a long-backed or long-legged quadruped in any peculiar manner; he exposes sheep with long and short wool to the same climate. He does not allow the most vigorous males to struggle for the females. He does not rigidly destroy all inferior animals, but protects during each varying season, as far as lies in his power, all his productions. He often begins his selection by some half-monstrous form; or at least by some modification prominent enough to catch the eye or to be plainly useful to him. Under Nature, the slightest differences of structure or constitution may well turn the nicely balanced scale in the struggle for life, and so be preserved. How fleeting are the wishes and efforts of man! how short his time! and consequently how poor will be his results, compared with those accumulated by Nature during whole geological periods! Can we wonder, then, that Nature's productions should be far "truer" in character than man's productions; that they should be infinitely better adapted to the most complex conditions of life, and should plainly bear the stamp of far higher workmanship?

It may metaphorically be said that natural selection is daily and hourly scrutinising, throughout the world, the slightest variations; rejecting those that are bad, preserving and adding up all that are good, silently and insensibly working, *whenever and wherever opportunity offers,* at the improvement of each organic being in relation to its organic and inorganic conditions of life.

If under changing conditions of life organic beings present individual differences in almost every part of their structure, and this cannot be disputed; if there be, owing to their geometrical rate of increase, a severe struggle for life at some age, season, or year, and this certainly cannot be disputed; then, considering the infinite complexity of the relations of all organic beings to each other and to their conditions of life, causing an infinite diversity in structure, constitution, and habits, to be advantageous to them, it would be a most extraordinary fact if no variations had ever occurred useful to each being's own welfare, in the same manner as so many variations have occurred useful to man. But if variations useful to any organic being ever do occur, assuredly individuals thus characterised will have the best chance of being preserved in the struggle for life; and from the strong principle of inheritance, these will tend to produce offspring similarly characterised. This principle of preservation, or the survival of the fittest, I have called Natural Selection. It leads to the improvement of each creature in relation to its organic and inorganic conditions of life; and consequently, in most cases, to what must be regarded as an advance in organisation. Nevertheless, low and simple forms will long endure if well fitted for their simple conditions of life.

Natural selection, on the principle of qualities being inherited at corresponding ages, can modify the egg, seed, or young, as easily as the adult. Amongst many animals, sexual selection will have given its aid to ordinary selection, by assuring to the most vigorous and best adapted males the greatest number of offspring. Sexual selection will also give characters useful to the males alone, in their struggles or rivalry with other males; and these characters will be transmitted to one sex or to both sexes, according to the form of inheritance which prevails.

Whether natural selection has really thus acted in adapting the various forms of life to their several conditions and stations, must be judged by the general tenor and balance of evidence given in the following chapters. But we have already seen how it entails extinction; and how largely extinction has acted in the world's history, geology plainly declares. Natural selection, also leads to divergence of character; for the more organic beings diverge in structure, habits, and constitution, by so much the more can a large number be supported on the area,—of which we see proof by looking to the inhabitants of any small spot, and to the productions naturalised in foreign lands. Therefore, during the modification of the descendants of any one species, and during the incessant struggle of all species to increase in numbers, the more diversified the descendants become, the better will be their chance of success in the battle for life. Thus the small differences distinguishing varieties of the same species, steadily tend to increase, till they equal the greater differences between species of the same genus, or even of distinct genera.

We have seen that it is the common, the widely-diffused and widely-ranging species, belonging to the larger genera within each class, which vary most; and these tend to transmit to their modified off-spring that superiority which now makes them dominant in their own countries. Natural selection, as has just been remarked, leads to divergence of character and to much extinction of the less improved and intermediate forms of life. On these principles, the nature of the affinities, and the generally well-defined distinctions between the innumerable organic beings in each class throughout the world, may be explained. It is a truly wonderful fact—the wonder of which we are apt to overlook from familiarity—that all animals and all plants throughout all time and space should be related to each other in groups, subordinate to groups, in the manner which we everywhere behold—namely, varieties of the same species most closely related, species of the same genus less closely and unequally related, forming sections and sub-genera, species of distinct genera much less closely related, and genera related in different degrees, forming sub-families, families, orders, sub-classes and classes. The several subordinate groups in any class cannot be ranked in a single file, but seem clustered round points, and these round other points, and so on in almost endless cycles. If species had been independently created, no explanation would have been possible of this kind of classification; but it is explained through inheritance and the complex action of natural selection, entailing extinction and divergence of character, as we have seen illustrated in the diagram.

The affinities of all the beings of the same class have sometimes been represented by a great tree. I believe this simile largely speaks the truth. The green and budding twigs may represent existing species; and those produced during former years may represent the long succession of extinct species. At each period of growth all the growing twigs have tried to branch out on all sides, and to overtop and kill the surrounding twigs and branches, in the same manner as species and groups of species have at all times overmastered other species in the great battle for life. The limbs divided into great branches, and these into lesser and lesser branches, were themselves once, when the tree was young, budding twigs, and this connection of the former and present buds by ramifying branches may well represent the classification of all extinct and living species in groups subordinate to groups. Of the many twigs which flourished when the tree was a mere bush, only two or three, now grown into great branches, yet survive and bear the other branches; so with the species which lived during long-past geological periods, very few have left living and modified descendants. From the first growth of the tree, many a limb and branch has decayed and dropped off; and these fallen branches of various sizes may represent those whole orders, families, and genera which have now no living representatives, and which are known to us only in a fossil state. As we here and there see a thin straggling branch springing from a fork low down in a tree, and which by some chance has been favoured and is still alive on its summit, so we occasionally see an animal like the Ornithorhynchus or Lepidosiren, which in some small degree connects by its affinities two large branches of life, and which has apparently been saved from fatal competition by having inhabited a protected station. As buds give rise by growth to fresh buds, and these, if vigorous, branch out and overtop on all sides many a feebler branch, so by generation I believe it has been with the great Tree of Life, which fills with its dead and broken branches the crust of the earth, and covers the surface with its ever-branching and beautiful ramifications. . . .

This final Darwin selection, pointed out in the prefatory remarks to this section, is from his "Conclusion" of *The Origin of Species.*

I see no good reason why the views given in this volume should shock the religious feelings of anyone. It is satisfactory, as showing how transient such impressions are, to remember that the greatest discovery ever made by man, namely, the law of the attraction of gravity, was also attacked by Leibnitz, "as subversive of natural, and inferentially of revealed, religion." A celebrated author and divine has written to me that "he has gradually learnt to see that it is just as noble a conception of the Deity to believe that He created a few original forms capable of self-development into other and needful forms, as to believe that He required a fresh act of creation to supply the voids caused by the action of His laws."

Why, it may be asked, until recently did nearly all the most eminent living naturalists and geologists disbelieve in the mutability of species? It cannot be asserted that organic beings in a state of nature are subject to no variation; it cannot be proved that the amount of variation in the course of long ages is a limited quality; no clear distinction has been, or can be, drawn between species and well-marked varieties. It cannot be maintained that species when inter-crossed are invariably sterile, and varieties invariably fertile; or that sterility is a special endowment and sign of creation. The belief that species were immutable productions was almost unavoidable as long as the history of the world was thought to be of short duration; and now that we have acquired some idea of the lapse of time, we are too apt to assume, without proof, that the geological record is so perfect that it would have afforded us plain evidence of the mutation of species, if they had undergone mutation.

But the chief cause of our natural unwillingness to admit that one species has given birth to clear and distinct species, is that we are always slow in admitting great changes of which we do not see the steps. The difficulty is the same as that felt by so many geologists, when Lyell first insisted that long lines of inland cliffs had been formed, the great valleys excavated, by the agencies which we see still at work. The mind cannot possibly grasp the full meaning of the term of even a million years; it cannot add up and perceive the full effects of many slight variations, accumulated during an almost infinite number of generations.

Although I am fully convinced of the truth of the views given in this volume under the form of an abstract, I by no means expect to convince experienced naturalists whose minds are stocked with a multitude of facts all viewed, during a long course of years, from a point of view directly opposite to mine. It is so easy to hide our ignorance under such expressions as the "plan of creation," "unity of design," &c., and to think that we give an explanation when we only re-state a fact. Anyone whose disposition leads him to attach more weight to unexplained difficulties than to the explanation of a certain number of facts will certainly reject the theory. A few naturalists, endowed with much flexibility of mind, and who have already begun to doubt the immutability of species, may be influenced by this volume; but I look with confidence to the future,—to young and rising naturalists, who will be able to view both sides of the question with impartiality. Whoever is led to believe that species are mutable will do good service by conscientiously expressing his conviction; for thus only can the load of prejudice by which this subject is overwhelmed be removed.

Several eminent naturalists have of late published their belief that a multitude of reputed species in each genus are not real species; but that other species are real, that is, have been independently created. This seems to me a strange conclusion to arrive at. They admit that a multitude of forms, which till lately they themselves thought were special creations, and which are still thus looked at by the majority of naturalists, and which consequently have all the external characteristic features of true species,—they admit that these have been produced by variation, but they refuse to extend the same view to other and slightly different forms. Nevertheless they do not pretend that they can define, or even conjecture, which are the created forms of life, and which are those produced by secondary laws. They admit variation as a *vera causa* in one case, they arbitrarily reject it in another, without assigning any distinction in the two cases. The day will come when this will be given as a curious illustration of the blindness of preconceived opinion. These authors seem no more startled at a miraculous act of creation than at an ordinary birth. But do they really believe that at innumerable periods in the earth's history certain elemental atoms have been commanded suddenly to flash into living tissues? Do they believe that at each supposed act of creation one individual or many were produced? Were all the infinitely numerous kinds of animals and plants created as eggs or seed, or as full grown? and in the case of mammals, were they created bearing the false marks of nourishment from the mother's womb? Undoubtedly some of these same questions cannot be answered by those who believe in the appearance or creation of only a few forms of life, or of some one form alone. It has been maintained by several authors that it is as easy to believe in the creation of a million beings as of one; but Maupertuis' philosophical axiom "of least action" leads the mind more willingly to admit the smaller number; and certainly we ought not to believe that innumerable beings within each great class have been created with plain, but deceptive, marks of descent from a single parent. . . .

Authors of the highest eminence seem to be fully satisfied with the view that each species has been independently created. To my mind it accords better with what we know of the laws impressed on matter by the Creator, that the production and extinction of the past and present inhabitants of the world should have been due to secondary causes, like those determining the birth and death of the individual. When I view all beings not as special creations, but as the lineal descendants of some few beings which lived long before the first bed of the Cambrian system was deposited, they seem to me to become ennobled. Judging from the past, we may safely infer that not one living species will transmit its unaltered likeness to a distant futurity. And of the species now living very few will transmit progeny of any kind to a far distant futurity; for the manner in which all organic beings are grouped, shows that the greater number of species in each genus, and all the species in many genera, have left no descendants, but have become utterly extinct. We can so far take a prophetic glance into futurity as to foretell that it will be the common and widely-spread species, belonging to the larger and dominant groups within each class, which will ultimately prevail and procreate new and dominant species. As all the living forms of life are the lineal descendants of those which lived long before the Cambrian epoch, we may feel certain that the ordinary succession by generation has never once been broken, and that no cataclysm has desolated the whole world. Hence we may look with some confidence to a secure future of great length. And as natural selection works solely by and for the good of each being, all corporeal and mental endowments will tend to progress towards perfection.

It is interesting to contemplate a tangled bank, clothed with many plants of many kinds, with birds singing on the bushes, with various insects flitting about, and with worms crawling through the damp earth, and to reflect that these elaborately constructed forms, so different from each other, and dependent upon each other in so complex a manner, have all been produced by laws acting around us.

These laws, taken in the largest sense, being Growth with Reproduction; Inheritance which is almost implied by reproduction; Variability from the indirect and direct action of the conditions of life, and from use and disuse: a Ratio of Increase so high as to lead to a Struggle for Life, and as a consequence to Natural Selection, entailing Divergence of Character and the Extinction of less-improved forms. Thus, from the war of nature, from famine and death, the most exalted object which we are capable of conceiving, namely, the production of the higher animals, directly follows. There is grandeur in this view of life, with its several powers, having been originally breathed by the Creator into a few forms or into one; and that, whilst this planet has gone cycling on according to the fixed law of gravity, from so simple a beginning endless forms most beautiful and most wonderful have been, and are being evolved.

19. SPENCER and JAMES:
The Significance of the Theory of Evolution

According to John Herman Randall, Jr., the coming of Darwinian thought is the major fresh impulse to philosophic thinking in the nineteenth century.* If we include under impulses both constructive and destructive ones, then his statement may conceivably be true. In any case, some kind of Darwinian impulse had an effect on the development of Herbert Spencer, self-educated prophet of the then very latest scientific new age.

Herbert Spencer (1820–1903) used his reading in the sciences as a springboard for prolific philosophical speculation; for him, philosophy derives from the sciences in the form of a synthesis of their fundamental principles. Even before the actual publication of Darwin's systematic theory of evolution, Spencer had induced from biology and general natural history the generalization that the universe progresses by way of increasing differentiation of its interlocking parts. What was for Darwin, in explicit statement at least, merely a theory of biological improvement incident upon evolution (for example, the advantage *vis-à-vis* manipulation of environment that two-legged, four-limbed animals have over four-legged ones), was for Spencer a metaphysical theory of universal progress—in the arts, in civilization, in the quality of human life. Spencer

* See his *The Career of Philosophy*, Vol. II, 1966, pp. viii–ix.

talks of society, for instance, as an evolving "organism." Furthermore, his claim that things are getting better and better is not founded on the determination that humans are getting happier or nicer, but only on the alleged fact that increasing adjustment to the environment and the increasing differentiation and complexity which ensues is lawful—that is, predictable and thus scientific. The goodness of science is overabounding; its merest touch sanctifies.

Finally, this universal progress is known to be "not an accident, not a thing within human control, but a beneficent necessity." Differentiation and individuation (and individualism) is good, and it happens quite independently of any human effort (in contrast to Hegel's and Green's view that the intervention of the state is necessary in promoting positive freedom and to Rousseau's view that education *in freedom is essential*). We are told that the ultimate reason for the progress of the world lies in "things themselves" which are forever unknowable by human consciousness.

Couched incongruously within Spencer's vast intellectual system is the alleged "littleness" of the human mind. Thus we find Spencer unwittingly reverting to salient doctrines of Leibniz and Spinoza (for example, liberalism: variety and individualism as values) and to Kant (unknowable thing-in-itself as limit to the mind), but without these thinkers' awareness of the role of mind and concept in determining these doctrines; also, for example, without Kant's moral philosophy to account for that thing-in-itself which is the self, and for human initiative and responsibility. In a word, we find a grandiose philosophy which claims to be "scientific" and "new," but which unwittingly reverts to previous philosophies, warms them up, and serves them in depleted form. To adapt an aphorism of Santayana's: To be ignorant of the history of philosophy is to be doomed to repeat it with a stutter.

Of course, Spencer's was not the only philosophy influenced by Darwinian biology; it also had an impact on the Americans, William James (1842–1910), Charles Peirce, the functionalists and pragmatists. On the whole, Darwin was a constructive influence upon James and Peirce, for they examined his ideas with a philosophically critical intelligence. According to William James—physiologist, psychologist and philosopher—Darwin and Spencer did a great service in showing that mind is not a "detached existent" but has a biological basis and a definite function in the natural environment. Yet James is profoundly critical of Spencer's philosophy of mind: "the adjustment (or correspondence) of inner to outer relations." James wonders how Spencer can talk about the environment, the "outer relations," unless he knows what the environment is, and if he *knows* this, then mind must already be involved at the outset in his knowing. We investigate mind ("internal relations") as already related to the known object, suggests James, and not in a pretended examination of it from within—a "within" set over and against a naïvely presupposed "external" reality.

Moreover, James goes on, Spencer's notion of mind as adjustment or correspondence to the environment is absurd. The term "correspondence" is ambiguous, but on none of its meanings can a sound philosophy of mind be built. If it means survival of the organism, then a moth, say, which has some awareness of a flame and flies into it and dies will be said to have no mind, while another which has no awareness of the flame and does not fly into it and thus does survive will be said to have a mind—an absurdity. If the term means a registering of the environment, we must talk about the process of knowing and cannot rest content with the image of a mind which corresponds to an environment like a glove corresponds to a hand or like a photograph corresponds to an object, for gloves and even cameras really know nothing; and we cannot begin by talking about a registering alone, but about the relationship between registering and registered, and thus about reality.

As far as Spencer's ethics go, James regards it as "unexampled insipidity."* It is false that what adjusts and survives is always good, thus constituting progress. Some environments are not worth surviving in; life within them is not worth the cost in immorality. The same applies to societies—he is attacking "social Darwinism"; some societies which survive are not good. So much for the belief in progress when adjustment and survival are the criteria of value. It is hard not to agree with James that Spencer's optimism is a mere bubble.

Hence Spencer is not the only fruit of Darwinian impulse. But James and his followers cannot be appreciated in a Darwinian context alone, for they build on the full history of philosophic thought.

In the selection from Spencer's "Progress: Its Law and Cause" we see what he takes to be an example of progress through adjustment and differentiation: new modes of communication which make possible the spreading of thought into every nook and cranny of life: "There arises a wide dissemination of cheap literature through railway bookstalls, and of advertisements in railway carriages: both of them aiding ulterior progress." Today, as the communications of the mass media pile up around us, we need to know the quality of the thought communicated, not just its quantity and speed of dissemination (for as Spencer himself put it, in a more thoughtful moment, some knowledge is of more worth than some other). If we do not require quality, then the progress will actually be, like some motives, ulterior; and the thought communicated will actually be, like so many commodities of the modern age, cheap.

* William James, "The Dilemma of Determinism" (1884), in *The Will to Believe* (New York: Dover Books), p. 168.

As early as 1878 in his "Remarks on Spencer's Definition of Mind as Correspondence," included here in its entirety, William James' mature philosophy was clearly prefigured. The pragmatic theory of meaning and truth as well as James' functionalist and proto-phenomenological philosophy of mind issue from his critique of Spencer.* After what has already been said, James' view can be sketched as follows: Our knowledge of reality is a function of our active, selective interests; the only criterion of the truth of a thought is the occurrence of the train of experiential consequences which the thought ideally predicts. Thought is intrusive, ideal, creative, purposive and end-directed (teleological); it is not reducible to the "external" viewpoint of physiology, which ignores the world-as-it-appears-to-the-conscious-organism. In a word, all thought is artlike. James' philosophy is a remarkable realization—through pruning and limitation—of German romanticism and idealism. He is a partial exception to the general anxiety and disillusionment which closed the romantic age, and his thought offers us a glimpse of what a reconciliation between natural science and the general culture might look like.

The selection which follows is taken from Spencer's essay "Progress: Its Law and Consequences," 1857.

The current conception of progress is somewhat shifting and indefinite. Sometimes it comprehends little more than simple growth—as of a nation in the number of its members and the extent of territory over which it has spread. Sometimes it has reference to quantity of material products—as when the advance of agriculture and manufactures is the topic. Sometimes the superior quality of these products is contemplated: and sometimes the new or improved appliances by which they are produced. When, again, we speak of moral or intellectual progress, we refer to the state of the individual or people exhibiting it; while, when the progress of knowledge, of science, of art, is commented upon, we have in view certain abstract results of human thought and action. Not only, however, is the current conception of progress more or less vague, but it is in great measure erroneous. It takes in not so much the reality of progress as its accompaniments—not so much the substance as the shadow. That progress in intelligence seen during the growth of the child into the man, or the savage into the philosopher, is commonly regarded as consisting in the greater number of facts known and laws understood: whereas the actual progress consists in those internal modifications of which this

* For further documentation of the point, see my book *William James: The Phenomenological Breakthrough*, Indiana University Press.

increased knowledge is the expression. Social progress is supposed to consist in the produce of a greater quantity and variety of the articles required for satisfying men's wants; in the increasing security of person and property; in widening freedom of action: whereas, rightly understood, social progress consists in those changes of structure in the social organism which have entailed these consequences. The current conception is a teleological one. The phenomena are contemplated solely as bearing on human happiness. Only those changes are held to constitute progress which directly or indirectly tend to heighten human happiness. And they are thought to constitute progress simply *because* they tend to heighten human happiness. But rightly to understand progress, we must inquire what is the nature of these changes, considered apart from our interests. Ceasing, for example, to regard the successive geological modifications that have taken place in the earth, as modifications that have gradually fitted it for the habitation of man, and as *therefore* a geological progress, we must seek to determine the character common to these modifications—the law to which they all conform. And similarly in every other case. Leaving out of sight concomitants and beneficial consequences, let us ask what progress is in itself.

In respect to that progress which individual organisms display in the course of their evolution, this question has been answered by the Germans. The investigations of Wolff, Goethe, and Von Baer have established the truth that the series of changes gone through during the development of a seed into a tree, or an ovum into an animal, constitute an advance from homogeneity of structure to heterogeneity of structure. In its primary stage, every germ consists of a substance that is uniform throughout, both in texture and chemical composition. The first step is the appearance of a difference between two parts of this substance; or, as the phenomenon is called in physiological language, a differentiation. Each of these differentiated divisions presently begins itself to exhibit some contrast of parts; and by and by these secondary differentiations become as definite as the original one. This process is continuously repeated—is simultaneously going on in all parts of the growing embryo; and by endless such differentiations there is finally produced that complex combination of tissues and organs constituting the adult animal or plant. This is the history of all organisms whatever. It is settled beyond dispute that organic progress consists in a change from the homogeneous to the heterogeneous.

Now, we propose in the first place to show that this law of organic progress is the law of all progress. Whether it be in the development of the earth, in the development of life upon its surface, in the development of society, of government, of manufactures, of commerce, of language, literature, science, art, this same evolution of the simple into the complex, through successive differentiations, holds throughout. . . .

Whether an advance from the homogeneous to the heterogeneous is or is not displayed in the biological history of the globe, it is clearly enough displayed in the progress of the latest and most heterogeneous creature—man. It is alike true that, during the period in which the earth has been peopled, the human organism has grown more heterogeneous among the civilized divisions of the species; and that the species, as a whole, has been growing more heterogeneous in virtue of the multiplication of races and the differentiation of these races from each other.

In proof of the first of these positions we may cite the fact that, in the relative development of the limbs, the civilized man departs more widely from the general type of the placental mammalia than do the lower human races. While often possessing well-developed body and arms, the Papuan has extremely small legs: thus reminding us of the quadrumana, in which there is no great contrast in size between the hind and fore limbs. But in the European, the greater length and massiveness of the legs has become very marked—the fore and hind limbs are relatively more heterogeneous. Again, the greater ratio which the cranial bones bear to the facial bones illustrates the same truth. Among the vertebrata in general, progress is marked by an increasing heterogeneity in the vertebral column, and more especially in the vertebrae constituting the skull: the higher forms being distinguished by the relatively larger size of the bones which cover the brain, and the relatively smaller size of those which form the jaw, etc. Now, this characteristic, which is stronger in man than in any other creature, is stronger in the European than in the savage. Moreover, judging from the greater extent and variety of faculty he exhibits, we may infer that the civilized man has also a more complex or heterogeneous nervous system than the uncivilized man: and indeed the fact is in part visible in the increased ratio which his cerebrum bears to the subjacent ganglia.

If further elucidation be needed, we may find it in every nursery. The infant European has sundry marked points of resemblance to the lower human races; as in the flatness of the alæ of the nose, the depression of its bridge, the divergence and forward opening of the nostrils, the form of the lips, the absence of a frontal sinus, the width between the eyes, the smallness of the legs. Now, as the developmental process by which these traits are turned into those of the adult European, is a continuation of that change from the homogeneous to the heterogeneous displayed during the previous evolution of the embryo, which every physiologist will admit; it follows that the parallel developmental process by which the like traits of the barbarous races have been turned into those of the civilized races, has also been a continuation of the change from the homogeneous to the heterogeneous. The truth of the second position—that mankind, as a whole, have become more heterogeneous—is so obvious as scarcely to need illustration. Every work on Ethnology, by its divisions and subdivisions of races, bears testimony to it. Even were we to admit the hypothesis that mankind originated from several separate stocks, it would still remain true, that as, from each of these stocks, there have sprung many now widely different tribes, which are proved by philological evidence to have had a common origin, the race as a whole is far less homogeneous than it once was. Add to which, that we have in the Anglo-Americans an example of a new variety arising within these few generations; and that, if we may trust to the description of observers, we are likely soon to have another such example in Australia.

On passing from humanity under its individual form, to humanity as socially embodied, we find the general law still more variously exemplified. The change from the homogeneous to the heterogeneous is displayed equally in the progress of civilization as a whole, and in the progress of every tribe or nation; and is still going on with increasing rapidity. As we see in existing barbarous tribes, society in its first and lowest form is a homogeneous aggregation of individuals having like powers and like functions: the only marked difference of function being that which accompanies difference of sex. Every man is warrior, hunter, fisherman, tool-maker, builder; every woman performs the same drudgeries; every family is self-sufficing, and save for purposes of aggression and defence, might as well live apart from the rest. Very early, however, in the process of social evolution, we find an incipient differentiation between the governing and the governed. Some kind of chieftainship seems coeval with the first advance from the state of separate wandering families to that of a nomadic tribe. The authority of the strongest makes itself felt among a body of savages as in a herd of animals or a posse of schoolboys. At first, however, it is indefinite, uncertain; is shared by others of scarcely inferior power; and is unaccompanied by any difference in occupation or style of living: the first ruler kills his own game, makes his own weapons, builds his own hut, and economically considered, does not differ from others of his tribe. Gradually, as the tribe progresses, the contrast between the governing and the governed grows more decided. Supreme power becomes hereditary in one family; the head of that family, ceasing to provide for his own wants, is served by others; and he begins to assume the sole office of ruling. . . .

We may suspect *a priori* that in some law of change lies the explanation of this universal transformation of the homogeneous into the heterogeneous.

Thus much premised, we pass at once to the statement of the law, which is this: *Every active force produces more than one change— every cause produces more than one effect.* . . .

Observe, now, . . . a . . . consequence. There must arise not simply a tendency toward the differentiation of each race of organisms into several races; but also a tendency to the occasional production of a somewhat higher organism. Taken in the mass these divergent varieties which have been caused by fresh physical conditions and habits of life will exhibit changes quite indefinite in kind and degree; and changes that do not necessarily constitute an advance. Probably in most cases the modified type will be neither more nor less heterogeneous than the original one. In some cases the habits of life adopted being simpler than before, a less heterogeneous structure will result: there will be a retrogradation. But it *must* now and then occur, that some division of a species, falling into circumstances which give it rather more complex experiences, and demand actions somewhat more involved, will have certain of its organs further differentiated in proportionately small degrees—will become slightly more heterogeneous.

Thus, in the natural course of things, there will from time to time arise an increased heterogeneity both of the earth's flora and fauna, and of individual races included in them. Omitting detailed explanations, and allowing for the qualifications which cannot here be specified, we think it is clear that geological mutations have all along tended to complicate the forms of life, whether regarded separately or collectively. The same causes which have led to the evolution of the earth's crust from the simple into the complex, have simultaneously led to a parallel evolution of the life upon its surface. In this case, as in previous ones, we see that the transformation of the homogeneous into the heterogeneous is consequent upon the universal principle, that every active force produces more than one change.

The deduction here drawn from the established truths of geology and the general laws of life, gains immensely in weight on finding it to be in harmony with an induction drawn from direct experience. Just that divergence of many races from one race, which we inferred must have been continually occurring during geologic time, we know to have occurred during the prehistoric and historic periods, in man and domestic animals. And just that multiplication of effects which we concluded must have produced the first, we see has produced the last. Single causes, as famine, pressure of population, war, have periodically led to further dispersions of mankind and of dependent creatures: each such dispersion initiating new modifications, new varieties of type. Whether all the human races be or be not derived from one stock, philology makes it clear that whole groups of races now easily distinguishable from each other were originally one race—that the diffusion of one race into different climates and conditions of existence has produced many modified forms of it. . . .

If the advance of man toward greater heterogeneity is traceable to the production of many effects by one cause, still more clearly may the advance of society toward greater heterogeneity be so explained. Consider the growth of an industrial organization. When, as must occasionally happen, some individual of a tribe displays unusual aptitude for making an article of general use—a weapon, for instance—which was before made by each man for himself, there arises a tendency toward the differentiation of that individual into a maker of such weapon. His companions—warriors and hunters all of them—severally feel the importance of having the best weapons that can be made; and are therefore certain to offer strong inducements to this skilled individual to make weapons for them. He, on the other hand, having not only an unusual faculty, but an unusual liking, for making such weapons (the talent and the desire for any occupation being commonly associated), is predisposed to fulfil these commissions on the offer of an adequate reward: especially as his love of distinction is also gratified. This first specialization of function, once commenced, tends ever to become more decided. On the side of the weapon-maker continued practice gives increased skill—increased superiority to his products: on the side of his clients, cessation of practice entails decreased skill. Thus the influences that determine this division of labor grow stronger in both ways; and the incipient heterogeneity is, on the average of cases, likely to become permanent for that generation, if no longer. . . .

Our limits will not allow us to follow out this process in its higher complications: else might we show how the localization of special industries in special parts of a kingdom, as well as the minute subdivision of labor in the making of each commodity, are similarly determined. Or, turning to a somewhat different order of illustrations, we might dwell on the multitudinous changes—material, intellectual, moral—caused by printing; or the further extensive series of changes wrought by gunpowder. But leaving the intermediate phases of social development, let us take a few illustrations from its most recent and its passing phases. To trace the effects of steam-power, in its manifold applications to mining, navigation, and manufactures of all kinds, would carry us into unmanageable detail. Let us confine ourselves to the latest embodiment of steam-power—the locomotive engine.

This, as the proximate cause of our railway system, has changed the face of the country, the course of trade, and the habits of the people. Consider, first, the complicated sets of changes that precede the making of every railway—the provisional arrangements, the meetings, the registration, the trial section, the parliamentary survey, the lithographed plans, the books of reference, the local deposits and notices, the application to Parliament, the passing Standing Orders Committee, the first, second, and third readings; each of which brief heads indicates a multiplicity of transactions, and the development of sundry occupations—as those of engineers, surveyors, lithographers, parliamentary agents, share-brokers; and the creation of sundry others—as those of traffic-takers, reference-takers. Consider, next, the yet more marked changes implied in railway construction—the cuttings, embankings, tunnellings, diversions of roads; the building of bridges and stations; the laying down of ballast, sleepers, and rails; the making of engines, tenders, carriages and wagons: which processes, acting upon numerous trades, increase the importation of timber, the quarrying of stone, the manufacture of iron, the mining of coal, the burning of bricks: institute a variety of special manufactures weekly advertised in the *Railway Times;* and, finally, open the way to sundry new occupations as those of drivers, stokers, cleaners, platelayers, etc., etc. And then consider the changes, more numerous and involved still, which railways in action produce on the community at large. The organization of every business is more or less modified: ease of communication makes it better to do directly what was before done by proxy; agencies are established where previously they would not have paid; goods are obtained from remote wholesale houses instead of near retail ones, and commodities are used which distance once rendered inaccessible. Again, the rapidity and small cost of carriage tend to specialize more than ever the industries of different districts—to confine each manufacture to the parts in which, from local advantages, it can be best carried on. Further, the diminished cost of carriage, facilitating distribution, equalizes prices, and also, on the average, lowers prices: thus bringing divers articles within the means of those before unable to buy them, and so increasing their comforts and improving their habits. At the same time the practice of travelling is immensely extended. Classes who never before thought of it, take annual trips to the sea; visit their distant relations; make tours; and so we are benefited in body, feelings, and intellect. Moreover, the more prompt transmission of letters and of news produces further changes—makes the pulse of the nation faster. Yet more, there arises a wide dissemination of cheap literature through railway bookstalls, and of advertisements in railway carriages: both of them aiding ulterior progress.

And all the innumerable changes here briefly indicated are consequent on the invention of the locomotive engine. The social organism has been rendered more heterogeneous in virtue of the many new occupations introduced, and the many old ones further specialized; prices in every place have been altered; each trader has, more or less, modified his way of doing business; and almost every person has been affected in his actions, thoughts, emotions. . . .

Space permitting, we could willingly have pursued the argument in relation to all the subtler results of civilization. As before, we showed that the law of progress to which the organic and inorganic worlds conform, is also conformed to by language, sculpture, music, etc.; so might we here show that the cause which we have hitherto found to determine progress holds in these cases also. We might demonstrate in detail how, in science, an advance of one division presently advances other divisions—how astronomy has been immensely forwarded by discoveries in optics, while other optical discoveries have initiated microscopic anatomy, and greatly aided the growth of physiology—how chemistry has indirectly increased our knowledge of electricity, magnetism, biology, geology—how electricity has reacted on chemistry, and magnetism, developed our views of light and heat, and disclosed sundry laws of nervous action.

In literature the same truth might be exhibited in the manifold effects of the primitive mystery-play, not only as originating the modern drama, but as affecting through it other kinds of poetry and fiction; or in the still multiplying forms of periodical literature that have descended from the first newspaper, and which have severally acted and reacted on other forms of literature and on each other. The influence which a new school of painting—as that of the pre-Raffaelites—exercises upon other schools; the hints which all kinds of pictorial art are deriving from photography; the complex results of new critical doctrines, as those of Mr. Ruskin, might severally be dwelt upon as displaying the like multiplication of effects. But it would needlessly tax the reader's patience to pursue, in their many ramifications, these various changes: here become so involved and subtle as to be followed with some difficulty. . . .

However, to avoid committing ourselves to more than is yet proved, we must be content with saying that such are the law and the cause of all progress that is known to us. Should the nebular hypothesis ever be established, then it will become manifest that the universe at large, like every organism, was once homogeneous; that as a whole, and in every detail, it has unceasingly advanced toward greater heterogeneity; and that its heterogeneity is still increasing. It will be seen that as in each event of to-day, so from the beginning, the decomposition of every expended force into several forces has been perpetually producing a higher complication; that the increase of heterogeneity so brought about is still going on, and must continue to go on; and that thus progress is not an accident, not a thing within human control, but a beneficent necessity.

A few words must be added on the ontological bearings of our argument. Probably not a few will conclude that here is an attempted solution of the great questions with which philosophy in all ages has perplexed itself. Let none thus deceive themselves. Only such as know not the scope and the limits of science can fall into so grave an error. The foregoing generalizations apply, not to the genesis of things in themselves but to their genesis as manifested to the human consciousness. After all that has been said, the ultimate mystery remains just as it was. The explanation of that which is explicable does but bring out into greater clearness the inexplicableness of that which remains behind. However we may succeed in reducing the equation to its lowest terms, we are not thereby enabled to determine the unknown quantity: on the contrary, it only becomes more manifest that the unknown quantity can never be found.

Little as it seems to do so, fearless inquiry tends continually to give a firmer basis to all true religion. The timid sectarian, alarmed at the progress of knowledge, obliged to abandon one by one the superstitions of his ancestors, and daily finding his cherished beliefs more and more shaken, secretly fears that all things may some day be explained, and has a corresponding dread of science; thus evincing the profoundest of all infidelity—the fear lest the truth be bad. On the other hand, the sincere man of science, content to follow wherever the evidence leads him, becomes by each new inquiry more profoundly convinced that the universe is an insoluble problem. Alike in the external and the internal worlds, he sees himself in the midst of perpetual changes, of which he can discover neither the beginning nor the end. If, tracing back the evolution of things, he allows himself to entertain the hypothesis that all matter once existed in a diffused form, he finds it utterly impossible to conceive how this came to be so; and equally, if he speculates on the future, he can assign no limit to the grand succession of phenomena ever unfolding themselves before him. On the other hand, if he looks inward, he perceives that both terminations of the thread of consciousness are beyond his grasp: he cannot remember when or how consciousness commenced, and he cannot examine the consciousness that at any moment exists; for only a state of consciousness that is already past can become the object of thought, and never one which is passing.

When, again, he turns from the succession of phenomena, external or internal, to their essential nature, he is equally at fault. Though he may succeed in resolving all properties of objects into manifestations of force, he is not thereby enabled to realize what force is; but finds, on the contrary, that the more he thinks about it the more he is baffled. Similarly, though analysis of mental actions may finally bring him down to sensations as the original materials out of which all thought is woven, he is none the forwarder; for he cannot in the least comprehend sensation—cannot even conceive how sensation is possible. Inward and outward things he thus discovers to be alike inscrutable in their ultimate genesis and nature. He sees that the materialist and spiritualist controversy is a mere war of words; the disputants being equally absurd—each believing he understands that which it is impossible for any man to understand. In all directions his investigations eventually bring him face to face with the unknowable; and he ever more clearly perceives it to be the unknowable. He learns at once the greatness and the littleness of human intellect—its power in dealing with all that comes within the range of experience; its impotence in dealing with all that transcends experience. He feels, with a vividness which no others can, the utter incomprehensibleness of the simplest fact, considered in itself. He alone truly *sees* that absolute knowledge is impossible. He alone *knows* that under all things there lies an impenetrable mystery.

The following essay by James was published as "Remarks on Spencer's Definition of Mind as Correspondence," *Journal of Speculative Philosophy*, 1878.

As a rule it may be said that, at a time when readers are so overwhelmed with work as they are at the present day, all purely critical and destructive writing ought to be reprobated. The half-gods generally refuse to go, in spite of the ablest criticism, until the gods actually *have* arrived; but then, too, criticism is hardly needed. But there are cases in which every rule may be broken. "What!" exclaimed Voltaire, when accused of offering no substitute for the Christianity he attacked, *"je vous délivre d'une bête féroce, et vous me demandez par quoi je la remplace!"* Without comparing Mr. Spencer's definition of Mind either to Christianity or to a *"bête féroce,"* it may certainly be said to be very far-reaching in its consequences, and, according to certain standards, noxious; whilst probably a large proportion of those hard-headed readers who subscribe to the *Popular Science Monthly* and *Nature,* and whose sole philosopher Mr. Spencer is, are fascinated by it without being in the least aware what its consequences are.

The defects of the formula are so glaring that I am surprised it should not long ago have been critically overhauled. The reader will readily recollect what it is. In part III of his *Principles of Psychology,* Mr. Spencer, starting from the supposition that the most essential truth concerning mental evolution will be that which allies it to the evolution nearest akin to it, namely, that of Life, finds that the formula *"adjustment of inner to outer relations,"* which was the definition of life, comprehends also "the entire process of mental evolution." In a series of chapters of great apparent thoroughness and minuteness he shows how all the different grades of mental perfection are expressed by the degree of extension of this adjustment, or, as he here calls it, "correspondence," in space, time, specialty, generality, and integration. The polyp's tentacles contract only to immediately present stimuli, and to almost all alike. The mammal will store up food for a day, or even for a season; the bird will start on its migration for a goal hundreds of miles away; the savage will sharpen his arrows to hunt next year's game; while the astronomer will proceed, equipped with all his instruments, to a point thousands of miles distant, there to watch, at a fixed day, hour, and minute, a transit of Venus or an eclipse of the Sun.

The picture drawn is so vast and simple, it includes such a multitude of details in its monotonous frame-work, that it is no wonder that readers of a passive turn of mind are, usually, more impressed by it than by any portion of the book. But on the slightest scrutiny its solidity begins to disappear. In the first place, one asks, what right has one, in a formula embracing professedly the "entire process of mental evolution," to mention only phenomena of cognition, and to omit all sentiments, all aesthetic impulses, all religious emotions and personal affections? The ascertainment of outward fact constitutes only one species of mental activity. The genus contains, in addition to purely cognitive judgments, or judgments of the actual—judgments that things do, as a matter of fact, exist so or so—an immense number of emotional judgments: judgments of the ideal, judgments that things *should* exist thus and not so. How much of our mental life is occupied with this matter of a better or a worse? How much of it involves preferences or repugnances on our part? We cannot laugh at a joke, we cannot go to one theatre rather than another, take more trouble for the sake of our own child than our neighbor's; we cannot long for vacation, show our best manners to a foreigner, or pay our pew rent, without involving in the premises of our action some element which has nothing whatever to do with simply cognizing the actual, but which, out of alternative possible actuals, selects one and cognizes that as the ideal. In a word, "Mind," as we actually find it, contains all sorts of laws—those of logic, of fancy, of wit, of taste, decorum, beauty, morals, and so forth, as well as of perception of fact. Common sense estimates mental excellence by a combination of all these standards, and yet how few of them correspond to anything that actually *is*—they are laws of the Ideal, dictated by subjective *interests* pure and simple. Thus the greater part of Mind, quantitatively considered, refuses to have anything to do with Mr. Spencer's definition. It is quite true that these ideal judgments are treated by him with great ingenuity and felicity at the close of his work—indeed, his treatment of them there seems to me to be its most admirable portion. But they are there handled as separate items having no connection with that extension of the "correspondence" which is maintained elsewhere to be the all-sufficing law of mental growth.

Most readers would dislike to admit without coercion that a law was adequate which obliged them to erase from literature (if by literature were meant anything worthy of the title of "mental product") all works except treatises on natural science, history, and statistics. Let us examine the reason that Mr. Spencer appears to consider coercive.

It is this: That, since every process grows more and more complicated as it develops, more swarmed over by incidental and derivative conditions which disguise and adulterate its original simplicity, the only way to discover its true and essential form is to trace it back to its earliest beginning. There it will appear in its genuine character pure and undefiled. Religious, aesthetic, and ethical judgments, having grown up in the course of evolution, by means that we can very plausibly divine, of course may be stripped off from the main stem of intelligence and leave that undisturbed. With a similar intent Mr. Tylor says: "Whatever throws light on the origin of a conception throws light on its validity." Thus, then, there is no resource but to appeal to the polyp, or whatever shows us the form of evolution just *before* intelligence, and what that, and only what that, contains will be the root and heart of the matter.

But no sooner is the reason for the law thus enunciated than many objections occur to the reader. In the first place, the general principle seems to lead to absurd conclusions. If the embryologic line of appeal can alone teach us the genuine essences of things, if the polyp is to dictate our law of mind to us because he came first, where are we to stop? He must himself be treated in the same way. Back of him lay the not-yet-polyp, and, back of all, the universal mother, fire-mist. To seek there for the reality, of course would reduce all thinking to nonentity, and, although Mr. Spencer would probably not regard this conclusion as a *reductio ad absurdum* of his principle, since it would only be another path to his theory of the Unknowable, less systematic thinkers may hesitate. But, waiving for the moment the question of principle, let us admit that relatively to *our* thought, at any rate, the polyp's thought is pure and undefiled. Does the study of the polyp lead us distinctly to Mr. Spencer's formula of correspondence? To begin with, if that formula be meant to include disinterested scientific curiosity, or "correspondence" in the sense of cognition, with no ulterior selfish end, the polyp gives it no countenance whatever. He is as innocent of scientific as of moral and aesthetic enthusiasm; he is the most narrowly teleological of organisms; reacting, so far as he reacts at all, only for self-preservation.

This leads us to ask what Mr. Spencer exactly means by the word correspondence. Without explanation, the word is wholly indeterminate. Everything corresponds in some way with everything else that co-exists in the same world with it. But, as the formula of correspondence was originally derived from biology, we shall possibly find in our author's treatise on that science an exact definition of what he means by it. On seeking there, we find nowhere a definition, but numbers of synonyms. The inner relations are "adjusted," "conformed," "fitted," "related," to the outer. They must "meet" or "balance" them. There must be "concord" or "harmony" between them. Or, again, the organism must "counteract" the changes in the environment. But these words, too, are wholly indeterminate. The fox is most beautifully "adjusted" to the hounds and huntsmen who pursue him; the limestone "meets" molecule by molecule the acid which corrodes it; the man is exquisitely "conformed" to the *trichina* which invades him, or to the typhus poison which consumes him; and the forests "harmonize" incomparably with the fires that lay them low. Clearly, a further specification is required; and, although Mr. Spencer shrinks strangely from enunciating this specification, he everywhere works his formula so as to imply it in the clearest manner.

Influence on physical well-being or survival is his implied criterion of the rank of mental action. The moth which flies into the candle, instead of away from it, "fails," in Spencer's words, to "correspond" with its environment; but clearly, in this sense, pure cognitive inference of the existence of heat after a perception of light would not suffice to constitute correspondence; while a moth which, on feeling the light, should merely vaguely fear to approach it, but have no proper image of the heat, would "correspond." So that the Spencerian formula, to mean anything definite at all, must, at least, be re-written as follows: "Right or intelligent mental action consists in the establishment, corresponding to outward relations, of such inward relations and reactions as will favor the survival of the thinker, or, at least, his physical well-being."

Such a definition as this is precise, but at the same time it is frankly teleological. It explicitly postulates a distinction between mental action pure and simple, and *right* mental action; and furthermore, it proposes, as criteria of this latter, certain ideal ends—those of physical prosperity or survival, which are pure *subjective interests* on the animal's part, brought with it upon the scene and corresponding to no relation already there.* No mental action is right or intelligent which fails to fit this standard. No correspondence can pass muster till it shows its subservience to these ends. Corresponding itself to no actual outward thing; referring merely to a future which *may* be, but which these interests now say *shall* be; purely ideal, in a word, they judge, dominate, determine all correspondences between the inner and the outer. Which is as much as to say that *mere* correspondence with the outer world is a notion on which it is wholly impossible to base a definition of mental action. Mr. Spencer's occult reason for leaving unexpressed the most important part of the definition he works with probably lies in its apparent implication of subjective spontaneity. The mind, according to his philosophy, should be pure product, absolute derivative from the non-mental. To make it dictate conditions, bring independent interests into the game which may determine what we shall call correspondence, and what not, might, at first sight, appear contrary to the notion of evolution which forbids the introduction at any point of an absolutely new factor. In what sense the existence of survival interest does postulate such a factor we shall hereafter see. I think myself that it is possible to express all its outward results in non-mental terms. But the unedifying look of the thing, its simulation of an independent mental teleology, seems to have frightened Mr. Spencer here, as elsewhere, away from a serious

* These interests are the real *a priori* element in cognition. By saying that their pleasures and pains have nothing to do with correspondence, I mean simply this: To a large number of terms in the environment there may be inward correlatives of a neutral sort as regards feeling. The "correspondence" is already there. But, now, suppose some to be accented with pleasure, others with pain; that is a fact additional to the correspondence, a fact with no outward correlative. But it immediately orders the correspondences in this way: that the pleasant or interesting items are singled out, dwelt upon, developed into their farther connections, whilst the unpleasant or insipid ones are ignored or suppressed. The future of the Mind's development is thus mapped out in advance by the way in which the lines of pleasure and pain run. The interests precede the outer relations noticed. Take the utter absence of response of a dog or a savage to the greater mass of environing relations. How can you alter it unless you previously *awaken an interest*—i.e., produce a susceptibility to intellectual pleasure in certain modes of cognitive exercise? Interests, then, are an all-essential factor which no writer pretending to give an account of mental evolution has a right to neglect.

scrutiny of the facts. But let us be indulgent to his timidity, and assume that survival was all the while a "mental reservation" with him, only excluded from his formula by reason of the comforting sound it might have to Philistine ears.

We should then have, as the embodiment of the highest ideal perfection of mental development, a creature of superb cognitive endowments, from whose piercing perceptions no fact was too minute or too remote to escape; whose all-embracing foresight no contingency could find unprepared; whose invincible flexibility of resource no array of outward onslaught could overpower; but in whom all these gifts were swayed by the single passion of love of life, of survival at any price. This determination filling his whole energetic being, consciously realized, intensified by meditation, becomes a fixed idea, would use all the other faculties as its means, and, if they ever flagged, would by its imperious intensity spur them and hound them on to ever fresh exertions and achievements. There can be no doubt that, if such an incarnation of earthly prudence existed, a race of beings in whom this monotonously narrow passion for self-preservation were aided by every cognitive gift, they would soon be kings of all the earth. All known human races would wither before their breath, and be as dust beneath their conquering feet.

But whether any Spencerian would hail with hearty joy their advent is another matter. Certainly Mr. Spencer would not; while the common sense of mankind would stand aghast at the thought of them. Why does common opinion abhor such a being? Why does it crave greater "richness" of nature in its mental ideal? Simply because, to common sense, survival is only one out of many interests— *primus inter pares,* perhaps, but still in the midst of peers. What are these interests? Most men would reply that they are all that makes survival worth securing. The social affections, all the various forms of play, the thrilling intimations of art, the delights of philosophic contemplation, the rest of religious emotion, the joy of moral self-approbation, the charm of fancy and of wit—some or all of these are absolutely required to make the notion of mere existence tolerable; and individuals who, by their special powers, satisfy these desires are protected by their fellows and enabled to survive, though their mental constitution should in other respects by lamentably ill-"adjusted" to the outward world. The story-teller, the musician, the theologian, the actor, or even the mere charming fellow, have never lacked means of support, however helpless they might individually have been to conform with those outward relations which we know as the powers of nature. The reason is very plain. To the individual man, as a social being, the interests of his fellow are a part of his environment. If his powers correspond to the wants of this social environment, he may survive, even though he be ill-adapted to the natural or "outer" environment. But these wants are pure subjective ideals, with nothing outward to correspond to them. So that, as far as the individual is concerned, it becomes necessary to modify Spencer's survival formula still further, by introducing into the term environment a reference, not only to existent things, but also to ideal wants. It would have to run in some such way as this: "Excellence of the individual mind consists in the establishment of inner relations more and more extensively conformed to the outward facts of nature, and to the ideal wants of the individual's fellows, but all of such a character as will promote survival or physical prosperity."

But here, again, common sense will meet us with an objection. Mankind desiderate certain qualities in the individual which are incompatible with his chance of survival being a maximum. Why do we all so eulogize and love the heroic, recklessly generous, and disinterested type of character? These qualities certainly imperil the survival of their possessor. The reason is very plain. Even if headlong courage, pride, and martyr-spirit do ruin the individual, they benefit the community as a whole whenever they are displayed by one of its members against a competing tribe. "It is death to you, but fun for us." Our interest in having the hero as he is, plays indirectly into the hands of our survival, though not of his.

This explicit acknowledgment of the survival interests of the tribe, as accounting for many interests in the individual which seem at first sight either unrelated to survival or at war with it, seems, after all, to bring back unity and simplicity into the Spencerian formula. Why, the Spencerian may ask, may not all the luxuriant foliage of ideal interests—aesthetic, philosophic, theologic, and the rest—which co-exist along with that of survival, be present in the tribe and so form part of the individual's environment, merely by virtue of the fact that they minister in an indirect way to the survival of the tribe as a whole? The disinterested scientific appetite of cognition, the sacred philosophic love of consistency, the craving for luxury and beauty, the passion for amusement, may all find their proper significance as processes of mind, strictly so-called, in the incidental utilitarian discoveries which flow from the energy they set in motion. Conscience, thoroughness, purity, love of truth, susceptibility to discipline, eager delight in fresh impressions, although none of them are traits of Intelligence *in se,* may thus be marks of a general mental energy, without which victory over nature and over other human competitors would be impossible. And, as victory means survival, and survival is the criterion of Intelligent "Correspondence," these qualities, though not expressed in the fundamental law of mind, may yet have been all the while understood by Mr. Spencer to form so many secondary consequences and corollaries of that law.

But here it is decidedly time to take our stand and refuse our aid in propping up Mr. Spencer's definition by any further good-natured translations and supplementary contributions of our own. It is palpable at a glance that a mind whose survival interest could only be adequately secured by such a wasteful array of energy squandered on side issues would be immeasurably inferior to one like that which we supposed a few pages back, in which the monomania of tribal preservation should be the one all-devouring passion.

Surely there is nothing in the essence of intelligence which should oblige it forever to delude itself as to its own ends, and to strive towards a goal successfully only at the cost of consciously appearing to have far other aspirations in view.

A furnace which should produce along with its metal fifty different varieties of ash and slag, a planing-mill whose daily yield in shavings far exceeded that in boards, would rightly be pronounced inferior to one of the usual sort, even though more energy should be displayed in its working, and at moments some of that energy be directly effective. If ministry to survival be the sole criterion of mental excellence, then luxury and amusement, Shakespeare, Beethoven, Plato, and Marcus Aurelius, stellar spectroscopy, diatom markings, and nebular hypotheses are by-products on too wasteful a scale. The slag-heap is too big—it abstracts more energy than it contributes to the ends of the machine; and every serious evolutionist ought resolutely to bend his attention henceforward to the reduction in number and amount of these outlying interests, and the diversion of the energy they absorb into purely prudential channels.

Here, then, is our dilemma: One man may say that the law of mental development is dominated solely by the principle of conservation; another, that richness is the criterion of mental evolution; a third, that pure cognition of the actual is the essence of worthy thinking—but who shall pretend to decide which is right? The umpire would have to bring a standard of his own upon the scene, which would be just as subjective and personal as the standards used by the contestants. And yet some standard there must be, if we are to attempt to define in any way the worth of different mental manifestations.

Is it not already clear to the reader's mind that the whole difficulty in making Mr. Spencer's law work lies in the fact that it is not really a constitutive, but a regulative, law of thought which he is erecting, and that he does not frankly say so? Every law of Mind must be either a law of the *cogitatum* or a law of the *cogitandum*. If it be a law in the sense of an analysis of what we *do* think, then it will include error, nonsense, the worthless as well as the worthy, metaphysics, and mythologies as well as scientific truths which mirror the actual environment. But such a law of the *cogitatum* is already well known. It is no other than the association of ideas according to their several modes; or, rather, it is this association definitively perfected by the inclusion of the teleological factor of interest by Mr. Hodgson in the fifth chapter of his masterly "Time and Space."

That Mr. Spencer, in the part of his work which we are considering, has no such law as this in view is evident from the fact that he has striven to give an original formulation to such a law in another part of his book,* in that chapter, namely, on the associability of relations, in the first volume, where the apperception of times and places, and the suppression of association by similarity, are made to explain the facts in a way whose operose ineptitude has puzzled many a simple reader.

Now, every living man would instantly define right thinking as thinking in correspondence with reality. But Spencer, in saying that right thought is that which conforms to existent outward relations, and this exclusively, undertakes to decide what the reality *is*. In other words, under cover of an apparently formal definition he really smuggles in a material definition of the most far-reaching import. For the Stoic, to whom *vivere convenienter naturæ* was also the law of mind, the reality was an archetypal Nature; for the Christian, whose mental law is to discover the will of God, and make one's actions correspond thereto, *that* is the reality. In fact, the philosophic problem which all the ages have been trying to solve in order to make thought in some way correspond with it, and which disbelievers in philosophy call insoluble, is just that: What is the reality? All the

* H. Spencer, *Principles of Psychology* (*sic*), 1855. Ed.

thinking, all the conflict of ideals, going on in the world at the present moment is in some way tributary to this quest. To attempt, therefore, with Mr. Spencer, to decide the matter merely incidentally, to forestall discussion by a definition—to carry the position by surprise, in a word—is a proceeding savoring more of piracy than philosophy. No, Spencer's definition of what we ought to think cannot be suffered to lurk in ambush; it must stand out explicitly with the rest, and expect to be challenged and give an account of itself like any other ideal norm of thought.

We have seen how he seems to vacillate in his determination of it. At one time, "scientific" thought, mere passive mirroring of outward nature, purely registrative cognition; at another time, thought in the exclusive service of survival, would seem to be his ideal. Let us consider the latter ideal first, since it has the polyp's authority in its favor: "We must survive—that end must regulate all our thought." The poor man who said to Talleyrand, *"Il faut bien que je vive!"* expressed it very well. But criticise this ideal, or transcend it as Talleyrand did by his cool reply, *"Je n'en vois pas la necessité,"* and it can say nothing more for itself. *A priori* it is a mere brute teleological affirmation on a par with all others. Vainly you should hope to prove it to a person bent on suicide, who has but the one longing—to escape, to cease. Vainly you would argue with a Buddhist or a German pessimist, for they feel the full imperious strength of the desire, but have an equally profound persuasion of its essential wrongness and mendacity. Vainly, too, would you talk to a Christian, or even to any believer in the simple creed that the deepest meaning of the world is moral. For they hold that mere conformity with the outward—worldly success and survival—is not the absolute and exclusive end. In the *failures* to "adjust"—in the rubbish-heap, according to Spencer —lies, for them, the real key to the truth—the sole mission of life being to teach that the outward actual is not the whole of being.

And now—if, falling back on the scientific ideal, you say that to *know* is the one τέλος of intelligence—not only will the inimitable Turkish cadi in Layard's Nineveh praise God in your face that he seeks not that which he requires not, and ask, "Will much knowledge create thee a double belly?"—not only may I, if it please me, legitimately refuse to stir from my fool's paradise of theosophy and mysticism, in spite of all your calling (since, after all, your true knowledge and my pious feeling have alike nothing to back them save their seeming good to our respective personalities)—not only this, but to the average sense of mankind, whose ideal of mental nature is best expressed by the word "richness," your statistical and cognitive intelligence will seem insufferably narrow, dry, tedious, and unacceptable.

The truth appears to be that every individual man may, if it please him, set up his private categorical imperative of what rightness or excellence in thought shall consist in, and these different ideals, instead of entering upon the scene armed with a warrant—whether derived from the polyp or from a transcendental source—appear only as so many brute affirmations left to fight it out upon the chessboard among themselves. They are, at best, postulates, each of which must depend on the general consensus of experience as a whole to bear out its validity. The formula which proves to have the most massive destiny will be the true one. But this is a point which can only be solved *ambulando*, and not by any *a priori* definition. The attempt to forestall the decision is free to all to make, but all make it at their risk. Our respective hypotheses and postulates help to shape the course of thought, but the only thing which we all agree in assuming is, that thought will be coerced away from them if they are wrong. If Spencer to-day says, "Bow to the actual," whilst Swinburne spurns "compromise with the nature of things," I exclaim, *"Fiat justitia, pereat mundus,"* and Mill says, "To hell I will go, rather than 'adjust' myself to an evil God," what umpire can there be between us but the future? The idealists and the empiricists confront each other like Guelphs and Ghibellines, but each alike waits for adoption, as it were, by the course of events.

In other words, we are all fated to be *a priori* teleologists whether we will or not. Interests which we bring with us, and simply posit or take our stand upon, are the very flour out of which our mental dough is kneaded. The organism of thought, from the vague dawn of discomfort or ease in the polyp to the intellectual joy of Laplace among his formulas, is teleological through and through. Not a cognition occurs but feeling is there to comment on it, to stamp it as of greater or less worth. Spencer and Plato are *ejusdem farinæ*. To attempt to hoodwink teleology out of sight by saying nothing about it, is the vainest of procedures. Spencer merely takes sides with the τέλος he happens to prefer, whether it be that of physical well-being or that of cognitive registration. He represents a particular teleology. Well might teleology (had she a voice) exclaim with Emerson's Brahma:

> "If the red slayer think he slays,
> Or if the slain think he is slain,

> They know not well the subtle ways
> I keep, and pass and turn again.
>
> . . . .
>
> "They reckon ill who leave me out;
> When me they fly, I am the wings;
> I am the doubter and the doubt," . . .

But now a scientific man, feeling something uncanny in this omnipresence of a teleological factor dictating *how* the mind shall correspond—an interest seemingly tributary to nothing non-mental—may ask us what we meant by saying sometime back that in one sense it is perfectly possible to express the existence of interests in non-mental terms. We meant simply this: That the reactions or outward consequences of the interests could be so expressed. The interest of survival which has hitherto been treated as an ideal *should-be,* presiding from the start and marking out the way in which an animal must react, is, from an outward and physical point of view, nothing more than an objective future implication of the reaction (if it occurs) as an actual fact. If the animal's brain acts fortuitously in the right way, he survives. His young do the same. The reference to survival in no way preceded or conditioned the intelligent act; but the fact of survival was merely bound up with it as an incidental consequence, and may, therefore, be called accidental, rather than instrumental, to the production of intelligence. It is the same with all other interests. They are pleasures and pains incidentally implied in the workings of the nervous mechanism, and, therefore, in their ultimate origin, non-mental; for the idiosyncrasies of our nervous centres are mere "spontaneous variations," like any of those which form the ultimate data for Darwin's theory. A brain which functions so as to insure survival may, therefore, be called intelligent in no other sense than a tooth, a limb, or a stomach, which should serve the same end—the sense, namely, of appropriate; as when we say "that is an intelligent device," meaning a device fitted to secure a certain end which we assume. If *nirvana* were the end, instead of survival, then it is true the means would be different, but in both cases alike the end would not precede the means, or even be coeval with them, but depend utterly upon them, and follow them in point of time. The fox's cunning and the hare's speed are thus alike creations of the non-mental. The τέλος they entail is no more an agent in one case than another, since in both alike it is a resultant. Spencer, then, seems justified in not admitting it to appear as an irreducible ultimate factor of Mind, any more than of Body.

This position is perfectly unassailable so long as one describes the phenomena in this manner from without. The τέλος in that case can only be hypothetically, not imperatively, stated: *if* such and such be the end, then such brain functions are the most intelligent, just as such and such digestive functions are the most appropriate. But such and such cannot be declared *as* the end, except by the commenting mind of an outside spectator. The organs themselves, in their working at any instant, cannot but be supposed indifferent as to what product they are destined fatally to bring forth, cannot be imagined whilst fatally producing one result to have at the same time a notion of a different result which should be their truer end, but which they are unable to secure.

Nothing can more strikingly show, it seems to me, the essential difference between the point of view of consciousness and that of outward existence. We can describe the latter only in teleological terms, hypothetically, or else by the addition of a supposed contemplating mind which measures what it sees going on by its private teleological standard, and judges it intelligent. But consciousness itself is not merely intelligent in this sense. It is *intelligent intelligence*. It seems both to supply the means and the standard by which they are measured. It not only *serves* a final purpose, but *brings* a final purpose—posits, declares it. This purpose is not a mere hypothesis— "*if* survival is to occur, then brain must so perform," etc.—but an imperative decree: "Survival *shall* occur, and, therefore, brain *must* so perform!" It seems hopelessly impossible to formulate anything of this sort in non-mental terms, and this is why I must still contend that the phenomena of subjective "interest," as soon as the animal consciously realizes the latter, appears upon the scene as an absolutely new factor, which we can only suppose to be latent thitherto in the physical environment by crediting the physical atoms, etc., each with a consciousness of its own, approving or condemning its motions.

This, then, must be our conclusion: That no law of the *cogitandum,* no normative receipt for excellence in thinking, can be authoritatively promulgated. The only formal canon that we can apply to mind which is unassailable is the barren truism that it must think rightly. We can express this in terms of correspondence by saying that thought must correspond with truth; but whether that truth be actual or ideal is left undecided.

We have seen that the invocation of the polyp to decide for us that it is actual (apart from the fact that he does not decide in that way) is based on a principle which refutes itself if consistently carried out. Spencer's formula has crumbled into utter worthlessness in our hands, and we have nothing to replace it by except our several individual hypotheses, convictions, and beliefs. Far from being vouched for by the past, these are verified only by the future. They are all of them, in some sense, laws of the ideal. They have to keep house together, and the weakest goes to the wall. The survivors constitute the right way of thinking. While the issue is still undecided, we can only call them our prepossessions. But, decided or not, "go on" we each must for one set of interests or another. The question for each of us in the battle of life is, "Can we *come out* with it?" Some of these interests admit to-day of little dispute. Survival, physical well-being, and undistorted cognition of what is, will hold their ground. But it is truly strange to see writers like Messrs. Huxley and Clifford, who show themselves able to call most things in question, unable, when it comes to the interest of cognition, to touch it with their solvent doubt. They assume some mysterious imperative laid upon the mind, declaring that the infinite ascertainment of facts is its supreme duty, which he who evades is a blasphemer and child of shame. And yet these authors can hardly have failed to reflect, at some moment or other, that the disinterested love of information, and still more the love of consistency in thought (that true scientific *æstrus*), and the ideal fealty to Truth (with a capital T), are all so many particular forms of aesthetic interest, late in their evolution, arising in conjunction with a vast number of similar aesthetic interests, and bearing with them no *a priori* mark of being worthier than these. If we may doubt one, we may doubt all. How shall I say that knowing fact with Messrs. Huxley and Clifford is a better use to put my mind to than feeling good with Messrs. Moody and Sankey, unless by slowly and painfully finding out that in the long run it works best?

I, for my part, cannot escape the consideration, forced upon me at every turn, that the knower is not simply a mirror floating with no foot-hold anywhere, and passively reflecting an order that he comes upon and finds simply existing. The knower is an actor, and co-efficient of the truth on one side, whilst on the other he registers the truth which he helps to create. Mental interests, hypotheses, postulates, so far as they are bases for human action—action which to a great extent transforms the world—help to *make* the truth which they declare. In other words, there belongs to mind, from its birth upward, a spontaneity, a vote. It is in the game, and not a mere looker-on; and its judgments of the *should-be,* its ideals, cannot be peeled off from the body of the *cogitandum* as if they were excrescences, or meant, at most, survival. We know so little about the ultimate nature of things, or of ourselves, that it would be sheer folly dogmatically to say that an ideal rational order may not be real. The only objective criterion of reality is coerciveness, in the long run, over thought. Objective facts, Spencer's outward relations, are real only because they coerce sensation. Any interest which should be coercive on the same massive scale would be *eodem jure* real. By its very essence, the reality of a thought is proportionate to the way it grasps us. Its intensity, its seriousness—its interest, in a word—taking these qualities, not at any given instant, but as shown by the total upshot of experience. If judgments of the *should-be* are fated to grasp us in this way, they are what "correspond." The ancients placed the conception of Fate at the bottom of things—deeper than the gods themselves. "The fate of thought," utterly barren and indeterminate as such a formula is, is the only unimpeachable regulative Law of Mind.

V.

Evolution and Anxiety:
Transition to the Present Age

20. HÖLDERLIN and BAUDELAIRE:
Human Estrangement and World-Weariness

This volume is intended to be read in sequence, and if it has been, only little remains to be said by an editor at this point. The general anxiety which closes the age of romanticism and evolution and which ushers in the age of the present stems from the apprehension that even when the traditional concepts of humane western thought are modernized (romanticized)—those of rationality, freedom, community and moral virtue —even then these concepts will be inadequate to render the revolutions in politics and science intelligible and to direct the tools of technology; man cut off from his historical moorings in an orienting network of concepts and at the mercy of dark impulses within himself loses control of his life and finds existence meaningless.

Traditionally, the good life has been considered possible only on the supposition of the efficacy of consciousness: for example, the efficacy of deliberation in a world that makes conscious sense. With the undermining of consciousness goes the undermining of tradition. Marx and Darwin, and as we shall see, Schopenhauer, Kierkegaard, Nietzsche and and Dostoevsky each took a slice from the fundament of consciousness. Unless a subconscious is exposed which not only makes sense in its own terms but which can bolster consciousness in *some* way (and I think that despite their penetrating insights the romantics did not accomplish enough in this field), then all that will remain of romanticism is a shallow-rooted enthusiasm that withers in the heat of the day. Already in *Hyperion* (1799) from the much-ignored Friedrich Hölderlin (1770– 1843) we hear talk of "the Nothing": a human spirit overextended, hollow and dry like a severed vine, disenchanted. Consciousness is limited, cut off, whereas what is required is a world which is its own: Diotima says to Hyperion: It was no man that you wanted, believe me, you wanted a world. A world which is consciousness's own encompassing object, soaked with value and replete with nourishment, is just what consciousness does not find. What is found, says Hyperion, is a world in which not even a beautiful dream can flourish.*

* *Hyperion: or the Hermit in Greece,* translated by W. Trask (New York: Frederick Ungar Publishing Co., 1965), pp. 29, 57, 80.

Nowhere is optimistic monism more severely attacked than by Hölderlin, the disappointed romantic. In "Hyperion's Song"* he places a gulf between gods and men:

> You wander high in the light
> Over the tender floor, O blessed spirits!
> Glistening airs of the gods
> Lightly caress you
> Like the musician's fingers
> On saintly strings.
>
> Fateless, like the slumbering
> Babe, breathe the heavenly ones;
> Virginally preserved
> In its modest bud
> Their spirit
> Eternally blooms
> And their blessèd eyes
> Gaze in their long and
> Lucid stillness.
>
> Yet we are destined
> Never to come to rest;
> They falter, they fall,
> These suffering mortals,
> In blindness from
> One hour to the next
> Like water hurled from
> Cliff upon cliff
> Down the whole year long into
> The unfathomed.

When we come to the later French poet Charles Baudelaire (1821–1867), consciousness has encased itself, as it were, and openly shuns contact with much of the "natural" world. Of course, by this time the discomfiting question fairly screams for reply: What *is* natural for man? What is natural for a being whose consciousness and imagination can withdraw into itself and work upon its own materials merely? So selective and special can consciousness be that it can find beauty in evil (see Baudelaire's "Flowers of Evil"); thus the poet gives a strange twist to the romantic idea that beauty is a symbol of the moral ideal and that it

---

* *Some Poems of Hölderlin*, translated by Frederic Prokosch, published by New Directions. Reprinted with the kind permission of Mr. Prokosch.

binds up the totality of our experience by reflecting the infinite in the finite: the morally good is not paramount in the reflection—indeed it may be glaring in its absence. The romantic drive for integration is deeply disturbed in Baudelaire. This is illustrated in his "poem in prose," "Anyplace Out of the World."*

Life is a hospital, in which every patient is gripped by the desire to change his bed. To suffer by the fire is one's preference; another is sure he would recover if he were by the window.

It seems to me I should be ever happy if I were someplace else, and this question of moving is one that I am constantly talking over with my soul.

"Tell me, my soul, my poor chilled soul, what do you say to living in Lisbon? It must be very warm there, and like a lizard you would bask happily. It is by the sea; they say that it is built of marble, and that the people have such a horror of vegetation that they tear up all the trees. There is a land after your own soul; a land composed of light and mineral, and with liquid to reflect them."

My soul does not answer.

"Since you love rest, and love to see moving things, will you come and live in that heavenly land, Holland? Maybe you would be happy in a country which you have so frequently admired in pictures. You would love forests of masts, and ships anchored at the doors of houses—what do you say to Rotterdam?"

My soul keeps silent.

"Or perhaps Java appears to you more attractive? Well, we shall find the mind of Europe married to tropical beauty right there."

Not a word. Can my soul be dead?

"Have you sunk then into so deep a stupor that only your pain gives you pleasure? If so, let us go to the lands that are made in the image of death. Poor soul, I know precisely the place for us! We will book passage to Torneo. Still further we will go—to the last limits of the Baltic. And if it be possible, still further from life; we will find our home at the Pole. There the sun only grazes the earth, and the slow alternations of light and night expel variety and bring in the half of nothingness, monotony. We can take great baths of darkness there; while, for our pleasure, the Aurora Borealis shall from time to time scatter its rosy sheaves before us, like reflections of fireworks in hell!"

Finally my soul bursts into speech, and wisely she cries out to me, "Anyplace, anyplace, out of the world!"

* Translated by Bruce Wilshire.

21. SCHOPENHAUER: The Tragedy of the Human Will

With Arthur Schopenhauer (1788–1860) the strand of anxiety emerged early in the nineteenth century and in strictly philosophical form, although Schopenhauer did not gain attention until the middle of the century. What to Schiller, surveying the future in the light of the French Revolution, seemed a protracted struggle on behalf of progress, seemed to Schopenhauer a struggle on behalf of nothing at all. He was convinced that the belief in moral progress was an illusion: Despite all our new science, all our revolutions, all our art, the brutal will to survive with all its hatreds and fears has run along in its subterranean bed essentially unchanged. Consciousness and reason are like foam on a river flicked around by the wind; the current runs elsewhere. As the reader will see from the first page of his *The World as Will and Idea* (1819) below, Schopenhauer stands in the company of Fichte, Schelling and Hegel insofar as he is an idealist; but his eye for both the tragic and the tawdry, along with his unique interpretation of Kant, makes him a strangely incongruous figure, a mordant pessimist.

Like Kant, he declares that discursive and empirical consciousness reveals only the lock-step of phenomena (which were for Schopenhauer causal laws determined by the principle of sufficient reason). Unlike Kant, he believes that the thing-in-itself (noumenon) is not unknown but is directly intuited by us—if we have the will to face it—in the push and pressure of our everyday behavior; it is our frantic will to survive and be happy, and it is irrational, *i.e.*, it is wedded to objects which we know do not satisfy but which we cannot give up. It is only in properly appreciated art (note the romantic theme) that there is any hope for the intellect to escape its servitude to the will.

Schopenhauer speaks for himself:

> The life of every individual, if we survey it as a whole and in general, and only lay stress upon its most significant features, is really always a tragedy, but gone through in detail, it has the character of a comedy. For the deeds and vexations of the day, the restless irritation of the moment, the desires and fears of the week, the mishaps of every hour, are all through chance, which is ever bent upon some jest, scenes of a comedy. . . . Thus, as if fate would add derision to the misery of our existence, our life must contain all the woes of tragedy, and yet we cannot even assert the dignity of tragic characters. . . .

It is perfectly clear, whether we agree with him or not—not a word need be added to ease comprehension.

Indeed, the four figures with which we close this volume—Schopenhauer, Kierkegaard, Nietzsche, Dostoevsky—are writers all so brilliant and all so essentially sad that it might almost make one think that there is some causal connection between sadness and the ability to write brilliantly!

The selections are taken from *The World as Will and Idea*, Vol. I, translated by Haldane and Kemp, London: K. Paul, Trench, Trübner, 1896.

FROM THE FIRST BOOK

"The world is my idea:"—this is a truth which holds good for everything that lives and knows, though man alone can bring it into reflective and abstract consciousness. If he really does this, he has attained to philosophical wisdom. It then becomes clear and certain to him that what he knows is not a sun and an earth, but only an eye that sees a sun, a hand that feels an earth; that the world which surrounds him is there only as idea, *i.e.*, only in relation to something else, the consciousness, which is himself. If any truth can be asserted *a priori,* it is this: for it is the expression of the most general form of all possible and thinkable experience: a form which is more general than time, or space, or causality, for they all presuppose it; and each of these, which we have seen to be just so many modes of the principle of sufficient reason, is valid only for a particular class of ideas; whereas the antithesis of object and subject is the common form of all these classes, is that form under which alone any idea of whatever kind it may be, abstract or intuitive, pure or empirical, is possible and thinkable. No truth therefore is more certain, more independent of all others, and less in need of proof than this, that all that exists for knowledge, and therefore this whole world, is only object in relation to subject, perception of a perceiver, in a word, idea. This is obviously true of the past and the future, as well as of the present, of what is farthest off, as of what is near; for it is true of time and space themselves, in which alone these distinctions arise. All that in any way belongs or can belong to the world is inevitably thus conditioned through the subject, and exists only for the subject. The world is idea.

This truth is by no means new. It was implicitly involved in the sceptical reflections from which Descartes started. Berkeley, however, was the first who distinctly enunciated it, and by this he has rendered a permanent service to philosophy, even though the rest of his teaching should not endure. Kant's primary mistake was the neglect of this principle. . . . How early again this truth was recognised by the wise men of India, appearing indeed as the fundamental tenet of the Vedânta philosophy ascribed to Vyasa, is pointed out by Sir William Jones in the last of his essays: "On the philosophy of the Asiatics" (Asiatic Researches, vol. iv. p. 164), where he says, "The fundamental tenet of the Vedanta school consisted not in denying the existence of matter, that is, of solidity, impenetrability, and extended figure (to deny which would be lunacy), but in correcting the popular notion of it, and in contending that it has no essence independent of mental perception; that existence and perceptibility are convertible terms." These words adequately express the compatibility of empirical reality and transcendental ideality.

In this first book, then, we consider the world only from this side, only so far as it is idea. The inward reluctance with which anyone accepts the world as merely his idea, warns him that this view of it, however true it may be, is nevertheless one-sided, adopted in consequence of some arbitrary abstraction. And yet it is a conception from which he can never free himself. The defectiveness of this view will be corrected in the next book by means of a truth which is not so immediately certain as that from which we start here; a truth at which we can arrive only by deeper research and more severe abstraction, by the separation of what is different and the union of what is identical. This truth, which must be very serious and impressive if not awful to everyone, is that a man can also say and must say, "the world is my will." . . .

From the Second Book

What now impels us to inquiry is just that we are not satisfied with knowing that we have ideas, that they are such and such, and that they are connected according to certain laws, the general expression of which is the principle of sufficient reason. We wish to know the significance of these ideas; we ask whether this world is merely idea; in which case it would pass by us like an empty dream or a baseless vision, not worth our notice; or whether it is also something else, something more than idea, and if so, what. Thus much is certain, that this something we seek for must be completely and in its whole nature different from the idea; that the forms and laws of the idea must therefore be completely foreign to it; further, that we cannot arrive at it from the idea under the guidance of the laws which merely combine objects, ideas, among themselves, and which are the forms of the principle of sufficient reason.

Thus we see already that we can never arrive at the real nature of things from without. However much we investigate, we can never reach anything but images and names. We are like a man who goes round a castle seeking in vain for an entrance, and sometimes sketching the façades. And yet this is the method that has been followed by all philosophers before me.

In fact, the meaning for which we seek of that world which is present to us only as our idea, or the transition from the world as mere idea of the knowing subject to whatever it may be besides this, would never be found if the investigator himself were nothing more than the pure knowing subject (a winged cherub without a body). But he is himself rooted in that world; he finds himself in it as an *individual,* that is to say, his knowledge, which is the necessary supporter of the whole world as idea, is yet always given through the medium of a body, whose affections are, as we have shown, the starting-point for the understanding in the perception of that world. His body is, for the pure knowing subject, an idea like every other idea, an object among objects. Its movements and actions are so far known to him in precisely the same way as the changes of all other perceived objects, and would be just as strange and incomprehensible to him if their meaning were not explained for him in an entirely different way. Otherwise he would see his actions follow upon given motives with the constancy of a law of nature, just as the changes of other objects follow upon causes, stimuli, or motives. But he would not understand the influence of the motives any more than the connection between every other effect which he sees and its cause. He would then call the inner nature of these manifestations and actions of his body which he did not understand a force, a quality, or a character, as he pleased, but he would have no further insight into it. But all this is not the case; indeed the answer to the riddle is given to the subject of knowledge who appears as an individual, and the answer is *will*. This and this alone gives him the key to his own existence, reveals to him the significance, shows him the inner mechanism of his being, of his action, of his movements. The body is given in two entirely different ways to the subject of knowledge, who becomes an individual only through his identity with it. It is given as an idea in intelligent perception, as an object among objects and subject to the laws of objects. And it is also given in quite a different way as that which is immediately known to everyone, and is signified by the word *will*. Every true act of his will is also at once and without exception a movement of his body. The act of will and the movement of the body are not two different things objectively known, which the bond of causality unites; they do not stand in the relation of cause and effect; they are one and the same, but they are given in entirely different ways,—immediately, and again in perception for the understanding. The action of the body is nothing but the act of the will objectified, *i.e.*, passed into perception. It will appear later that this is true of every movement of the body, not merely those which follow upon motives, but also involuntary movements which follow upon mere stimuli, and, indeed, that the whole body is nothing but objectified will, *i.e.*, will becomes idea. All this will be proved and made quite clear in the course of this work. In one respect, therefore, I shall call the body the *objectivity of will;* . . . Thus in a certain sense we may also say that will is the knowledge *a priori* of the body and the body is the knowledge *a posteriori* of the will. . . .

From the Third Book

We should see the will express itself here in the lowest grade as blind striving, an obscure, inarticulate impulse, far from susceptible of being directly known. It is the simplest and the weakest mode of its objectification. But it appears as this blind and unconscious striving in the whole of unorganised nature, in all those original forces of which it is the work of physics and chemistry to discover and to study the laws, and each of which manifests itself to us in millions of phenomena which are exactly similar and regular, and show no trace of individual character, but are mere multiplicity through space and time, *i.e.*, through the *principium individuationis,* as a picture is multiplied through the facets of a glass.

From grade to grade objectifying itself more distinctly, yet still completely without consciousness as an obscure striving force, the will acts in the vegetable kingdom also, in which the bond of its phenomena consists no longer properly of causes, but of stimuli; and, finally, also in the vegetative part of the animal phenomenon, in the production and maturing of the animal, and in sustaining its inner economy, in which the manifestation of will is still always necessarily determined by stimuli. The ever-ascending grades of the objectification of will bring us at last to the point at which the individual that expresses the Idea could no longer receive food for its assimilation through mere movement following upon stimuli. For such a stimulus must be waited for, but the food has now come to be of a more special and definite kind, and with the ever-increasing multiplicity of the individual phenomena, the crowd and confusion has become so great that they interfere with each other, and the chance of the individual that is moved merely by stimuli and must wait for its food would be too unfavourable. From the point, therefore, at which the animal has delivered itself from the egg or the womb in which it vegetated without consciousness, its food must be sought out and selected. For this purpose movement following upon motives, and therefore consciousness, becomes necessary, and consequently it appears as an agent, μηχανη, called in at this stage of the objectification of will for the conservation of the individual and the propagation of the species. It appears represented by the brain or a large ganglion, just as every other effort or determination of the will which objectifies itself is represented by an organ, that is to say, manifests itself for the idea as an organ. But with this means of assistance, this μηχανη, the *world as idea* comes into existence at a stroke, with all its forms, object and subject, time, space, multiplicity, and causality. The world now shows its second side. Till now *mere will,* it becomes also *idea,* object of the knowing subject. The will, which up to this point followed its tendency in the dark with unerring certainty, has at this grade kindled for itself a light as a means which became necessary for getting rid of the disadvantage which arose from the throng and the complicated nature of its manifestations, and which would have accrued precisely to the most perfect of them. The hitherto infallible certainty and regularity with which it worked in unorganised and merely vegetative nature, rested upon the fact that it alone was active in its original nature, as blind impulse, will, without assistance, and also without interruption, from a second and entirely different world, the world as idea, which is indeed only the image of its own inner being, but is yet of quite another nature, and now encroaches on the connected whole of its phenomena. Hence its infallible certainty comes to an end. Animals are already exposed to illusion, to deception. They have, however, merely ideas of perception, no conceptions, no reflection, and they are therefore bound to the present; they cannot have regard for the future. It seems as if this knowledge without reason was not in all cases sufficient for its end, and at times required, as it were, some assistance. For the very remarkable phenomenon presents itself, that the blind working of the will and the activity enlightened by knowledge encroach in a most astonishing manner upon each other's spheres in two kinds of phenomena. In the one case we find in the very midst of those actions of animals which are guided by perceptive knowledge and its motives one kind of action which is accomplished apart from these, and thus through the necessity of the blindly acting will. I refer to those mechanical instincts which are guided by no motive or knowledge, and which yet have the appearance of performing their work from abstract rational motives. The other case, which is opposed to this, is that in which, on the contrary, the light of knowledge penetrates into the workshop of the blindly active will, and illuminates the vegetative functions of the human organism. I mean clairvoyance. Finally, when the will has attained to the highest grade of its objectification, that knowledge of the understanding given to brutes to which the senses supply the data, out of which there arises mere perception confined to what is immediately present, does not suffice. That complicated, many-sided, imaginative being, man, with his many needs, and exposed as he is to innumerable dangers, must, in order to exist, be lighted by a double knowledge; a higher power, as it were, of perceptive knowledge must be given him, and also reason, as the faculty of framing abstract conceptions. With this there has appeared reflection, surveying the future and the past, and, as a consequence, deliberation, care, the power of premeditated action independent of the present, and finally, the full and distinct consciousness of one's own deliberate volition as such. Now if with mere knowledge of perception there arose the possibility of illusion and deception, by which the previous infallibility of the blind striving of will was done away with, so that mechanical and other instincts, as expressions of unconscious will, had to lend their help in the midst of those that were conscious, with the entrance of reason that certainty and infallibility of the expressions of will (which at the other extreme in unorganised nature appeared as strict conformity to law) is almost entirely lost; instinct disappears altogether; deliberation, which is supposed to take the place of everything else, begets (as was shown in the First Book) irresolution and uncertainty; then error becomes possible, and in many cases obstructs the adequate objectification of the will in action. For although in the character the will has already taken its definite and unchangeable bent or direction, in accordance with which volition, when occasioned by the presence of a motive, invariably takes place, yet error can falsify its expressions, for it introduces illusive motives that take the place of the real ones which they resemble; as, for example, when superstition forces on a man imaginary motives which impel him to a course of action directly opposed to the way in which the will would otherwise express itself in the given circumstances. Agamemnon slays his daughter; a miser dispenses alms, out of pure egotism, in the hope that he will some day receive an hundred-fold; and so on.

Thus knowledge generally, rational as well as merely sensuous, proceeds originally from the will itself, belongs to the inner being of the higher grades of its objectification as a mere $\mu\eta\chi\alpha\nu\eta$, a means of supporting the individual and the species, just like any organ of the body. Originally destined for the service of the will for the accomplishment of its aims, it remains almost throughout entirely subjected to its service: it is so in all brutes and in almost all men. Yet we shall see in the Third Book how in certain individual men knowledge can deliver itself from this bondage, throw off its yoke, and, free from all the aims of will, exist purely for itself, simply as a clear mirror of the world, which is the source of art. Finally, in the Fourth Book, we shall see how, if this kind of knowledge reacts on the will, it can bring about self-surrender, *i.e.*, resignation, which is the final goal, and indeed the inmost nature of all virtue and holiness, and is deliverance from the world. . . .

FROM THE FOURTH BOOK

In the aesthetical mode of contemplation we have found *two inseparable constituent parts*—the knowledge of the object, not as individual thing but as Platonic Idea, that is, as the enduring form of this whole species of things; and the self-consciousness of the knowing person, not as individual, but as *pure will-less subject of knowledge*. The condition under which both these constituent parts appear always united was found to be the abandonment of the method of knowing which is bound to the principle of sufficient reason, and which, on the other hand, is the only kind of knowledge that is of value for the service of the will and also for science. Moreover, we shall see that the pleasure which is produced by the contemplation of the beautiful arises from these two constituent parts, sometimes more from the one, sometimes more from the other, according to what the object of the æsthetical contemplation may be.

All *willing* arises from want, therefore from deficiency, and therefore from suffering. The satisfaction of a wish ends it; yet for one wish that is satisfied there remain at least ten which are denied. Further, the desire lasts long, the demands are infinite; the satisfaction is short and scantily measured out. But even the final satisfaction is itself only apparent; every satisfied wish at once makes room for a new one; both are illusions; the one is known to be so, the other not yet. No attained object of desire can give lasting satisfaction, but merely a fleeting gratification; it is like the alms thrown to the beggar, that keeps him alive to-day that his misery may be prolonged till the morrow. Therefore, so long as our consciousness is filled by our will, so long as we are given up to the throng of desires with their constant hopes and fears, so long as we are the subject of willing, we can never have lasting happiness nor peace. It is essentially all the same whether we pursue or flee, fear injury or seek enjoyment; the care for the constant demands of the will, in whatever form it may be, continually occupies and sways the consciousness; but without peace no true well-being is possible. The subject of willing is thus constantly stretched on the revolving wheel of Ixion, pours water into the sieve of the Danaids, is the ever-longing Tantalus.

But when some external cause or inward disposition lifts us suddenly out of the endless stream of willing, delivers knowledge from the slavery of the will, the attention is no longer directed to the motives of willing, but comprehends things free from their relation to the will, and thus observes them without personal interest, without subjectivity, purely objectively, gives itself entirely up to them so far as they are ideas, but not in so far as they are motives. Then all at once the peace which we were always seeking, but which always fled from us on the former path of the desires, comes to us of its own accord, and it is well with us. It is the painless state which Epicurus prized as the highest good and as the state of the gods; for we are for the moment set free from the miserable striving of the will; we keep the Sabbath of the penal servitude of willing; the wheel of Ixion stands still.

But this is just the state which I described above as necessary for the knowledge of the Idea, as pure contemplation, as sinking oneself in perception, losing oneself in the object, forgetting all individuality, surrendering that kind of knowledge which follows the principle of sufficient reason, and comprehends only relations; the state by means of which at once and inseparably the perceived particular thing is raised to the Idea of its whole species, and the knowing individual to the pure subject of will-less knowledge, and as such they are both taken out of the stream of time and all other relations. It is then all one whether we see the sun set from the prison or from the palace.

Inward disposition, the predominance of knowing over willing, can produce this state under any circumstances. This is shown by those admirable Dutch artists who directed this purely objective perception to the most insignificant objects, and established a lasting monument of their objectivity and spiritual peace in their pictures of *still life,* which the aesthetic beholder does not look on without emotion; for they present to him the peaceful, still, frame of mind of the artist, free from will, which was needed to contemplate such insignificant things so objectively, to observe them so attentively, and to repeat this perception so intelligently; and as the picture enables the onlooker to participate in this state, his emotion is often increased by the contrast between it and the unquiet frame of mind, disturbed by vehement willing, in which he finds himself. In the same spirit, landscape-painters, and particularly Ruisdael, have often painted very insignificant country scenes, which produce the same effect even more agreeably.

All this is accomplished by the inner power of an artistic nature alone; but that purely objective disposition is facilitated and assisted from without by suitable objects, by the abundance of natural beauty which invites contemplation, and even presses itself upon us. Whenever it discloses itself suddenly to our view, it almost always succeeds in delivering us, though it may be only for a moment, from subjectivity, from the slavery of the will, and in raising us to the state of pure knowing. This is why the man who is tormented by passion, or want, or care, is so suddenly revived, cheered, and restored by a single free glance into nature: the storm of passion, the pressure of desire and fear, and all the miseries of willing are then at once, and in a marvellous manner, calmed and appeased. For at the moment at which, freed from the will, we give ourselves up to pure will-less knowing, we pass into a world from which everything is absent that influenced our will and moved us so violently through it. This freeing of knowledge lifts us as wholly and entirely away from all that, as do sleep and dreams; happiness and unhappiness have disappeared; we are no longer individual; the individual is forgotten; we are only pure subject of knowledge; we are only that *one* eye of the world which looks out from all knowing creatures, but which can become perfectly free from the service of will in man alone. Thus all difference of individuality so entirely disappears, that it is all the same whether the perceiving eye belongs to a mighty king or to a wretched beggar; for neither joy nor complaining can pass that boundary with us. So near us always lies a sphere in which we escape from all our misery; but who has the strength to continue long in it? As soon as any single relation to our will, to our person, even of these objects of our pure contemplation, comes again into consciousness, the magic is at an end; we fall back into the knowledge which is governed by the principle of sufficient reason; we know no longer the Idea, but the particular thing, the link of a chain to which we also belong, and we are again abandoned to all our woe. Most men remain almost always at this standpoint because they entirely lack objectivity, *i.e.*, genius. Therefore they have no pleasure in being alone with nature; they need company, or at least a book. For their knowledge remains subject to their will; they seek, therefore, in objects, only some relation to their will, and whenever they see anything that has no such relation, there sounds within them, like a ground bass in music, the constant inconsolable cry, "It is of no use to me"; thus in solitude the most beautiful surroundings have for them a desolate, dark, strange, and hostile appearance. . . .

Before us there is certainly only nothingness. But that which resists this passing into nothing, our nature, is indeed just the will to live, which we ourselves are as it is our world. That we abhor annihilation so greatly is simply another expression of the fact that we so strenuously will life, and are nothing but this will, and know nothing besides it. But if we turn our glance from our own needy and embarrassed condition to those who have overcome the world, in whom the will, having attained to perfect self-knowledge, found itself again in all, and then freely denied itself, and who then merely wait to see the last trace of it vanish with the body which it animates; then, instead of the restless striving and effort, instead of the constant transition from wish to fruition, and from joy to sorrow, instead of the never-satisfied and never-dying hope which constitutes the life of the man who wills, we shall see that peace which is above all reason, that perfect calm of the spirit, that deep rest, that inviolable confidence and serenity, the mere reflection of which in the countenance, as Raphael and Correggio have represented it, is an entire and certain gospel; only knowledge remains, the will has vanished. We look with deep and painful longing upon this state, beside which the misery and wretchedness of our own is brought out clearly by the contrast. Yet this is the only consideration which can afford us lasting consolation, when, on the one hand, we have recognised incurable suffering and endless misery as essential to the manifestation of will, the world; and, on the other hand, see the world pass away with the abolition of will, and retain before us only empty nothingness. Thus, in this way, by contemplation of the life and conduct of saints, whom it is certainly rarely granted us to meet with in our own experience, but who are brought before our eyes by their written history, and, with the stamp of inner truth, by art, we must banish the dark impression of that nothingness which we discern behind all virtue and holiness as their final goal, and which we fear as children fear the dark; we must not even evade it like the Indians, through myths and meaningless words, such as re-absorption in Brahma or the Nirvana of the Buddhists. Rather do we freely acknowledge that what remains after the entire abolition of will is for all those who are still full of will certainly nothing; but, conversely, to those in whom the will has turned and has denied itself, this our world, which is so real, with all its suns and milky-ways—is nothing.*

22. KIERKEGAARD: Dread in Human Existence

Like Marx, the Danish thinker Sören Kierkegaard (1813–1855) rebelled against Hegel, and for a similar reason. Hegel is too cerebral; he needs to be "realized" and made directly relevant to existence. But unlike Marx, who never gave up a basic rationalism (it was only the objects of systematizing thought that had to be recast), Kierkegaard maintained that reality simply could not be thought by reason at all. And by reality he meant primarily individual human existence.

In the case of the existing person, conscious of the future into which he is thrust, reality cannot be a perfect union of essence and existence, argued Kierkegaard, because consciousness at any moment is always more than can ever be made an object for a subsequent reflective moment of that consciousness. That is, the essence of consciousness, or *what* it is, can never be fully grasped rationally. Reality is precisely this

* This is also just the Prajna-Paramita of the Buddhists, the "beyond all knowledge," *i.e.*, the point at which subject and object are no more.

geyserlike consciousness directed upon the future which overflows the categories of all rational reflection, slips around them, and is—to use his word—elusive. Directly contradicting Hegel, Kierkegaard asserts that the truth of inwardness is found in this gushing, elusive, prereflective state.

For Kierkegaard the elusive "more" in consciousness drives us on in our existence—indeed it is the heart of our existence—and it surprises us with needs, affinities, and leaps of faith in art, ethics and religion. The leap is greatest in religion, for here the object, God, is also in its own way elusive; that is, Christ our divine savior is the eternal and infinite incarnated in the finite and temporal, and this, says Kierkegaard, is a repulsive absurdity to reason. All that we can be sure of is the intensity, sincerity and commitment with which we believe, come what may, or the *how* of our believing and not the *what* believed. Thus Kierkegaard's unprecedented epistemological theory is that the truth of the individual is this committed, integrated, unshakable subjectivity. It is a theory which integrates belief, emotion and daily life in an era which deeply desired the integration; but it integrates these at the risk of producing a new split between the intellect and life.*

Thus Kierkegaard's work can be understood in part as a breakdown of the romantic ideal. The ideal was to find in the temporal process a rational and finite symbol for the totality of reality. Like Hölderlin, Kierkegaard sets a gulf between God and man.** In fact, he seems intent upon exacerbating the breakdown of the romantic ideal of unity, for he conceives the infinite and eternal God in the most static, Aristotelian terms imaginable. Temporal man is depicted as yearning for salvation in the embrace of this distant eternal God; but he dreads Him as well, since He is unknown to reason and, for noneternal man, He is forever not-yet. Dread is fear of the unknown and the not-yet; we both want and do not want the object dreaded; it is an ambivalent "sympathetic antipathy and antipathetic sympathy."

Nearly all the ideals of romanticism are either shipwrecked or exaggerated in Kierkegaard: reason, totality, spontaneity, community and emotion. For this thinker, the heart of consciousness is opaque and turbulent; it blows before our gaze like bubbles, possibilities for our life—choices, contingencies—which structure our existence, but are not-yet, are just nothing. Demoniacal dread is dread of the not-yet when the not-yet is the unacknowledged and unachieved good. To modify a line from Shakespeare: We are of such stuff as dreams are made on, and our little life is rounded with a cry.

---

* See his *Concluding Unscientific Postscript* (Princeton University Press, 1941), especially pp. 74–76, 99–113, 116, 160, 267–279, 296.
** *Ibid.*, p. 296.

These passages are taken from Kierkegaard's *The Concept of Dread* (1844).*

Innocence is ignorance. In his innocence man is not determined as spirit but is soulishly determined in immediate unity with his natural condition. Spirit is dreaming in man. This view is in perfect accord with that of the Bible, and by refusing to ascribe to man in the state of innocence a knowledge of the difference between good and evil it condemns all the notions of merit Catholicism has imagined.

In this state there is peace and repose; but at the same time there is something different, which is not dissension and strife, for there is nothing to strive with. What is it then? Nothing. But what effect does nothing produce? It begets dread. This is the profound secret of innocence, that at the same time it is dread. Dreamingly the spirit projects its own reality, but this reality is nothing, but this nothing constantly sees innocence outside of it.

Dread is a qualification of the dreaming spirit, and as such it has its place in psychology. When awake, the difference between myself and my other† is posited; sleeping, it is suspended; dreaming, it is a nothing vaguely hinted at. The reality of the spirit constantly shows itself in a form which entices its possibility, but it is away as soon as one grasps after it, and it is a nothing which is able only to alarm. More it cannot do so long as it only shows itself. One almost never sees the concept dread dealt with in psychology, and I must therefore call attention to the fact that it is different from fear and similar concepts which refer to something definite, whereas dread is freedom's reality as possibility for possibility.‡ One does not therefore find dread in the beast, precisely for the reason that by nature the beast is not qualified by spirit.

When we consider the dialectical determinants in dread, it appears that they have precisely the characteristic ambiguity of psychology.

* Translated by Walter Lowrie. Reprinted by permission of Princeton University Press. Copyright © 1944 by Princeton University Press.

† "My other" is my eternal life or spirit. It is in the state of innocency that the spirit, as in a dream, manifests itself as possibility. That is, one senses freedom. (Trans.)

‡ From the context, what one expects is "possibility for freedom," and the Danish editors do not hesitate to say that this is what is meant. To establish their point, they refer to p. 81 [of original edition—Ed.] where we read that "The possibility of freedom manifests itself before freedom" and to p. 99 where it is recalled that dread has been defined as "freedom's appearance before itself in possibility." In *Sickness unto Death* S. K. uses "possibility" and "freedom" interchangeably. (Trans.)

Dread is a *sympathetic antipathy and an antipathetic sympathy*. One easily sees, I think, that this is much more truly a psychological subject than is the concupiscence of which we have spoken. Language confirms this completely. One speaks of a sweet dread, a sweet feeling of apprehension, one speaks of a strange dread, a shrinking dread, etc.

The dread which is posited in innocence is, in the first place, not guilt; in the second place, it is not a heavy burden, not a suffering which cannot be brought into harmony with the felicity of innocence. If we observe children, we find this dread more definitely indicated as a seeking after adventure, a thirst for the prodigious, the mysterious. The fact that there are children in whom this is not found proves nothing, for neither in the beast does it exist, and the less spirit, the less dread. This dread belongs to the child so essentially that it cannot do without it; even though it alarms him, it captivates him nevertheless by its sweet feeling of apprehension. In all nations in which the childish character is preserved as the dreaming of the spirit this dread is found, and the deeper it is, the more profound is the nation. It is only a prosaic stupidity which thinks that this is a disorganization. Dread has here the same significance melancholy has at a far later point where freedom, after having passed through imperfect forms of its history, has to come to itself in a deeper sense.

Just as the relation of dread to its object, to something which is nothing (language in this instance also is pregnant: it speaks of being in dread of nothing), is altogether ambiguous, so will the transition here from innocence to guilt be correspondingly so dialectical that the explanation is and must be psychological. The qualitative leap is outside of ambiguity, but he who through dread becomes guilty is innocent, for it was not he himself but dread, an alien power, which laid hold of him, a power he did not love but dreaded—and yet he is guilty, for he sank in the dread which he loved even while he feared it. There is nothing in the world more ambiguous, and therefore this is the only psychological explanation, although (to repeat what I have said) it never occurs to it to want to be the explanation which explains the qualitative leap. Every theory about the prohibition tempting Adam or the seducer deceiving him has only for a superficial observation sufficient ambiguity, while it perverts ethics, introduces a quantitative determination, and would by the help of psychology pay man a compliment from which everyone who is ethically developed would beg to be excused, regarding it as a new and deeper seduction.

Everything turns upon dread coming into view. Man is a synthesis of the soulish and the bodily. But a synthesis is unthinkable if the two are not united in a third factor. This third factor is the spirit. In the state of innocence man is not merely an animal, for if at any time of his life he was merely an animal, he never would become a man. So then the spirit is present, but in a state of immediacy, a dreaming state. Forasmuch as it is present, it is in one way a hostile power, for it constantly disturbs the relation between soul and body, a relation which endures, and yet does not endure, inasmuch as it has endurance only by means of the spirit. On the other hand, it is a friendly power which has precisely the function of constituting the relationship. What then is man's relation to this ambiguous power? How is spirit related to itself and to its situation? It is related as dread. The spirit cannot do away with itself; nor can it grasp itself so long as it has itself outside of itself. Neither can man sink down into the vegetative life, for he is determined as spirit. He cannot flee from dread, for he loves it; really he does not love it, for he flees from it. Innocence has now reached its apex. It is ignorance, but not an animal brutality, but an ignorance which is qualified by spirit, but which precisely is dread, because its ignorance is about nothing. Here there is no knowledge of good and evil, etc., but the whole reality of knowledge is projected in dread as the immense nothing of ignorance.

Innocence still *is*, but one word suffices, and with that ignorance is concentrated. Innocence of course cannot understand this word; but dread has as it were obtained its first prey; instead of nothing, innocence gets an enigmatic word. So when it is related in Genesis that God said to Adam, "Only of the tree of the knowledge of good and evil thou shalt not eat," it is a matter of course that Adam did not really understand this word. For how could he have understood the difference between good and evil, seeing that this distinction was in fact consequent upon the enjoyment of the fruit?

When one assumes that the prohibition awakens the desire, one posits a knowledge instead of ignorance; for Adam would have had to have a knowledge of freedom, since his desire was to use it. The explanation therefore anticipates what was subsequent. The prohibition alarms Adam [induces a state of dread] because the prohibition awakens in him the possibility of freedom. That which passed innocence by as the nothing of dread has now entered into him, and here again it is a nothing, the alarming possibility of *being able*. What it is he is able to do, of that he has no conception; to suppose that he had some conception is to presuppose, as commonly is done, what came later, the distinction between good and evil. There is only the possibility of being able, as a higher form of ignorance, as a heightened expression of dread, because this in a more profound sense is and is not, because in a more profound sense he loves it and flees from it.

After the word of prohibition follows the word of judgment: "Thou shalt surely die." What it means to die, Adam of course cannot conceive; but if one assumes that these words were said to him, there is nothing to prevent his having a notion of the terrible. Indeed even the beast is able to understand the mimic expression and movement in the speaker's voice, without understanding the word. In case one lets the prohibition awaken desire, one may also let the word about punishment awaken a deterring conception. However, this confuses things. The terrible becomes in this instance merely dread; for Adam has not understood what was said, and here again we have only the ambiguity of dread. The infinite possibility of being able (awakened by the prohibition) draws closer for the fact that this possibility indicates a possibility as its consequence.

Thus innocence is brought to its last extremity. It is in dread in relation to the prohibition and the punishment. It is not guilty, and yet it is in dread, as though it were lost. . . .

The demoniacal is dread of the good. In the state of innocence freedom was not posited as freedom, its possibility appears in the dread of the individuality. In the demoniacal the situation is reversed. Freedom is posited as unfreedom, for freedom is lost. The possibility of freedom is in turn dread. The difference is absolute; for the possibility of freedom manifests itself here in relation to unfreedom, which is exactly the opposite of innocence, which is a determinant oriented towards freedom.

The demoniacal is unfreedom which would shut itself off. This, however, is an impossibility; it always maintains a relationship, and even when this has apparently disappeared it is nevertheless there, and dread manifests itself at once in the instant of contact with the good (cf. what was said above about the accounts in the New Testament).*

The demoniacal is *shut-upness* [*det Indesluttede,* or *Indesluttedhed*] *unfreely revealed.* These two traits denote, as they should, the same thing; for the shut-up is precisely the mute, and if it has to

---

* Kierkegaard refers to Biblical accounts of demon-possessed persons who experienced dread at the sight of Jesus. (Ed.)

express itself, this must come about against its will when the freedom lying prone in unfreedom revolts upon coming into communication with freedom outside and now betrays unfreedom in such a way that it is the individual who betrays himself against his will in dread. The word "shut-up" must therefore be taken here in a perfectly definite sense, for in the sense of reserve, in which it is commonly used,* it may denote the highest freedom. Brutus, Henry V of England as Prince of Wales, etc., were in this sense shut-up until the time came when it was evident that their shut-upness was a pact with the good. Such a shut-upness was therefore identical with expansion, and never is there an individuality which in the finer and nobler sense of the word is more expanded than he who is shut-up within the womb of a great idea. Freedom is precisely the expansive. It is in opposition to this I would employ the word "shut-up," κατ᾽ ἐξοχήν, for "unfreedom." Commonly a more metaphysical term is used for the evil. It is called "negating." The ethical term precisely corresponding to that, when one contemplates the effect thereof upon the individual, is shut-upness. The demoniacal does not shut itself up *with* something, but shuts *itself* up; and in this lies the mystery of existence, the fact that unfreedom makes a prisoner precisely of itself. Freedom is constantly communicating (it will do no harm to take into account even the religious significance of this word†); unfreedom becomes more and more shut-up and wants no communication. This can be observed in all spheres. It shows itself in hypochondriacs, in crotcheteers, it shows itself in the highest passions when by a profound misunderstanding they introduce silence as a system. When freedom then comes in contact with shut-upness it becomes afraid [*angest*]. In

---

* I.e., the Danish word *Indesluttedhed*, for which, alas, we have no equivalent in English. "Concludedness" is a word that has been suggested to me because etymologically it *might* have this meaning; but the reader will perceive that it would not fit here in every instance, perhaps in none. In translating other works of S. K. where this word occurs less frequently, I have been accustomed to use "close reserve," also "morbid reserve," even "introversion"; but here where this concept is the principal theme and is illuminated from every side I could not be so easygoing. But it is a dreadful alternative to have to say "shut-upness." At this point, having plagued the reader long enough with this word, and having got beyond the passage where *Indesluttedhed* is carefully defined, I feel free to return to "close reserve." The German translator is in no difficulty, for he has the word *Verschlossenheit*. Of the French translators, M. Gateau uses the term *hermétisme* commonly, but also *taciturne* and *réservé*, whereas M. Tisseau employs at least a dozen words: *l'esprit renfermé, repliement de l'esprit, mutisme,* and I cannot recall what all. (Trans.)

† I.e., communicating in the Sacrament of the Lord's Supper. Trans.

common speech we have an expression which is exceedingly suggestive. We say of a person that he will not come out with it. The shut-up is precisely the mute; the spoken word is precisely the saving thing, that which delivers from the mute abstraction of the shut-up. Let the demoniacal here mean *x*; freedom's relation to it from without, *x*: the law for the revelation of the demoniacal is that against its will it comes out with it. For by speech is implied a communication. A demoniac in the New Testament says therefore to Christ, τί ἐμοὶ καὶ σοί;* he goes on to say that Christ has come to destroy him (dread of the good). Or a demoniac beseeches Christ to go another way.† (When dread is dread of the evil, cf. §I,‡ the individual seeks refuge in salvation.)

Life presents examples of this abundantly in all possible spheres and in all possible degrees. A hardened criminal will not go to confession (the demoniacal consists precisely in this, that the man is not willing to communicate with the good through the chastisement of suffering). There is a method applicable to such a case which perhaps is rarely used: it is silence and the power of the eye. If an inquisitor has the requisite physical strength and spiritual elasticity to hold out, though it were for sixteen hours, he will at last be rewarded by the admission breaking out involuntarily. No man who has a bad conscience can endure silence. Put him in solitary confinement, and he will become apathetic. But this silence, while the judge is present, and the clerk waiting to inscribe the confession in the record, is the most searching interrogation and the most terrible torture, and yet lawful; but it is by no means so easy to bring this about as one may suppose. The only power which can compel shut-upness to speak is either a higher demon (for every devil has his turn to reign) or the good which is absolutely able to be silent. And if here in this examination by silence any artfulness would put the man in embarrassment, the inquisitor himself will become ashamed, and it will prove that he at last becomes afraid of himself and must break the silence. Confronted with a subordinate demon, or with subordinate human beings whose God-consciousness is not strongly developed, shut-upness triumphs absolutely, because the former is not able to hold out, and the latter, in all innocence, are accustomed to live from hand to mouth and keep

---

* Mark 5:7. We translate it, "What have I to do with thee?" Cp. Luke 8:28. (Trans.)

† In Mark 5:17 the people of Gedara beseech Christ to depart from their coasts, but there seems to be no reference in the Gospels to a demoniac's having besought Christ to go another way. (Trans.)

‡ Not included in this selection from *The Concept of Dread*. (Ed.)

the heart on the tongue. It is incredible what power resolute reserve is capable of exercising over such men, how they end by begging and imploring for merely one word to break the stillness, but it is also shocking to crush the weak under foot in this fashion. It may be thought perhaps that such things occur only among princes and Jesuits, that to get a clear notion of it one must think of Domitian, Cromwell, the Duke of Alba, or a general of the Jesuit Order, which is almost an appellative term for this. Not at all, it occurs much more frequently. However, one must be cautious in passing judgment upon the phenomenon; for, although the phenomenon is the same, the reason for it may be exactly the opposite, since the individual who subjects others to the despotism and torture of shut-upness might himself wish to speak, might himself be waiting for a higher demon who could bring the revelation forth. But the torturer may also be selfishly related to his shut-upness. But about this I could write a whole book, in spite of the fact that I have not (after the custom and established convention of observers in our age) been either in Paris or London—as if there was such a lot to be learned there besides talk and the wisdom of traveling salesmen. If only one pays attention to oneself, an observer will with five men, five women, and ten children have enough for the discovery of all possible states of the human soul. What I should have to say in such a book would have some importance, especially for everyone who has to deal with children or has any relation with them. It is of infinite importance that a child be brought up with a conception of the lofty shut-upness [reserve], and be saved from the mistaken kind. In an external respect it is easy to perceive when the moment has arrived that one ought to let the child walk alone; in a spiritual respect it is not so easy. In a spiritual respect the problem is very difficult, and one cannot exempt oneself from responsibility by keeping a nursemaid and buying a gocart. The art is to be constantly present and yet not to be present, to let the child be allowed to develop itself, while nevertheless one has constantly a survey clearly before one. The art is to leave the child to itself in the very highest measure and on the greatest possible scale, and to express this apparent abandonment in such a way that, unobserved, one at the same time knows everything. One can quite well find time for this even if one is a royal functionary. If only one will, one can do everything. And the father who educates or does everything for the child entrusted to him, but has not prevented him from becoming shut-up, has incurred a great accountability.

The demoniacal is the shut-up, the demoniacal is dread of the good. We will now let the shut-up be X, an unknown quantity, and let its content too be X, which may denote the most terrible thing or the most insignificant, the most appalling thing, the presence of which in life is perhaps not dreamt of by many, or the bagatelle to which nobody pays any attention. What then may be the significance of the good regarded as an X? It signifies revelation. Revelation may in turn signify the sublimest thing (redemption in the most eminent sense) and the most insignificant (the utterance of a casual remark)—this must not disturb us, the category remains the same. The phenomena have this in common, that they are demoniacal, even though the differences are dizzy ones. "Revelation" in this context is the good, for revelation is the first utterance of salvation. Here applies the old saying, that if one dare utter the word, the enchantment of the magic spell is broken, and hence it is that the somnambulist wakes when his name is called.

The collisions of shut-upness in connection with revelation may in turn be infinitely various, with countless nuances, for the vegetative luxuriance of the spiritual life does not fall short of that in nature, and the spiritual states are more countless in their diversity than are the flowers. Shut-upness may wish for revelation, wish that it might be effected from without, that this might happen to it. (This is a misunderstanding, since it is a womanish relation to the freedom posited in revelation and to the freedom which posits revelation. Unfreedom may very well remain even though the state of the shut-up becomes happier.) It may will revelation to a certain degree, but keep back a little vestige, only to begin all over again with shut-upness. (This is the case with subordinate natures which can do nothing *en gros*.) It may will revelation, but *incognito*. (This is the most subtle contradiction of shut-upness. Nevertheless, examples of it are to be found in poetic existences.) Revelation may have already conquered, shut-upness ventures to employ its last expedient and is cunning enough to transform revelation itself into a mystification, and shut-upness has won.*

But I dare not continue. How could I ever finish if I were merely to indicate these states algebraically, not to speak of describing them, or if I would break the silence of shut-upness in order to let its mono-

---

* It is easy to see that shut-upness *eo ipso* signifies a lie, or, if you prefer, untruth. But untruth is precisely unfreedom, it is dread of revelation. Hence the devil is called the father of lies. That there is a great difference between a lie and an untruth, between lies and lies, and between untruth and untruth, I have always conceded, but the category is the same. (Trans.)

logues become audible? For its talk is precisely monologue, and hence when we would characterize a shut-up we say that he talks to himself. But here I essay only to give everything "an understanding but no tongue," as said the shut-up Hamlet warningly to his two friends.

However, I will indicate one collision, the contradiction of which is as terrible as is shut-upness itself. What the shut-up keeps hidden in his close reserve may be so terrible that he dare not utter it even in his own hearing, because it seems to him as though by this very utterance he were committing a new sin, or as though it would tempt him again. In order that this phenomenon may occur the individual must be such a blending of purity and impurity as seldom is encountered. It is therefore most likely to occur when the individual at the time of accomplishing the terrible act was not master of himself. For example, a man in a state of intoxication may have done what he remembers only obscurely, yet knows that it was so wild a thing that it is almost impossible for him to recognize himself. The same may also be the case with a man who once was insane and has retained a memory of that previous state. What decides whether the phenomenon is demoniacal is the attitude of the individual towards revelation, whether he is willing to permeate that fact with freedom, assume the responsibility of it in freedom. If he is not willing to do that, then the phenomenon is demoniacal. This distinction must be held sharply, for even the man who merely wishes revelation is nevertheless essentially demoniacal. He has in fact two wills, one of them subordinate, impotent, which wills revelation, and a stronger will which wills to be shut up; but the fact that this is the stronger shows that essentially he is demoniacal. Close reserve is involuntary revelation. The weaker the individuality originally is, or in proportion as the elasticity of freedom is consumed in the service of close reserve, the more certainly will the secret break out at last. The most trivial contact, a glance in passing, etc. is sufficient to start that terrible monologue; or it may be comical, depending upon the content of the close reserve. The ventriloquism may be plainly declarative, or it may be indirect, as when an insane man points to another person and says, "He is very objectionable to me, he's probably insane." Revelation may declare itself in words when the unfortunate man ends by intruding upon everyone his hidden secret. It may declare itself by a look, by a glance; for there is a glance of the eye by which a man involuntarily reveals what is hidden. There is an accusing glance which reveals what one almost dreads to understand; a contrite, imploring glance which hardly tempts curiosity to peer into this involuntary telegraphy. Depending upon the content of close reserve, all this in turn may be almost comical, when what dread reveals against its will are ludicrous incidents, pettiness, vanity, pranks, petty envy, little crotchets about medicine and health, etc.

The demoniacal is the sudden. The sudden is a new expression for close reserve seen in another aspect. The demoniacal is characterized as the shut-up when one reflects upon the content, it is characterized as the sudden when one reflects upon time. Close reserve was the effect of the negating retrenchment of the ego in the individuality. Reservedness closed itself constantly more and more against communication. But communication is in turn the expression for continuity, and the negation of continuity is the sudden. One might suppose that close reserve would have an extraordinary continuity. But exactly the opposite is the case, although in comparison with the soft and vapid dispersion of oneself which ends with the sense impression, this has an appearance of continuity. The continuity which close reserve may have can be compared with the vertigo we may suppose a top must feel as it revolves perpetually upon its pivot. In case this close reserve does not carry the thing so far as to become completely insane, insanity being the pitiful *perpetuum mobile* of monotonous indifference, the individuality will still retain a certain continuity with the rest of human life. Against the foil of this continuity, that apparent continuity of close reserve will display itself as the sudden. One instant it is there, the next it is gone, and no sooner is it gone than it is there again as large as life. It cannot be embroidered upon any continuity, nor woven into it, but what expresses itself thus is precisely the sudden.

In case the demoniacal were something somatic, there never would be the sudden. When a fever, insanity, etc., comes back again, one discovers at last a law, and this law in some degree annuls the sudden. But the sudden recognizes no law. It does not properly belong among natural phenomena but is psychic, is the expression of unfreedom.

Like the demoniacal, the sudden is dread of the good. The good in this context means continuity, for the first expression of salvation is continuity. While the life of the individual goes on in a certain degree in continuity with the rest of human life, close reserve maintains itself in him as continuity's abracadabra which communicates only with itself and therefore does not cease to be the sudden.

Depending upon the content of close reserve, the sudden may signify the terrible, but also, for the observer, the effect may appear comic. In this connection we must note that every individual has a little of this suddenness, just as every individual has a little bit of *l'idée fixe*.

I will not follow this out further, but to uphold my category I will recall the fact that the sudden is always due to dread of the good, because there is something which freedom is not willing to permeate. Among the formations which lie in dread of the evil it is weakness which corresponds to what we here call "the sudden."

If in a different way we would make clear to ourselves how it is the demoniacal is the sudden, we may from a purely aesthetic point of view consider the question how the demoniacal can best be represented on the stage. If one would present Mephistopheles, it is well enough to give him lines to recite, if one wishes to use him as an efficient force in the dramatic action, rather than depict his character properly. In that case Mephistopheles is not really represented but is vaguely indicated as a malicious, witty, intriguing pate. This is a volatilization which a popular legend has already improved upon. It recounts that the devil sat and speculated for 3000 years how to overthrow man—then finally he found it out. Here the accent is placed upon the 3000 years, and the picture this produces in the mind is precisely that of the brooding shut-upness of the demoniacal. If one would not volatilize Mephistopheles in the way above indicated, one may choose another mode of representation. In this it will appear that Mephistopheles is essentially mimic.* Even the terrible words which rise out of the abyss of malice are incapable of producing such an effect as does the suddenness of the leap which lies within the compass of mimic art. Even were the word more terrible, even though it were a Shakespeare, a Byron, a Shelley, that breaks the silence, the word always conserves its saving power; for even all despair and all the horror of evil expressed in one word is not so horrible as silence. Mimic art is able to express the sudden, though this does not imply that this art as such is the sudden. In this respect Bournonville as Master of the Ballet deserves great credit for his representation of

---

* The author of *Either/Or* has called attention to the fact that Don Juan is essentially musical. Precisely in the same sense it is true of Mephistopheles that he is essentially mimic. Theatrical art has suffered the same fate as music: it has been supposed that everything could become theatrical and everything musical. We have a ballet, it is called *Faust*. If the composer had really understood what is implied by interpreting *Faust* mimically, it never would have occurred to him to turn *Faust* into a ballet. (Trans.)

Mephistopheles. The horror which seizes one on seeing Mephistopheles leap in through the window and remain stationary in the attitude of the leap! This bound within the leap, recalling the plunge of the bird of prey and the bound of the wild beast, which are doubly terrifying because commonly they break forth from complete immobility, produces therefore an infinite impression. Hence Mephistopheles must walk as little as possible, for the walk itself is in a way a transition to the leap, suggests a presentiment of its possibility. This first appearance of Mephistopheles in the ballet of *Faust* is not a *coup de théâtre* but a very profound thought. Words and speech, short as they may be, have yet always, if we regard the thing abstractly, a certain continuity, because it is in time they are heard. But the sudden is completely detached from continuity, whether it be with the past or with the future. So it is with Mephistopheles. No one has yet seen him—when there he stands, wholly himself from head to feet, and speed cannot be expressed more strongly than by the fact that he stands there with one leap. If this passes into a walk, the effect is weakened. By the fact that Mephistopheles is represented in this fashion, his appearance upon the scene produces the effect of the demoniacal, which comes more suddenly than the thief in the night, for one commonly thinks of the thief as moving stealthily. By this then Mephistopheles reveals his nature, which, like the demoniacal nature, is the sudden. Thus in its forward movement the demoniacal is the sudden, thus it springs into existence in a man, and thus man himself is sudden in so far as he is demoniacal, whether it be that this power has possessed him wholly or that only a little part of it is present in him. Thus the demoniacal always is, and thus suddenly does unfreedom become dread, and such too is the movement of its dread. Hence the aptness of the demoniacal for the mimic art, not in the sense of the beautiful but of the sudden, the abrupt, something which life often gives us opportunity to observe.

The demoniacal is the vacuous, the tedious. Having called attention, apropos of the sudden, to the aesthetic problem of how to represent the demoniacal on the stage, I will raise the same question again in order to throw light upon the affirmation I have made here. When a demon is allowed to speak, and there is someone then who would impersonate him, the actor who has such a problem to solve must be clear about the categories. He knows that the demoniacal is essentially mimic; the sudden, however, is not attainable because that would interrupt the lines. So he will not botch the thing, with the notion that by blurting out the words, etc., he might be capable of producing any genuine effect. Therefore he rightly chooses exactly the opposite, namely, the tedious. The continuity which corresponds to the sudden is what one might call "extinction." Tediousness, the impression of being extinct, is in fact a continuity in nothingness. Now we can interpret a little differently the figure stated in the popular legend. The 3000 years are not now stressed in order to emphasize the sudden, but this prodigious space of time calls forth an apprehension of the horrible emptiness and vacuity of the evil. Freedom is quietness in continuity; the opposite of this is the sudden, but it may also be the quiet which invariably comes to mind when we see a man who looks as if he had been long dead and buried.

23. NIETZSCHE: The New Man and the New Morality

Friedrich Nietzsche (1844–1900) was deeply influenced by the romantics. We find in his work the desire to be whole and the sense that the self becomes whole only through an unselfish giving to the world in art and love. And yet Nietzsche must try very hard to believe that man's consciousness, so susceptible to corruption and ulterior motive, can fasten strongly enough on values potent enough to prevent his love of power from going awry, and becoming destructive. Nietzsche issues a challenge to patience, cunning, intelligence, self-control, care; in his word, spirit. He calls for a new man, a man capable of becoming whole—a superman. He offers no guarantee, however, that the challenge will be answered.

Nietzsche's response to Darwin is significant. As is typical of the English, Nietzsche claims, Darwin forgets spirit, or what is distinctly human, and as a result his theory is incorrect when applied to human beings.* Nietzsche reasons like this: When the distinctly human level is reached in evolution, the struggle for existence is seldom a mere struggle for survival in the midst of brute attack and poverty, but rather there is a subtle struggle for power in the midst of profusion and riches. Survival of the fittest does not happen in a society that keeps alive the physically weak with modern medicine and surgical techniques, while the physically strong die in battles and speeding machines. Less-endowed individuals, the weak, compensate for their weaknesses by developing their cunning and their spirit; therefore it is the weak who dominate the struggle for power rather than the "naturally strong"—whatever that slippery phrase

* See *Twilight of the Idols*, para. 14.

might mean for a human being. Deftly, then, Nietzsche puts his finger on the weakest part of Darwin's theory of evolution: the indeterminacy of key concepts when applied to man, like "strength," "struggle," and "the fittest." Nietzsche impresses us with the supervening urgency of attacking the ethical problem before we expedite simplistic plans for eliminating the "weak" and breeding the "strong" through genetic psychological or other techniques. The problem is philosophical, not biological or psychological. It involves the massively difficult question of just what a good human being is.

Now, let us be very careful with Nietzsche's concept of Superman (or Over-man), since it has been terribly abused, particularly by the Nazis. All he means, I think, is that we must become stronger in the sense that we must become morally better if civilization is to survive in the modern age. We can no longer play with weapons like children play with toys; the results would be too awful for words. Man must grow up —and this takes super-discipline and super-courage.

This first selection from *Thus Spake Zarathustra** (1883–1885) expresses Nietzsche's belief that physical weakness leads to compensation and spiritual gain. Zarathustra is also a "cripple at the bridge." Expressed also is Nietzsche's contention that psychological deformity and the eccentricity of the professionalized man is the truly lamentable thing (the "inverse cripple").

One day as Zarathustra crossed over the great bridge, cripples and beggars ringed him about, and a hunchback spoke to him thusly:

"Behold Zarathustra! The people learn from you and begin to believe in your doctrine; but before it is entirely believed one thing more must be done—you must first win over us cripples! Here you have a beautiful selection and, truly, an opportunity with more than one handle. You can heal the blind and make the lame walk, and from them that have too much behind you can take a little away. I mean that would be the right way to make the cripples believe in Zarathustra."

But Zarathustra replied thus to him who spoke: "If one takes away the hump from the hunchback, one takes away his spirit—thus the people teach. And if one gives the blind his eyes, he will see so many bad things on the earth that he will curse the man who heals him. But he who makes the lame man run, inflicts upon him the greatest injury. For hardly can he run, when his vices run away with him—so the people teach about cripples. And why should not Zarathustra learn from the people, when the people learn from Zarathustra?

* Translated by Bruce Wilshire.

"But since I have been among men the thing of least importance to me is that one person lacks an eye, another an ear, a third a leg, and that others have lost the tongue, or the nose, or the head.

"I see and have seen worse things, and many things so hideous that I should neither like to speak of such matters nor keep silent about some of them: men who lack everything, except they have too much of one thing—men who are nothing more than a big eye, or a big mouth, or a big paunch, or something else big—inverse cripples, I call them.

"And when I emerged from my solitude and crossed over this bridge for the first time, I could not trust my eyes, but looked again and again, and finally said, 'That is an ear! An ear as big as a man!' I looked even harder: Actually, underneath the ear, something was moving, something pitifully small, wretched and thin. To be sure, this immense ear was perched on a small thin stalk—the stalk, however, was a man! He who put a glass to his eye could even make out a small envious face; also, that a bloated little soul was dangling from the stalk. The people, though, told me that this great ear was not only a human being, but a great one, a genius. But I never believe the people when they speak of great men, and I hold to my belief that this was an inverse cripple, who had too little of everything, and too much of one thing."

When Zarathustra had spoken thus to the hunchback and to those for whom the hunchback was the mouthpiece, he turned to his disciples in deep dejection and said, "Really, friends, I walk among men as among the fragments and limbs of men. This is what seems terrible to me, that I find man broken up, and scattered about, as on a battlefield or a butcherfield. And when my eye flees from the present to the past, it finds always the same: fragments and limbs and accidents—but no men!

"The present and past upon earth—oh my friends—is what I find most unendurable; and I should not know how to live if I were not also a prophet of what must come. A prophet, a willer, a creator, a future himself and also a bridge to the future—and, sadly, also a cripple, as it were, at this bridge—all this is Zarathustra. . . ."

The second selection, "Of Old and New Tablets," from *Zarathustra* reveals Nietzsche's concern to find new codes of morality, applicable to the new possibilities of the modern age, which shall replace the old broken ones. For they must be replaced.

1

Here I sit and wait, old broken tablets around me, new half-written ones as well. When will my time come?—the time of my descent and going under: for once again I will go unto men. For that I now wait, since first must the sign come to me that it is *my* time: the laughing lion with the flock of doves. Between times I talk to myself as one who has time. Nobody tells me anything new, so I tell myself about myself.

2

When men I approached, I found them sitting on an old delusion: They all thought they had long known what was good and evil for men. An old tiresome business seemed to them all talk about virtue, and he who wished to sleep well spoke of good and evil before going to bed.

This sleepiness I disturbed when I taught that *no one yet knows* what is good and evil, unless it be the creative one. It is he who creates man's goal and gives the earth its meaning and its future. That anything is good and evil is his creation.

And I directed them to overturn their old academic chairs, and wherever that old delusion had sat. I directed them to laugh at their great moralists, saints, poets and saviors of the world. I directed them to laugh at their gloomy sages and at whoever had sat on the tree of life like a black scarecrow. On their great highway of graves I sat, and amidst corpses and vultures I laughed at their past and all its rotting, decaying glory.

Truly, like fools and preachers of penitence, I raised a hue and cry over their greatness and smallness. That their best is still so small! That their greatest evil is still so small!—at that I laughed.

My wise yearning—born in the mountains—a wild wisdom truly! —cried and laughed in me. Like a rustling of wings this great yearning of mine. And often it carried me up, away and far, in the middle of my laughter; then I flew quivering like an arrow in sun-drunken rapture:—Out into distant futures, which no dream has yet dreamed, into warmer souths than artists have yet conceived, where dancing gods are ashamed of all clothes (to speak in parables and to limp and stutter like poets; and I am really ashamed that I must still be a poet).

Where all becoming seemed to me the dance of gods and the roguishness of gods, and the world loosed and unbridled and fleeing back to itself; as an eternal fleeing and seeking of one another of many gods—as their happy disputes and their conversing again together—as their convergence.

Where all time seemed to me a happy mockery of moments, and where necessity was freedom itself playing happily with the thorn of freedom.

Where I also found again my old devil and arch-enemy, the spirit of gravity and all that he created: constraint, law, necessity, consequence, purpose, will—and good and evil. For must there not be that which one dances *over*, and away from? Must there not be moles and grave dwarfs for the sake of the light and the lightest?

3

It was there also that I picked up from the path the word Superman, and that man is something that must be surpassed. That man is a bridge and not a goal—rejoicing over his noons and evenings as ways to new dawns. The Zarathustra word of great noon, and whatever else I hung up over man like the last red glow of evening.

Truly, new stars did I let them see, along with new nights. And over clouds and day and night did I spread out laughter like a bright-colored canopy. I taught them all my poetry and striving: to compose and collect into unity what in man is fragment, riddle and awful accident. As composer, reader of riddles, and redeemer of chance did I teach them to create the future—and all that *has been* to redeem by creating. The past of man to redeem, and every "it was" to transform until the will says, "But so I willed it! So I shall will it!"—this did I call redemption and this alone did I teach them to call redemption.

Now I await my redemption—that I may go to them for the last time. For once again I will go unto them; among them I want to go under; in dying will I give them my richest gift. From the sun did I learn this: The joyful one goes down and out of inexhaustible riches pours gold into the sea, so that even the poorest fisherman rows with golden oars! For this I once saw and did not tire of weeping in beholding it.

Like the sun will Zarathustra also go down. Now he sits here and waits, surrounded by old broken tablets and new tablets as well—half written.

4

Look, here is a new tablet. But where are my brothers who will accompany me to the valley and carry it into hearts of flesh? Thus my great love of the farthest cries out: *Do not spare your neighbor!* Man is something that must be surpassed.

There are various ways and manners of surpassing: see about that yourself! But only a buffoon thinks: "Man can also be leaped over." Surpass yourself even in your neighbor: and do not allow yourself to be given what you can seize. What you do, nobody can do to you in return. Look, there is no reward.

He who cannot command himself shall obey. And many can command themselves, but much is still lacking before they can obey themselves.

5

So noble souls will have it: They do not want to have anything for nothing, least of all, life. He who is of the rabble wishes to live for nothing; we others, however, to whom life has given itself—we are always thinking what we can best give *in return*! And truly, it is a noble dictum: "What life promises us, that promise will we keep to life!"

One should not wish to enjoy where one does not contribute to the joy. And one should not *wish* to enjoy!

For enjoyment and innocence are the most bashful things. Neither like to be sought. One should *have* them—but one should *seek* for guilt and pain!

6

Oh my brothers, firstlings are always sacrificed. We, however, are firstlings. We all bleed at secret sacrificial altars; we all burn and roast in honor of old idols. What is best in us is still young: it excites old palates. Our flesh is tender, our skin is only lamb's skin. How could we fail to excite old idol-priests!

In ourselves lives he still, the old idol-priest, who broils our best for his banquet. Oh my brothers, how could firstlings fail to be sacrifices!

But so our kind wants it; and I love those who do not want to preserve themselves. The ones that go down I love with my whole love: for they go beyond.

7

To be true—only a few are able! And those who can, will not! Least of all, however, can the good be true. Oh, those good ones!

Good men never speak the truth. To be good in this way is a disease of the spirit.

They yield and submit themselves, those good ones; their heart repents and their soul obeys. However, he who obeys *does not listen to himself!*

All that is called evil by the good, must come together so that one truth may be born. Oh my brothers, are you evil enough for *this* truth? The audacious daring, the prolonged distrust, the cruel No, the tedium, the cutting into the quick—how seldom do *these* come together! But from such seeds is truth produced.

All science has grown up so far alongside bad conscience. Break, break, you lovers of knowledge, the old tablets!

8

When the water is spanned by planks, when gangways and railings arch over the river, truly, he who says, "Everything is in flux," is not believed. Even the simpletons contradict him. "What?" the simpletons say. "All in flux? After all, planks and railings are *over* the river! Over the river all is stable, all the bridges and bearings, all the values of things, all 'good' and 'evil': these are all *stable!*"

And when the hard winter comes, the river-animal tamer, then even the quickest-witted learn distrust, and truly, not only the simpletons say, "Does not everything *stand still?*"

"In the last analysis, everything stands still"—that is truly a winter doctrine, good cheer for an unproductive period, a grand comfort for winter-sleepers and fireside-loungers.

"In the last analysis, everything stands still"—: but *contrary* thereto, preaches the thawing wind! The thawing wind, a bull which is no plowing bull, a furious destroying bull with angry horns breaks the ice! The ice, however, *breaks bridges!*

Oh my brothers, *now* is not everything in flux? Have not all railings and bridges fallen into the water? Who could still cling to "good" and "evil"?

"Woe to us! Hail to us! The thawing wind blows!"—so preach in every street my brothers.

9

There is an old illusion which is called good and evil. Until now the orbit of this illusion has revolved around soothsayers and stargazers. Once one *believed* in soothsayers and stargazers, and therefore one believed, "Everything is fate: thou shalt for thou must!"

Then again man distrusted all soothsayers and stargazers, and therefore did one believe, "Everything is freedom: you can, for you will!"

Oh my brothers, until now there has been only illusion about the stars and the future—not knowledge. Therefore until now there has been only illusion about good and evil—not knowledge!

10

"Thou shalt not steal! Thou shalt not slay!"—such precepts were once called holy; before them did one bow the knee and head, and take off one's shoes.

But I ask you: Where have there ever been better robbers and killers in the world than such holy precepts?

Is there not in all life itself robbing and killing? And for such precepts to be called holy, was not *truth* itself thereby slain?

Or was it the preaching of death, which contradicted and contravened all life, which was called holy? Oh my brothers, break, break the old tablets!

11

It is my pity for all the past that I see it is abandoned,—Abandoned to the pleasure, the spirit, the madness of each generation that comes along and reinterprets all that has been its bridge!

A great tyrant might come along, a shrewd monster who might constrain and torture all that is past—according to his own pleasure —until it becomes a bridge to him, a harbinger and herald and cockcrow.

This however is the other danger and my other pity: he who is of the rabble thinks back to his grandfather—with his grandfather, however, does time stop. Thus is all the past abandoned: since it might happen someday that the rabble become master, and drown all time in shallow waters.

Therefore, oh my brothers, a *new nobility* is needed, which shall be the opponent of all rabble and tyrant rule, and which shall write again the word "noble" on new tablets.

For many noble ones are needed, and noble ones of many kinds, that there may be a nobility. Or as I once in a parable spoke: "Even this is divinity, that there are gods, but no God."

12

Oh my brothers, I dedicate you and direct you to a new nobility: you shall become the procreators and cultivators and sowers of the future. . . .

In your children shall you *make amends* for being the children of your fathers: all the past shall you thus redeem! This new tablet I place over you!

Our final Nietzsche selection, entitled "The Sooth Sayer," is also from *Zarathustra*. It reveals the possibility that Zarathustra's infirmity will be too much to overcome through the compensatory activity it generates and that it will drag him down. One suspects that the death of which Zarathustra dreams—the coffin full of horrors and the ashes being carried to the mountains—is his own. Notice the final line: Zarathustra looks at the disciple who interprets the dream to mean the death of another and shakes his head.

"—and I saw a great sadness come over mankind. The best were fed up with their work.

"A teaching appeared, a faith ran with it: 'All is empty, all is the same, all has happened before.'

"And from the hills it echoed: 'All is empty, all is the same, all has happened before.'

"Indeed we have harvested: but why did all our fruit turn rotten and brown? What fell down last night from the evil moon?

"In vain was all our work, our wine has turned to poison, an evil eye sears our fields and hearts.

"We have all become dry; and if fire should fall on us, we should turn to ashes—indeed we have wearied the fire itself.

"All our springs have dried up, even the sea has withdrawn. All the ground cracks open, but the depths will not swallow.

" 'Alas, where is there still a sea in which one might drown?'—so sounds our wailing across shallow swamps.

"Really, we have become too tired to die; we wake and live on—in tombs!—"

So Zarathustra heard a soothsayer speak; and the prophecy touched his heart and changed him. He walked around sad and weary; and he became like those of whom the soothsayer had spoken.

"Actually," he said to his disciples, "a little while, and the long twilight comes. Alas, how shall I preserve my light through it!

"That it may not smother in this sadness! For it shall be a light to distant worlds, and also to the most distant nights!"

Thus Zarathustra went about grieved in his heart, and for three days he took neither food nor drink, had no rest and lost his speech. At last he fell into a deep sleep. His disciples sat around him in long night watches, and waited anxiously to see if he would awaken and speak again and recover from his affliction.

And these are the words Zarathustra spoke when he awoke; his voice came to his disciples as from a great distance, however:

"Hear then the dream that I dreamed, you friends, and help me to understand it!

"The dream is still a riddle to me; its meaning is hidden and locked up within it and does not fly freely above it.

"I dreamed I had renounced all life. I had become a nightwatchman and grave guard, up there in the lonely mountain fortress of death.

"There I guarded his coffins. Full stood dusty vaults with the evidence of his victories. Overwhelmed life stared out at me from glass coffins.

"I breathed the smell of dusty eternities: sultry and dusty lay my soul. Who could have aired out his soul there?

"The brightness of midnight was always around me; loneliness crouched beside her; and as a third, death-rattle silence, the worst of my women friends.

"I carried the rustiest keys and used them to open the most creaking gates.

"The sound ran like a wickedly angry croaking through the long corridors when the gate's wings moved: fiendishly cried this bird, unhappy at being awakened.

"But it was more frightening and heart-strangling when again it was silent and still all around, and I sat alone in that malignant silence.

"So time passed with me, and slipped by, if time there still was: what do I know about that! But at last that which awakened me happened.

"Three times pealed blows at the gate like thunder; the vaults echoed and howled three times; then I went to the gate.

" 'Alpa,' I cried, 'who carries his ashes to the mountain? Alpa! Alpa! Who carries his ashes to the mountain?'

"And I pressed the key, and pulled at the gate, and exerted myself. But it opened not a finger's breadth:

"Then did a roaring wind tear the wings of the gate apart: whistling, whizzing and piercing it threw up a black coffin before me:

"And in the roaring and whistling and whizzing, the coffin burst open and out spilled a thousand peals of laughter.

"And a thousand caricatures of children, angels, owls, fools, and butterflies the size of children laughed, mocked and roared at me.

"Then I was terribly frightened; it threw me down. And I cried with horror as I have never cried before. And my own cry awakened me—and I came to my senses."

So Zarathustra told his dream, and then became silent; since he did not yet know the interpretation of his dream. But the disciple whom he loved most rose quickly, seized Zarathustra's hand, and said:

"Your life itself interprets to us this dream, O Zarathustra!

"Are you not yourself the wind which whistles shrilly, which bursts open the gates of the fortress of death?

"Are you not yourself the coffin full of many colored sarcasms and the angelic caricatures of life?

"Truly, like a thousand peals of children's laughter Zarathustra enters all death chambers, laughing at those nightwatchmen and guards of graves and at whoever else is rattling with sinister keys.

"With your laughter you will frighten and prostrate them; and your power over them will make them faint and wake them.

"And when the long twilight comes and the mortal weariness, even then you will not vanish from our firmament, you advocate of life!

"You have made us see new stars, and new glories of the night: truly, laughter itself you have spread over us like a many colored canopy.

"Now then will children's laughter always from coffins flow; now will a strong wind always come victoriously to all mortal weariness: you yourself are the pledge and prophet of this!

"Really, *this is what you dreamed of:* your enemies. That was your hardest dream.

"But as you woke from them and came to your senses, so they will awaken from themselves, and come to you."

So the disciple spoke; and all the others then thronged about Zarathustra, grasped him by the hands, and tried to persuade him to leave his bed and his sadness, and return to them. However, Zara-thustra sat upright on his couch with an absent look in his eyes. Like one returning from a long trip abroad, he looked at his disciples and examined their features. But still he did not know them. When they lifted him to his feet—note well—his eyes suddenly changed; he understood all that had happened, stroked his beard, and said in a strong voice:

"All right, there is time for this too! But see to it, my disciples, that we have a good meal, and without delay. So do I mean to atone for bad dreams!

"The soothsayer shall sit by my side and eat and drink: and truly I will yet show him a sea in which he can drown himself!"—

Thus spoke Zarathustra. But then he gazed long into the face of him who had played the dream interpreter, and shook his head.—

24. DOSTOEVSKY: The Ineffectual Freedom of Consciousness

It is a long way from Rousseau to Dostoevsky (1821–1881). If we plotted the development of the age exclusively on a line connecting the two thinkers, then we would have to conclude that no other age runs through its development and exhausts itself so rapidly. Although intel-lectual history is exceedingly more complex than anything that can be plotted on a single line or adumbrated in a single theme, still there is value in comparing the two thinkers

Rousseau thought that man was structured by natural tendencies and that there were natural consummations of these tendencies. Rousseau thought therefore that education should be largely negative; that is, that it should prevent any impeding of natural tendencies, which left alone become natural perfections and values. He assumed that the child's con-sciousness of his own natural ends—potential satisfactions, values and consummations—would be sufficient motivation toward striving to attain them.

Dostoevsky's underground man is not conscious of any dynamic tendency to become anything; he feels no sap springing up in his trunk; he cannot become anything, not even a mouse or an insect. Whether or not there are any natural tendencies of development is quite irrelevant, for his consciousness is detached from any such tendencies and rec-ognizes none. Moreover, the underground man's free and unruly consciousness desecrates every symbol of consummation and perfection, simply because the man feels a need to prove that he is *free* to desecrate it. This need is one tendency Rousseau did not predict. Nothing contains this underground man, nothing commands, magnetizes or controls his loyalty, and that is precisely what disgusts him about the impotent symbols in traditional society.

Is there anything natural about a man equipped with such a consciousness? Where on earth can he feel at home? These are questions left to us by Dostoevsky, and they have never been better put, I think, than in his *Notes from the Underground* (Part One) (1864):*

I†

I am a sick man . . . I am a spiteful man. I am an unpleasant man. I think my liver is diseased. However, I don't know beans about my disease, and I am not sure what is bothering me. I don't treat it and never have, though I respect medicine and doctors. Besides, I am extremely superstitious, let's say sufficiently so to respect medicine. (I am educated enough not to be superstitious, but I am.) No, I refuse to treat it out of spite. You probably will not understand that. Well, but *I* understand it. Of course, I can't explain to you just whom I am annoying in this case by my spite. I am perfectly well aware that I cannot "get even" with the doctors by not consulting them. I know better than anyone that I thereby injure only myself and no one else. But still, if I don't treat it, it is out of spite. My liver is bad, well then—let it get even worse!

I have been living like that for a long time now—twenty years. I am forty now. I used to be in the civil service, but no longer am. I was a spiteful official. I was rude and took pleasure in being so. After all, I did not accept bribes, so I was bound to find a compensation in that, at least. (A bad joke but I will not cross it out. I wrote it

---

* From the book *Notes from Underground and the Grand Inquisitor.* Translated by Ralph E. Matlaw. Copyright © 1960 by E. P. Dutton & Co., Inc., New York. Reprinted by permission of the publishers.

† The author of these notes and the "Notes" themselves are, of course, imaginary. Nevertheless, such persons as the writer of these notes, not only may, but positively must, exist in our society, considering those circumstances under which our society was in general formed. I wanted to expose to the public more clearly than it is done usually, one of the characters of the recent past. He is one of the representatives of the current generation. In this excerpt entitled "Underground," this person introduces himself, his views, and, as it were, tries to explain the reasons why he appeared and was bound to appear in our midst. In the following excerpt, the actual notes of this person about several events in his life, will appear. (*Fyodor Dostoevsky*)

thinking it would sound very witty; but now that I see myself that I only wanted to show off in a despicable way, I will purposely not cross it out!) When petitioners would come to my desk for information I would gnash my teeth at them, and feel intense enjoyment when I succeeded in distressing some one. I was almost always successful. For the most part they were all timid people—of course, they were petitioners. But among the fops there was one officer in particular I could not endure. He simply would not be humble, and clanked his sword in a disgusting way. I carried on a war with him for eighteen months over that sword. At last I got the better of him. He left off clanking it. However, that happened when I was still young. But do you know, gentlemen, what the real point of my spite was? Why, the whole trick, the real vileness of it lay in the fact that continually, even in moments of the worst spleen, I was inwardly conscious with shame that I was not only not spiteful but not even an embittered man, that I was simply frightening sparrows at random and amusing myself by it. I might foam at the mouth, but bring me some kind of toy, give me a cup of tea with sugar, and I would be appeased. My heart might even be touched, though probably I would gnash my teeth at myself afterward and lie awake at night with shame for months after. That is the way I am.

I was lying when I said just now that I was a spiteful official. I was lying out of spite. I was simply indulging myself with the petitioners and with the officer, but I could never really become spiteful. Every moment I was conscious in myself of many, very many elements completely opposite to that. I felt them positively teeming in me, these opposite elements. I knew that they had been teeming in me all my life, begging to be let out, but I would not let them, would not let them, purposely would not let them out. They tormented me till I was ashamed; they drove me to convulsions, and finally, they bored me, how they bored me! Well, are you not imagining, gentlemen, that I am repenting for something now, that I am asking your forgiveness for something? I am sure you are imagining that. However, I assure you it does not matter to me if you are.

Not only could I not become spiteful, I could not even become anything: neither spiteful nor kind, neither a rascal nor an honest man, neither a hero nor an insect. Now, I am living out my life in my corner, taunting myself with the spiteful and useless consolation that an intelligent man cannot seriously become anything and that only a fool can become something. Yes, an intelligent man in the nineteenth century must and morally ought to be pre-eminently a characterless creature; a man of character, an active man, is pre-eminently a limited creature. That is the conviction of my forty years. I am forty years old now, and forty years, after all, is a whole lifetime; after all, that is extreme old age. . . .

After all, people who know how to revenge themselves and to take care of themselves in general, how do they do it? After all, when they are possessed, let us suppose, by the feeling of revenge, then for the time there is nothing else but that feeling left in their whole being. Such a man simply rushes straight toward his object like an infuriated bull with its horns down, and nothing but a wall will stop him. (By the way: facing the wall, such people—that is, the straightforward persons and men of action—are genuinely nonplussed. For them a wall is not an evasion, as for example for us people who think and consequently do nothing; it is not an excuse for turning aside, an excuse for which our kind is always very glad, though we scarcely believe in it ourselves, usually. No, they are nonplussed in all sincerity. The wall has for them something tranquilizing, morally soothing, final—maybe even something mysterious . . . but of the wall later.) Well, such a direct person I regard as the real normal man, as his tender mother Nature wished to see him when she graciously brought him into being on the earth. I envy such a man till I am green in the face. He is stupid. I am not disputing that, but perhaps the normal man should be stupid, how do you know? Perhaps it is very beautiful, in fact. And I am all the more convinced of that suspicion, if one can call it so, by the fact that if, for instance, you take the antithesis of the normal man, that is, the hyperconscious man, who has come, of course, not out of the lap of nature but out of a retort (this is almost mysticism, gentlemen, but I suspect this, too), this retort-made man is sometimes so nonplussed in the presence of his antithesis that with all his hyperconsciousness he genuinely thinks of himself as a mouse and not a man. It may be a hyperconscious mouse, yet it is a mouse, while the other is a man, and therefore, etc. And the worst is, he himself, his very own self, looks upon himself as a mouse. No one asks him to do so. And that is an important point. Now let us look at this mouse in action. Let us suppose, for instance, that it feels insulted, too (and it almost always does feel insulted), and wants to revenge itself too. There may even be a greater accumulation of spite in it than in *l'homme de la nature et de la vérité*. The base, nasty desire to repay with spite whoever has offended it, rankles perhaps even more nastily in it than in *l'homme de la nature et de la vérité*, because *l'homme de a nature et de la vérité* through his innate stupidity looks upon his revenge as justice pure and simple; while in consequence of his hyperconsciousness the mouse does not believe in the justice of it. To come at last to the deed itself, to the very act of revenge. Apart from the one fundamental nastiness the unfortunate mouse succeeds in creating around it so many other nastinesses in the form of doubts and questions, adds to the one question so many unsettled questions, that there inevitably works up around it a sort of fatal brew, a stinking mess, made up of its doubts, agitations and lastly of the contempt spat upon it by the straightforward men of action who stand solemnly about it as judges and arbitrators, laughing at it till their healthy sides ache. Of course the only thing left for it is to dismiss all that with a wave of its paw, and, with a smile of assumed contempt in which it does not even believe itself, creep ignominiously into its mouse-hole. There, in its nasty, stinking, underground home our insulted, crushed and ridiculed mouse promptly becomes absorbed in cold, malignant and, above all, everlasting spite. For forty years together it will remember its injury down to the smallest, most shameful detail, and every time will add, of itself, details still more shameful, spitefully teasing and irritating itself with its own imagination. It will be ashamed of its own fancies, but yet it will recall everything, it will go over it again and again, it will invent lies against itself pretending that those things might have happened, and will forgive nothing. Maybe it will begin to revenge itself, too, but, as it were, piecemeal, in trivial ways, from behind the stove, incognito, without believing either in its own right to vengeance, or in the success of its revenge, knowing beforehand that from all its efforts at revenge it will suffer a hundred times more than he on whom it revenges itself, while he probably will not even feel it. On its deathbed it will recall it all over again, with interest accumulated over all the years. But it is just in that cold, abominable half-despair, half-belief, in that conscious burying oneself alive for grief in the underworld for forty years, in that hyperconsciousness and yet to some extent doubtful hopelessness of one's position, in that hell of unsatisfied desires turned inward, in that fever of oscillations, of resolutions taken forever and regretted again a minute later—that the savor of that strange enjoyment of which I have spoken lies. It is so subtle, sometimes so difficult to analyze consciously, that somewhat limited people, or simply people with strong nerves, will not understand anything at all in it. "Possibly," you will add on your own account with a grin, "people who have never received a slap in the face will not understand it either," and in that way you will politely hint to me that I, too, perhaps, have been slapped in the face in my life, and so I speak as an expert. I'll bet that you are thinking that. But set your minds at rest, gentlemen, I have not received a slap in the face, though it doesn't matter to me at all what you may think about it. Possibly, I even myself regret that I have given so few slaps in the face during my life. But enough, not another word on the subject of such extreme interest to you.

I will continue calmly about people with strong nerves who do not understand a certain refinement of enjoyment. Though in certain circumstances these gentlemen bellow their loudest like bulls, though this, let us suppose, does them the greatest honor, yet, as I have already said, confronted with the impossible they at once resign themselves. Does the impossible mean the stone wall? What stone wall? Why, of course, the laws of nature, the conclusions of natural science, of mathematics. As soon as they prove to you, for instance, that you are descended from a monkey, then it is no use scowling, accept it as a fact. When they prove to you that in reality one drop of your own fat must be dearer to you than a hundred thouand of your fellow creatures, and that this conclusion is the final solution of all so-called virtues and duties and all such ravings and prejudices, then you might as well accept it, you can't do anything about it, because two times two is a law of mathematics. Just try refuting it.

"But really," they will shout at you, "there is no use protesting; it is a case of two times two makes four! Nature does not ask your permission, your wishes, and whether you like or dislike her laws does not concern her. You are bound to accept her as she is, and consequently also all her conclusions. A wall, you see, is a wall—etc. etc." Good God! but what do I care about the laws of nature and arithmetic, when, for some reason, I dislike those laws and the fact that two times two makes four? Of course I cannot break through a wall by battering my head against it if I really do not have the strength to break through it, but I am not going to resign myself to it simply because it is a stone wall and I am not strong enough.

As though such a stone wall really were a consolation, and really did contain some word of conciliation, if only because it is as true as two times two makes four. Oh, absurdity of absurdities! How much better it is to understand it all, to be conscious of it all, all the impossibilities and the stone walls, not to resign yourself to a single one of those impossibilities and stone walls if it disgusts you to resign yourself; to reach, through the most inevitable, logical combinations, the most revolting conclusions on the everlasting theme that you are yourself somehow to blame even for the stone wall, though again it is as clear as day you are not to blame in the least, and therefore grinding your teeth in silent impotence sensuously to sink into inertia, brooding on the fact that it turns out that there is even no one for you to feel vindictive against, that you have not, and perhaps never will have, an object for your spite, that it is a sleight-of-hand, a bit of juggling, a card-sharper's trick, that it is simply a mess, no knowing what and no knowing who, but in spite of all these uncertainties, and jugglings, still there is an ache in you, and the more you do not know, the worse the ache.

IV

"Ha, ha, ha! Next you will find enjoyment in a toothache," you cry with a laugh.

"Well? So what? There is enjoyment even in a toothache," I answer. I had a toothache for a whole month and I know there is. In that case, of course, people are not spiteful in silence, they moan; but these are not sincere moans, they are malicious moans, and the maliciousness is the whole point. The sufferer's enjoyment finds expression in those moans; if he did not feel enjoyment in them he would not moan. It is a good example, gentlemen, and I will develop it. The moans express in the first place all the aimlessness of your pain, which is so humiliating to your consciousness; the whole legal system of Nature on which you spit disdainfully, of course, but from which you suffer all the same while she does not. They express the consciousness that you have no enemy, but that you do have a pain; the consciousness that in spite of all the dentists in the world you are in complete slavery to your teeth; that if someone wishes it, your teeth will leave off aching, and if he does not, they will go on aching another three months; and that finally if you still disagree and still protest, all that is left you for your own gratification is to thrash yourself or beat your wall with your fist as hard as you can, and absolutely nothing more. Well then, these mortal insults, these jeers on the part of someone unknown, end at last in an enjoyment which sometimes reaches the highest degree of sensuality. I beg you, gentlemen, to listen sometimes to the moans of an educated man of the nineteenth century who is suffering from a toothache, particularly on the second or third day of the attack, when he has already begun to moan not as he moaned on the first day, that is, not simply because he has a toothache, not just as any coarse peasant might moan, but as a man affected by progress and European civilization, a man who is "divorced from the soil and the national principles," as they call it these days. His moans become nasty, disgustingly spiteful, and go on for whole days and nights. And, after all, he himself knows that he does not benefit at all from his moans; he knows better than anyone that he is only lacerating and irritating himself and others in vain; he knows that even the audience for whom he is exerting himself and his whole family now listen to him with loathing, do not believe him for a second, and that deep down they understand that he could moan differently, more simply, without trills and flourishes, and that he is only indulging himself like that out of spite, out of malice. Well, sensuality exists precisely in all these consciousnesses and infamies. "It seems I am troubling you, I am lacerating your hearts, I am keeping everyone in the house awake. Well, stay awake then, you, too, feel every minute that I have a toothache. I am no longer the hero to you now that I tried to appear before, but simply a nasty person, a scoundrel. Well, let it be that way, then! I am very glad that you see through me. Is it nasty for you to hear my foul moans? Well, let it be nasty. Here I will let you have an even nastier flourish in a minute. . . ." You still do not understand, gentlemen? No, it seems our development and our consciousness must go further to understand all the intricacies of this sensuality. You laugh? I am delighted. My jokes, gentlemen, are of course in bad taste, uneven, involved, lacking self-confidence. But of course that is because I do not respect myself. Can a man with consciousness respect himself at all? . . .

You see, gentlemen, reason, gentlemen, is an excellent thing, there is no disputing that, but reason is only reason and can only satisfy man's rational faculty, while will is a manifestation of all life, that is, of all human life including reason as well as all impulses. And although our life, in this manifestation of it, is often worthless, yet it is life nevertheless and not simply extracting square roots. After all, here I, for instance, quite naturally want to live, in order to satisfy all my faculties for life, and not simply my rational faculty, that is, not simply one-twentieth of all my faculties for life. What does reason know? Reason only knows what it has succeeded in learning (some things it will perhaps never learn; while this is nevertheless no comfort, why not say so frankly?) and human nature acts as a whole, with everything that is in it, consciously or unconsciously, and, even if it goes wrong, it lives. I suspect, gentlemen, that you are looking at me with compassion; you repeat to me that an enlightened and developed man, such, in short, as the future man will be, cannot knowingly desire anything disadvantageous to himself, that this can be proved mathematically. I thoroughly agree, it really can—by mathematics. But I repeat for the hundredth time, there is one case, one only, when man may purposely, consciously, desire what is injurious to himself, what is stupid, very stupid—simply in order *to have the right* to desire for himself even what is very stupid and not to be bound by an obligation to desire only what is rational. After all, this very stupid thing, after all, this caprice of ours, may really be more advantageous for us, gentlemen, than anything else on earth, especially in some cases. And in particular it may be more advantageous than any advantages even when it does us obvious harm, and contradicts the soundest conclusions of our reason about our advantage—because in any case it preserves for us what is most precious and most important —that is, our personality, our individuality. Some, you see, maintain that this really is the most precious thing for man; desire can, of course, if it desires, be in agreement with reason; particularly if it does not abuse this practice but does so in moderation, it is both useful and sometimes even praiseworthy. But very often, and even most often, desire completely and stubbornly opposes reason, and . . . and . . . and do you know that that, too, is useful and sometimes even praiseworthy? Gentlemen, let us suppose that man is not stupid. (Indeed, after all, one cannot say that about him anyway, if only for the one consideration that, if man is stupid, then, after all, who is wise?) But if he is not stupid, he is just the same monstrously ungrateful! Phenomenally ungrateful. I even believe that the best definition of man is—a creature that walks on two legs and is ungrateful. But that is not all, that is not his worst defect; his worst defect is his perpetual immorality, perpetual—from the days of the Flood to the Schleswig-Holstein period of human destiny. Immorality, and consequently lack of good sense; for it has long been accepted that lack of good sense is due to no other cause than immorality. Try it, and cast a look upon the history of mankind. Well, what will you see? Is it a grand spectacle? All right, grand, if you like. The Colossus of Rhodes, for instance, that is worth something. Mr. Anaevsky may well testify that some say it is the work of human hands, while others maintain that it was created by Nature herself. Is it variegated? Very well, it may be variegated too. If one only took the dress uniforms, military and civilian, of all peoples in all ages—that alone is worth something, and if you take the undress uniforms you will never get to the end of it; no historian could keep up with it. Is it monotonous? Very well. It may be monotonous, too; they fight and fight; they are fighting now, they fought first and they fought last—you will admit that it is almost too montonous. In short, one may say anything about the history of the world—anything that might enter the most disordered imagination. The only thing one cannot say is that it is rational. The very word sticks in one's throat. And, indeed, this is even the kind of thing that continually happens. After all, there are continually turning up in life moral and rational people, sages, and lovers of humanity, who make it their goal for life to live as morally and rationally as possible, to be, so to speak, a light to their neighbors, simply in order to show them that it is really possible to live morally and rationally in this world. And so what? We all know that those very people sooner or later toward the end of their lives have been false to themselves, playing some trick, often a most indecent one. Now I ask you: What can one expect from man since he is a creature endowed with such strange qualities? Shower upon him every earthly blessing, drown him in bliss so that nothing but bubbles would dance on the surface of his bliss, as on a sea; give him such economic prosperity that he would have nothing else to do but sleep, eat cakes and busy himself with ensuring the continuation of world history and even then man, out of sheer ingratitude, sheer libel, would play you some loathsome trick. He would even risk his cakes and would deliberately desire the most fatal rubbish, the most uneconomical absurdity, simply to introduce into all this positive rationality his fatal fantastic element. It is just his fantastic dreams, his vulgar folly, that he will desire to retain, simply in order to prove to himself (as though that were so necessary) that men still are men and not piano keys, which even if played by the laws of nature themselves threaten to be controlled so completely that soon one will be able to desire nothing but by the calendar. And, after all, that is not all: even if man really were nothing but a piano key, even if this were proved to him by natural science and mathematics, even then he would not become reasonable, but would purposely do something perverse out of sheer ingratitude, simply to have his own way. And if he does not find any means he will devise destruction and chaos, will devise sufferings of all sorts, and will thereby have his own way. He will launch a curse upon the world, and, as only man can curse (it is his privilege, the primary distinction between him and other animals), then, after all, perhaps only by his curse will he attain his object, that is, really convince himself that he is a man and not a piano key! If you say that all this, too, can be calculated and tabulated, chaos and darkness and curses, so that the mere possibility of calculating it all beforehand would stop it all, and reason would reassert itself—then man would purposely go mad in order to be rid of reason and have his own way! I believe in that, I vouch for it, because, after all, the whole work of man seems really to consist in nothing but proving to himself continually that he is a man and not an organ stop. It may be at the cost of his skin! But he has proved it; he may become a caveman, but he will have proved it. And after that can one help sinning, rejoicing that it has not yet come, and that desire still depends on the devil knows what!

You will shout at me (that is, if you will still favor me with your shout) that, after all, no one is depriving me of my will, that all they are concerned with is that my will should somehow of itself, of its own free will, coincide with my own normal interests, with the laws of nature and arithmetic.

Bah, gentlemen, what sort of free will is left when we come to tables and arithmetic, when it will all be a case of two times two makes four? Two times two makes four even without my will. As if free will meant that!

IX

Gentlemen, I am joking, of course, and I know myself that I'm joking badly, but after all, you know, one can't take everything as a joke. I am, perhaps, joking with a heavy heart. Gentlemen, I am tormented by questions; answer them for me. Now you, for instance, want to cure men of their old habits and reform their will in accordance with science and common sense. But how do you know, not only that it is possible, but also that it is *desirable,* to reform man in that way? And what leads you to the conclusion that it is so *necessary* to reform man's desires? In short, how do you know that such a reformation will really be advantageous to man? And to go to the heart of the matter, why are you *so sure* of your conviction that not to act against his real normal advantages guaranteed by the conclusions of reason and arithmetic is always advantageous for man and must be a law for all mankind? After all, up to now it is only your supposition. Let us assume it to be a law of logic, but perhaps not a law of humanity at all. You gentlemen perhaps think that I am mad? Allow me to defend myself. I agree that man is pre-eminently a creative animal, predestined to strive consciously toward a goal, and to engage in engineering; that is, eternally and incessantly, to build new roads, *wherever they may lead.* But the reason why he sometimes wants to swerve aside may be precisely that he is *forced* to make that road, and perhaps, too, because however stupid the straightforward practical man may be in general, the thought nevertheless will sometimes occur to him that the road, it would seem, almost always does lead *somewhere,* and that the destination it leads to is less important than the process of making it, and that the chief thing is to save the well-behaved child from despising engineering, and so giving way to the fatal idleness, which, as we all know, is the mother of all vices. Man likes to create and build roads, that is beyond dispute. But why does he also have such a passionate love for destruction and chaos? Now tell me that! But on that point I want to say a few special words myself. May it not be that he loves chaos and destruction (after all, he sometimes unquestionably likes it very much, that is surely so) because he is instinctively afraid of attaining his goal and completing the edifice he is constructing? How do you know, perhaps he only likes that edifice from a distance, and not at all at close range, perhaps he only likes to build it and does not want to live in it, but will leave it, when completed, *aux animaux domestiques*—such as the ants, the sheep, and so on, and so on. Now the ants have quite a different taste. They have an amazing edifice of that type, that endures forever—the anthill.

With the anthill, the respectable race of ants began and with the anthill they will probably end, which does the greatest credit to their perseverance and staidness. But man is a frivolous and incongruous creature, and perhaps, like a chessplayer, loves only the process of the game, not the end of it. And who knows (one cannot swear to it), perhaps the only goal on earth to which mankind is striving lies in this incessant process of attaining, or in other words, in life itself, and not particularly in the goal which of course must always be two times two makes four, that is a formula, and after all, two times two makes four is no longer life, gentlemen, but is the beginning of death. Anyway, man has always been somehow afraid of this two times two makes four, and I am afraid of it even now. Granted that man does nothing but seek that two times two makes four, that he sails the oceans, sacrifices his life in the quest, but to succeed, really to find it—he is somehow afraid, I assure you. He feels that as soon as he has found it there will be nothing for him to look for. When workmen have finished their work they at least receive their pay, they go to the tavern, then they wind up at the police station—and there is an occupation for a week. But where can man go? Anyway, one can observe a certain awkwardness about him every time he attains such goals. He likes the process of attaining, but does not quite like to have attained, and that, of course, is terribly funny. In short, man is a comical creature; there seems to be a kind of pun in it all. But two times two makes four is, after all, something insufferable. Two times two makes four seems to me simply a piece of insolence. Two times two makes four is a fop standing with arms akimbo barring your path and spitting. I admit that two times two makes four is an excellent thing, but if we are going to praise everything, two times two makes five is sometimes also a very charming little thing.

And why are you so firmly, so triumphantly convinced that only the normal and the positive—in short, only prosperity—is to the advantage of man? Is not reason mistaken about advantage? After all, perhaps man likes something besides prosperity? Perhaps he likes suffering just as much? Perhaps suffering is just as great an advantage to him as prosperity? Man is sometimes fearfully, passionately in love with suffering and that is a fact. There is no need to appeal to universal history to prove that; only ask yourself, if only you are a man and have lived at all. As far as my own personal opinion is concerned, to care only for prosperity seems to me somehow even ill-bred. Whether it's good or bad, it is sometimes very pleasant to smash things, too. After all, I do not really insist on suffering or on prosperity either. I insist on my caprice, and its being guaranteed to me when necessary. Suffering would be out of place in vaudevilles, for instances; I know that. In the crystal palace it is even unthinkable; suffering means doubt, means negation, and what would be the good of a crystal palace if there could be any doubt about it? And yet I am sure man will never renounce real suffering, that is, destruction and chaos. Why, after all, suffering is the sole origin of consciousness. Though I stated at the beginning that consciousness, in my opinion, is the greatest misfortune for man, yet I know man loves it and would not give it up for any satisfaction. Consciousness, for instance, is infinitely superior to two times two makes four. Once you have two times two makes four, there is nothing left to do or to understand. There will be nothing left but to bottle up your five senses and plunge into contemplation. While if you stick to consciousness, even though you attain the same result, you can at least flog yourself at times, and that will, at any rate, liven you up. It may be reactionary, but corporal punishment is still better than nothing.

X

You believe in a crystal edifice that can never be destroyed; that is, an edifice at which one would neither be able to stick out one's tongue nor thumb one's nose on the sly. And perhaps I am afraid of this edifice just because it is of crystal and can never be destroyed and that one could not even put one's tongue out at it even on the sly.

You see, if it were not a palace but a chicken coop and rain started, I might creep into the chicken coop to avoid getting wet, and yet I would not call the chicken coop a palace out of gratitude to it for sheltering me from the rain. You laugh, you even say that in such circumstances a chicken coop is as good as a mansion. Yes, I answer, if one had to live simply to avoid getting wet.

But what is to be done if I have taken it into my head that this is not the only object in life, and that if one must live one may as well live in a mansion. That is my choice, my desire. You will only eradicate it when you have changed my desire. Well, do change it, tempt me with something else, give me another ideal. But in the meantime, I will not take a chicken coop for a palace. Let the crystal edifice even be an idle dream, say it is inconsistent with the laws of nature and that I have invented it only through my own stupidity, through some old-fashioned irrational habits of my generation. But what do I care if it is inconsistent? Does it matter at all, since it exists in my desires, or rather exists as long as my desires exist? Perhaps you are laughing again? Laugh away; I will put up with all your laughter rather than pretend that I am satisfied when I am hungry. I know, anyway, that I will not be appeased with a compromise, with an endlessly recurring zero, simply because it is consistent with the laws of nature and *really* exists. I will not accept as the crown of my desires a block of buildings with apartments for the poor on a lease of a thousand years and, to take care of any contingency, a dentist's shingle hanging out. Destroy my desires, eradicate my ideals, show me something better, and I will follow you. You may say, perhaps, that it is not worth your getting involved in it; but in that case, after all, I can give you the same answer. We are discussing things seriously; but if you won't deign to give me your attention, then, after all, I won't speak to you, I do have my underground.

But while I am still alive and have desires I would rather my hand were withered than to let it bring one brick to such a building! Don't remind me that I have just rejected the crystal edifice for the sole reason that one cannot put out one's tongue at it. I did not say it at all because I am so fond of putting my tongue out. Perhaps the only thing I resented was that of all your edifices up to now, there has not been a single one at which one could not put out one's tongue. On the contrary, I would let my tongue be cut off out of sheer gratitude if things could be so arranged that I myself would lose all desire to put it out. What do I care that things cannot be so arranged, and that one must be satisfied with model apartments? Why then am I made with such desires? Can I have been made simply in order to come to the conclusion that the whole way I am made is a swindle? Can this be my whole purpose? I do not believe it.

But do you know what? I am convinced that we underground folk ought to be kept in tow. Though we may be able to sit underground forty years without speaking, when we do come out into the light of day and break out we talk and talk and talk. . . .

"Then why have you written all this?" you will say to me.

"I ought to put you underground for forty years without anything to do and then come to you to find out what stage you have reached! How can a man be left alone with nothing to do for forty years?"

Epilogue:
Self-Limitation as the Ground of Hope

The romantics teach us that there is no meaning without mind and no mind without imagination. To encompass the present and the actual we must range beyond it in the possible. Consciousness itself marks both center and periphery. So, then, what can balance it but itself?

But what is consciousness? Hegel links it to reason and reason to absolute reality, and so exalts it to the level of divinity. Dostoevsky and Kierkegaard indicate its affinity with unreality, and so suggest its hazardous role in human existence.

Are not both extremes off center? Do not both positions scorn simple humility in the face of the real—the humility and respect that Kant tried to retain in his idea of the thing-in-itself after he had, for scientific purposes, made consciousness the center of the world? Is not this our problem: to transcend the present and the actual and still retain our respect for what we cannot fully know and cannot fully control? To transcend without reducing ourselves to ineffectual and humiliating flailing? To transcend without committing acts of terror against others? As the earlier romantics said, is not freedom self-imposed limitation?

I think that William James can help us here. A passage like the following might be mistaken for one of Kierkegaard's praises of the leap of faith, but there is a difference:

It is only by risking our persons from one hour to another that we live at all. And often enough our faith beforehand in an uncertified result *is the only thing that makes the result come true*. Suppose, for instance, that you are climbing a mountain, and have worked yourself into a position from which the only escape is by a terrible leap. Have faith that you can successfully make it, and your feet are nerved to its accomplishment. But mistrust yourself, and think of all the sweet things you have heard the scientists say of *maybes*, and you will hesitate so long that, at last, all unstrung and trembling, and launching yourself in a moment of despair, you roll in the abyss. In such a case (and it belongs to an enormous class), the part of wisdom as well as of courage is to *believe what is in the line of your needs*, for only by such belief is the need fulfilled. Refuse to believe, and you shall indeed be right, for you shall irretrievably perish. But believe, and again you shall be right, for you shall save yourself. You make one or the other of two possible universes true by your trust or mistrust,—both universes having been only *maybes*, in this particular, before you contributed your act.*

The difference between James and Kierkegaard lies in this: Despite James' talk of the act of faith as actualizing a possible universe, his words must be understood within the context of a philosophy of radical finitude. Kierkegaard's conception of human finitude and limitation is *non*-radical, even though he is severely critical of Hegel's pride: Kierkegaard tells us of an Infinite and Eternal God whom we must somehow contact, although the intellect rebels in the face of the task. An absolutist element enters into Dostoevsky as well, through the back door as it were: the underground man wants a world so perfect that he cannot stick his tongue out at things because he cannot feel disgusted with them. He wants heaven, not earth. But can there be *free men* in heaven?

James' philosophy of radical finitude is revealed in his essay "The Will to Believe," in which he limits even leaps of faith to issues that cannot be decided on presently available intellectual grounds; there is every reason to believe that he would have taken Kierkegaard's admission of the intellectual absurdity of Christianity (at least as Kierkegaard construed it) to constitute an available intellectual ground *against* belief. "Our passional nature not only lawfully may, but must, decide on option between propositions, whenever it is a genuine option that cannot by its nature be decided on intellectual

---

* "Is Life Worth Living?" in *The Will to Believe and Other Essays in Popular Philosophy*, p. 59. Dover Books.

grounds."* Notable, as well, James occasionally refers to a finite Deity.

But the most important aspect of James' philosophy of radical finitude is his pluralism or anti-monism; it contends that despite the fact that our experience is presented as a single continuous field, a whole, a view of the world—despite this, first, the whole universe cannot be summed up in a system of thought; and second, the whole does not necessarily determine the individual, and conversely, the individual does not necessarily determine the whole. The universe is open not only on its periphery, but there are open spots within it as well. There is room for the individual to rattle around; room to change the world a little if one wants to and has the courage to; or room to draw a few breaths in peace and just to dream. Hence along with irreducible individuality and freedom there also comes irreducible limitation.

I think it is only when we wilfully ignore our limitation that the life-giving power of the possible, the "maybe," becomes a poisonous disruption. Only when we forget that most mysteries are hidden in the tissue of everyday life, and are not grand and portentous, do we swing wildly from one extreme of mania to the other extreme of despair.

What appeared to the romantics to be high sentiment for action, all too frequently degenerated into sentimentality—a substitute for action. Could it be that too much emphasis was placed on the single moment and the single leap and that no faith was left over for the many little moments and many little leaps? In any case, today apathy is a problem for a multitude of us—decay of the will, pointlessness, together with its ironic reaction-formation: frantic and fanatical activity. One need not be a psychoanalyst to see that the late nineteenth-century thinkers' enlistment of will power to fight the instincts was a response to their fear that the will had no power at all. And one need not be avant-garde to believe that the plays of Samuel Beckett, in which the characters are paralyzed or mutilated or bound, or in which they play with their voices on tape recorders, are more than merely passing novelties. Mustn't we come to see that the will has *some* power which we must will to accept as enough? Isn't the circularity and autonomy of intentional self-limitation the only godlike thing that a nongod can have?

As much by their failure as by their successes, the romantics help us make the problem of our existence quite clear: We must learn

* "The Will to Believe," *op. cit.*, p. 11.

what is good to do and then we must manage to become enthused about doing it in a sane way. We need to find our joy somewhere in between the extremes of a wild celebration of all possibility and a pinched fear of any possibility; we find it in limiting ourselves to what is really possible to live with over many ordinary days in contact with many ordinary people. Freedom, community, autonomy, inwardness and emotion are the interrelated themes and tasks for our time just as for the romantics, but our experience of these themes and tasks is not the same as the romantics', for their rocky and painful experience of them is an additional theme which we experience in our own way. The romantics pictured the infinite as their outermost environing context; for us the infinite is embedded in the grit of an inescapably daily and inescapably contingent human existence. If we are to step beyond the romantics, it is possible only because of them; but to step beyond is to step into the finite.

Suggestions for Further Reading

Barrett, William, *Irrational Man*, New York, Doubleday, 1958
———, *What Is Existentialism?*, New York, Grove Press, 1964.
  Barrett's incisively written books reveal that romanticism is one of the roots of modern existentialism; his books provide one of the best introductions to the twentieth-century philosopher, Martin Heidegger.
Beyer, Werner, *The Enchanted Forest*, New York, Barnes & Noble, 1963.
  Beyer's scholarship discloses hitherto unrevealed Germanic influences on Coleridge.
Comte, Auguste, *Positive Philosophy*, trans. by Martineau, London, Trubner and Co., 1853.
  This is a famous work that should be read by all who are interested in modern intellectual history. Its intrinsic value, however, is exceedingly small—or so it seems to me.
Dostoevsky, Fyodor, *The Brothers Karamazov*, trans. by Garnett, New York, The Modern Library.
  The reader must grapple with this fascinating but enigmatic novel if he would have any hope of understanding Dostoevsky's thought as a whole.
Findlay, J. N., *Hegel Reexamined*, New York, Collier Books, 1962.
  That a contemporary British philosopher should write such a good book on Hegel signals, I think, a new dawn of philosophical interest and concern in historical matters. It is Hegel for non-Hegelians; it should have a wide audience.

Gode von Aesche, Alexander, *Natural Science in German Romanticism*, New York, Columbia University Press, 1941.

This is a mine of scholarship; it is well written and easily understood.

Heine, Heinrich, *Religion and Philosophy in Germany*, trans. by Snodgrass, Boston, Beacon Press, 1959.

This is a vastly entertaining and occasionally enlightening book by the famous German poet of the nineteenth century.

Hirsch, E. D., Jr., *Wordsworth and Schelling*, New Haven, Yale University Press, 1960.

Interdisciplinary books of this kind are much needed. Hirsch helps us see things whole.

Hook, Sidney, *From Hegel to Marx*, New York, Humanities Press, 1950.

This is a highly informative and readable book written by an expert.

Jolivet, Régis, *Introduction to Kierkegaard*, New York, E. P. Dutton, 1946.

It is beautifully designed to do just what its title indicates.

Loewenberg, J., *Hegel's Phenomenology: Dialogues on the Life of Mind*, La Salle, Ill., Open Court Publishing Co., 1965.

A life-long student of Hegel shares his thoughts in a conversational way. It is recommended for all those who find the usual textbook treatment of Hegel to be so much jargon.

Lowes, John Livingston, *The Road to Xanadu*, New York, Houghton Mifflin Co., 1930.

This justly famous work endeavors to trace the glistening paths of the romantic imagination. It is particularly concerned with Coleridge.

Löwith, Karl, *From Hegel to Nietzsche: The Revolution in Nineteenth Century Thought*, translated by D. Green, London, Constable, 1965.

This book rolls along like a Bruckner symphony: Löwith does not set off to reach new territory, but brilliantly surveys what he has already reached. He succeeds in making the reader feel at home in the nineteenth century.

Merz, J. T., *A History of European Thought in the 19th Century*, in four volumes, New York, Dover Press, 1965 (first published 1904–12).

The republishing of this massive work testifies to renewed scholarly interest in the nineteenth century.

Randall, John Herman, Jr., *The Career of Philosophy*, Vol. II, *From the German Enlightenment to the Age of Darwin*, New York, Columbia University Press, 1965.

This is a rewarding presentation and commentary for the more advanced reader.

Walzel, Oskar, *German Romanticism*, New York, Capricorn Books, 1966 (first published in 1932 by G. P. Putnam's Sons).

A helpful survey which is particularly good on Friedrich Schlegel.